TIME LIFE® BOOKS

*This volume is one of a series that explains and demonstrates
how to prepare various types of food, and that offers in each
book an international anthology of great recipes.*

Outdoor Cooking

BY
THE EDITORS OF TIME-LIFE BOOKS

TIME-LIFE BOOKS/ALEXANDRIA, VIRGINIA

Cover: Impaled on the rod of a rotisserie, a chicken turns above a drip pan positioned among live coals. While it roasts, the bird is basted with spoonfuls of liquid from the pan—a flavorful blend composed of the chicken's juices and fat, white wine, soy sauce and lemons.

Time-Life Books Inc.
is a wholly owned subsidiary of
TIME INCORPORATED

Founder: Henry R. Luce 1898-1967

Editor-in-Chief: Henry Anatole Grunwald
President: J. Richard Munro
Chairman of the Board: Ralph P. Davidson
Corporate Editor: Jason McManus
Group Vice President, Books: Joan D. Manley

TIME-LIFE BOOKS INC.

EDITOR: George Constable
Executive Editor: George Daniels
Director of Design: Louis Klein
Editorial Board: Roberta R. Conlan, Ellen Phillips, Gerry Schremp, Gerald Simons, Rosalind Stubenberg, Kit van Tulleken, Henry Woodhead
Editorial General Manager: Neal Goff
Director of Research: Phyllis K. Wise
Director of Photography: John Conrad Weiser

PRESIDENT: Reginald K. Brack Jr.
Senior Vice President: William Henry
Vice Presidents: George Artandi, Stephen L. Bair, Robert A. Ellis, Juanita T. James, Christopher T. Linen, James L. Mercer, Joanne A. Pello, Paul R. Stewart

THE GOOD COOK

Editor: Gerry Schremp
Designer: Ellen Robling
Chief Researcher: Barbara Levitt

Editorial Staff for Outdoor Cooking
Associate Editors: Adrian Allen (pictures), Anne Horan (text)
Text Editor: Sarah Brash
Researchers: Robert Carmack (techniques), Patricia McKinney (anthology), Denise Li, Ann Ready
Assistant Designer: Peg Schreiber
Copy Coordinators: Tonna Gibert, Nancy Lendved
Art Assistant: Mary L. Orr
Picture Coordinator: Alvin Ferrell
Editorial Assistants: Andrea Reynolds, Patricia Whiteford

Special Contributor: Leslie Marshall

Editorial Operations
Copy Room: Diane Ullius
Production: Anne B. Landry (director), Celia Beattie
Quality Control: James J. Cox (director), Sally Collins
Library: Louise D. Forstall

CHIEF SERIES CONSULTANT

Richard Olney, an American, has lived and worked for some three decades in France, where he is highly regarded as an authority on food and wine. Author of *The French Menu Cookbook* and of the award-winning *Simple French Food,* he has also contributed to numerous gastronomic magazines in France and the United States, including the influential journals *Cuisine et Vins de France* and *La Revue du Vin de France.* He has directed cooking courses in France and the United States and is a member of several distinguished gastronomic and oenological societies, including L'Académie Internationale du Vin, La Confrérie des Chevaliers du Tastevin and La Commanderie du Bontemps de Médoc et des Graves. Although he is chief consultant for the series, this volume was prepared under the guidance of American consultants.

CHIEF AMERICAN CONSULTANT

Carol Cutler is the author of a number of cookbooks, including the award-winning *The Six-Minute Soufflé and Other Culinary Delights.* During the 12 years she lived in France, she studied at the Cordon Bleu and the École des Trois Gourmandes, and with private chefs. She is a member of the Cercle des Gourmettes, a long-established French food society limited to just 50 members, and is also a charter member of Les Dames d'Escoffier, Washington Chapter.

SPECIAL CONSULTANT

Jeremiah Tower is a distinguished American restaurateur who lived in Europe for many years. He is associated with the Balboa Café and the Stars restaurant in San Francisco, and the Santa Fe Bar & Grill in Berkeley, California. He is a member of La Commanderie du Bontemps de Médoc et des Graves and of La Jurade de Saint-Émilion. He has been responsible for all of the step-by-step photographic sequences in this volume.

PHOTOGRAPHER

Aldo Tutino has worked in Milan, New York City and Washington, D.C. He has received a number of awards for his photographs from the New York Advertising Club.

INTERNATIONAL CONSULTANTS

GREAT BRITAIN: *Jane Grigson* has written a number of books about food and has been a cookery correspondent for the London *Observer* since 1968. *Alan Davidson* is the author of several cookbooks and the founder of Prospect Books, which specializes in scholarly publications about food and cookery. FRANCE: *Michel Lemonnier,* the cofounder and vice president of Les Amitiés Gastronomiques Internationales, is a frequent lecturer on wine and vineyards. GERMANY: *Jochen Kuchenbecker* trained as a chef, but worked for 10 years as a food photographer in several European countries before opening his own restaurant in Hamburg. *Anne Brakemeier* is the co-author of a number of cookbooks. THE NETHERLANDS: *Hugh Jans* has published cookbooks and his recipes appear in several Dutch magazines.

Correspondents: Elisabeth Kraemer-Singh (Bonn); Margot Hapgood, Dorothy Bacon (London); Susan Jonas, Miriam Hsia, Lucy T. Voulgaris (New York); Maria Vincenza Aloisi, Josephine du Brusle (Paris); Ann Natanson (Rome). Valuable assistance was also provided by: Enid Farmer (Boston); Anne Jackson, Debby Raad, Lesley Kinahan, Stephanie Lee (London).

CONTENTS

The Renaissance of an Ancient Art

Revered as a gift from the gods in eons past, fire has magical powers. After its leaping flames die down, its embers form an incandescent bed above which foods of almost every description can be grilled or roasted—and in the process become permeated by the delicate but distinctive fragrance of smoke. Depending on weather, the fire can burn outdoors or in a fireplace; depending on taste, the fare can be as plain as hamburgers or as fancy as a butterflied leg of lamb.

Achieving predictably delicious results when cooking any food over glowing embers is the subject of this book. The following pages address the basics: the equipment and how it works, the fire and how to build it, the marinades that aid in the preparation of foods, and the sauces and relishes that enhance their presentation. Four chapters then deal with the techniques for handling the primary ingredients: vegetables, meats, poultry, and fish and shellfish. A final chapter describes ways to manage such diverse foods as cheese and rabbit, and how to succeed in such ambitious undertakings as roasting a whole pig or staging a clambake. The second half of the volume consists of an anthology of the best published recipes for outdoor cooking.

International in scope, the recipes reflect the universality of the art. In every part of the world, the outdoors was man's first kitchen and an open fire his first stove; his first cooking method was to lay the food in the smoldering embers or impale it on sticks held over them. An early description of outdoor cooking appears in the *Iliad* of the Greek poet Homer, who recounts that Trojan warriors slew "a sheep of silvery whiteness" and "cut the meat carefully up into smaller pieces, spitted them, and drew them off again when they were well roasted."

For soldiers and civilians alike, such feasts became rarer as cities grew and Old World cooks took their fires indoors to clay ovens, fireplaces and—eventually—metal stoves. Outdoor cooking was left to hunters and fishermen, shepherds and adventurers.

In the New World, early explorers and settlers rediscovered the rewards of cooking over coals. The Spaniards found the Caribbean Indians cooking their game and fish on green-wood grills called *barbacoas,* which were suspended above pits heated with wood fires. The colonists of Virginia learned from the Indians to barbecue pigs in a similar manner, and the Pilgrims adopted the New England Indians' technique of baking clams and fish in pits lined with seaweed-covered stones.

Over the years, however, Americans also abandoned the open fire for the convenience of indoor kitchens. Barbecues and clambakes survived chiefly as community festivities, often gargantuan in scale. One 1840 Rhode Island clambake held to honor presidential candidate William Henry Harrison drew a crowd of 10,000. At a Kansas barbecue in June of 1850, the assembled multitude roasted and devoured six cattle, 20 hogs and more than 50 sheep, pigs and lambs—upward of four tons of meat.

Until the 1940s, however, only campers and picnickers regularly paid much attention to outdoor cooking. Then, exuberantly changing their life style, Americans traded their city apartments for suburban houses and turned their new backyards into outdoor living rooms. Cooking and eating alfresco became the vogue. No longer an occasional summer treat, cooking over coals developed into an everyday affair whose popularity has grown over the decades since.

Basically, modern techniques of outdoor cooking mirror ancient practices. Food is still grilled, but on a metal rack instead of a *barbacoa,* and the fire is contained in a metal bowl or box instead of a pit. Spitting is now done with a metal rod rather than a stick; an electric or battery-powered motor keeps the rod turning smoothly. Even the smoking of food, which at one time required building a shed, is accomplished today in a portable cooker.

Such refinements in equipment tame the fire, so the cook can concentrate attention on the preparation, embellishment and presentation of the food itself. The result, as the demonstrations in this book show, can be spectacular finished dishes with an elegant appearance and matchless flavor.

Because any food cooked over coals is innately rich, experience has proved that the most appropriate beverages to accompany it are light and simple ones. The most practical wine is rosé, which complements virtually everything from beef to pork, from poultry to seafood. Tavel from Provence is a good choice; so are California rosés made from Cabernet, Pinot Noir or Zinfandel grapes. Among white wines, Muscadet from the Loire Valley marries well with fish or shellfish, as do clear-tasting Schwarze Katz and Piesporter from Germany, the Chardonnays and Chablis from California and the Soaves from Italy. Among red wines, young Beaujolais has a strong, fresh bouquet that will harmonize with beef and poultry. Equally suitable are the French Côte du Rhônes and the California Cabernet Sauvignons.

But beverages for outdoor meals need not be restricted to wine. Cold beer, with its mildly bitter taste, is always welcome. And for those who prefer nonalcoholic beverages, iced tea is refreshing and flavorful, particularly if it is laced with slices of lemon or lime and sprigs of fresh mint.

A Guide to Outdoor Cooking Equipment

The battery of basic equipment used for cooking outdoors ranges from tiny collapsible boxes to huge masonry structures. Some equipment is designed for grilling only; some can incorporate rotisseries for spit-roasting, and some is intended primarily for smoking food. Some employs gas or electricity instead of—or in addition to—wood or charcoal.

Despite the obvious differences in their sizes, shapes and designs, all outdoor cooking equipment is based on two components: a firebox that holds the coals or other heat source and a rack or spit that holds food. As the five types of portable charcoal cookers below demonstrate, these elements can be put together in various ways.

The brazier *(far left)*, for example, is no more than a firebox and rack, and the fire is laid directly on the bottom of the firebox. In this model, the rack is supported on a central post that can be raised or lowered with a crank to adjust the temperature at which foods cook; in other models, the rack rests on notched brackets attached to the rim of the firebox, and the rack is adjusted by moving it from one set of notches to another. Long legs with wheels elevate the cooker to a convenient height. Some braziers also have a windscreen, or hood, that attaches to the firebox rim. Shaped like a half cylinder, the hood can be fitted with an electric or battery-powered rotisserie.

In a hibachi, by contrast, the fire is laid on a grate rather than on the bottom of the firebox. (The model shown second from left has a double grate.) The addition of a grate permits air flow under the coals, which consequently burn hotter and more evenly. Vents near the bottom of the firebox can be opened or closed to regulate the air supply and thus the rate of burning. Hibachis usually have brackets for adjusting the height of the racks.

Their small size makes them handy to use on a tabletop.

A kettle grill *(center, left)* also contains a grate for the fire and has firebox vents to regulate the heat. Its rack, however, is not adjustable. In the model shown, the vent closure doubles as a sweeper to push ashes into an ash catcher below the firebox. But the principal feature of the kettle grill is its vented cover. Grilling food under a cover shortens its cooking time by as much as 25 per cent and intensifies its smoky flavor.

A rotisserie grill *(center, right)* has a grate, vents in the firebox and a vented cover. The rack height can be adjusted by means of levers at the front of the grill. The rotisserie is supported by brackets that permit raising and lowering the spit rod. The model shown includes a cutting board that can be fixed to the edge of the firebox at either side.

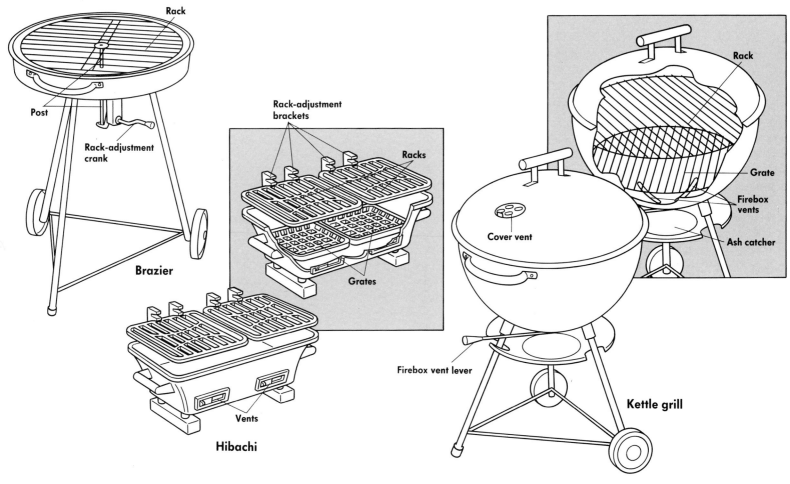

Brazier

Hibachi

Kettle grill

A charcoal-water smoker cooks food, but is not designed for preserving it. The smoker *(far right)* holds a pan for fuel and—above it—another pan for water and one or two racks for food. Its tight-fitting cover traps smoke released by the green hardwood that is used to augment the charcoal fire; meanwhile the water pan provides steam to keep the food on the racks above it moist *(pages 46-47)*. The model shown has a gauge to allow monitoring of the heat inside, and doors through which the charcoal and water supplies can be replenished. In addition to serving as a smoker, the device may be used as a grill if the cover and water pan are removed and the charcoal pan placed directly under a rack.

Choosing an outdoor cooker requires careful shopping. Except for the hibachi, which is often made of cast-iron, the fire-boxes and covers of outdoor grills and smokers are usually formed out of sheet steel. For durability and good heat reten-tion, the steel should be 20-gauge or heavier; hot coals may burn a hole in light-gauge steel. The finish may be ei-ther porcelain enamel or heat-resistant paint. Of the two, porcelain enamel will stand up better to rust and heat.

Wire racks should be coated with nick-el chrome, which resists flaking or pit-ting and thus keeps the wires easy to clean. Be sure that the rack is sturdy enough not to bend readily, lest it sag under the weight of food. Legs of portable cookers should be widely based for stabil-ity and firmly fastened to the firebox.

Before purchasing any grill or smoker, try out all of the vents, cranks, levers, hinges, wheels and other moving parts to make sure that they operate properly. Look for handles that are easy to grasp and will remain comfortably cool to the touch. Wood and phenolic plastic handles absorb less heat than metal ones.

Regular maintenance of a simple sort will extend the life of any cooker. One way of preserving the finish is to line the firebox with heavy-duty aluminum foil before building a fire, remembering to cut a hole in the foil where it overlies a vent. When the food is cooked and the fire is dead, the cooker is left to cool; then the rack or rotisserie and grate can be re-moved and the ashes wrapped in the foil and discarded. If the firebox is not lined with foil, the cold ashes can be shoveled out or the grill inverted to dump them.

After each use, clean the rack with a stiff wire brush to remove the cooked-on grease and food. Wash the spit rod and holding forks of a rotisserie with soapy hot water and dry them well with a towel.

Before storing a grill or smoker for the winter, wash it thoroughly and dry each part. Then place it, if possible, in a dry, protected area such as a garage or base-ment. If it must be stored outdoors, use a tarpaulin or plastic cover to ward off rust.

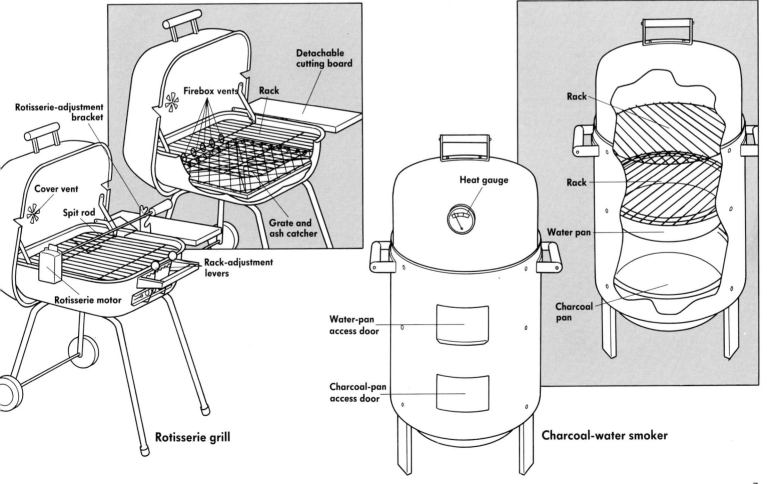

Rotisserie-adjustment bracket

Firebox vents

Rack

Detachable cutting board

Cover vent

Spit rod

Grate and ash catcher

Rack-adjustment levers

Rotisserie motor

Rotisserie grill

Heat gauge

Water-pan access door

Charcoal-pan access door

Rack

Rack

Water pan

Charcoal pan

Charcoal-water smoker

7

Handling Fuel and Fire

Successful cooking with coals depends on a good fire—hot enough to sustain a constant heat, but not so intense that it burns the food. And a good fire depends on the proper use of fuel.

For an outdoor grill, either lump charcoal or charcoal briquets will suffice. Lump charcoal, which is pure carbonized wood with no additives, is easy to light and burns fast. It produces a bed of usable embers in as little as 20 minutes, but may need to be replenished in another half hour—which can be a tricky job if it entails removing a hot rack.

Charcoal briquets are basically composed of pulverized charcoal bound with cornstarch, although these ingredients are often augmented by mineral coal, sodium nitrate to aid ignition, and lime to retard the rate of burning. Denser than lumps, briquets burn longer, but they are slower to ignite: They may take 40 minutes or more to produce usable embers.

Whether you use lump charcoal or briquets, most grilling will require a bed about 2 inches [5 cm.] deep and an inch or two [2½ or 5 cm.] larger all around than the area covered by the food. For spit-roasting or grilling over a drip pan, you will need enough coals to form rows about 4 inches [10 cm.] deep in front and in back of the pan. In either case, start by piling the charcoal in a mound so that the fire will spread quickly and evenly.

An electric starter is a convenient—and odorless—means for igniting the fire. Be careful to follow the package instructions to the letter; an overheated electric starter can burn out and melt. Petroleum-based liquids and jellies are handy alternatives, but may impart an undesirable taste to the food. Such products must be used with caution; once you get even the faintest glimmer of a fire under way, do not add any more starter lest a perilous flare-up result. Never use gasoline or kerosene: Both are dangerously explosive.

After the fire has taken hold and the coals have burned long enough to acquire a coat of white ash, the coals should be rearranged for grilling or for spit-roasting *(right)*. To judge whether coals have reached the proper temperature, hold the palm of your hand about 4 to 6 inches [10 to 15 cm.] from the fire. Then count the seconds (one thousand one, one thousand two, etc.). If you must withdraw your hand after two seconds, the fire is hot and suitable for searing foods quickly. If you can tolerate the heat for four seconds, the fire is medium hot and suitable for grilling or roasting.

Opening all the vents of a grill will increase the temperature of the fire; closing them partially will reduce it. Tapping the coals to remove their insulating cover of ash will increase the heat, so will pushing them close together; spreading coals apart will cool the fire.

Neither charcoal lumps nor briquets are safe to use in any enclosed space such as an indoor fireplace or a garage: Charcoal releases carbon monoxide in quantities that can be fatal. To grill or roast over coals at a fireplace indoors, use wood logs as your fuel. The flames will force whatever carbon monoxide the wood generates up the chimney. The logs will burn down to produce embers.

Hardwoods (such as hickory, oak and maple) are better than softwoods (poplar, spruce and Douglas fir), which burn down rapidly and shoot out sparks besides. Whatever wood you choose, the logs should have been dried for at least six months; freshly cut green wood contains too much moisture to burn well.

Allow 40 to 50 minutes for wood to reach a suitable ashy stage. You then can cook directly over the logs, if you encase the food in a long-handled grill basket or thread it onto long skewers. However, holding the basket or skewers in place is a hot and tiring task. Except for foods that cook rapidly, a better technique is to build a brick support for a rack *(pages 36-37)* or rotisserie *(pages 58-59)* on the hearth in front of the fireplace. For grilling, rake out embers to form a 2-inch [5-cm.] layer between the bricks; for spit-roasting, the fire will give enough heat.

A Log Fire for Cooking on the Hearth

1 **Laying the fire.** Open the damper and place crumpled newspapers under the grate. Arrange three crisscrossed layers of kindling in the grate.

2 **Adding logs.** Place a split log toward the back of the grate. Lay a second log parallel to the first, leaving 2 or 3 inches [5 or 8 cm.] between them.

3 **Adding kindling.** Place several pieces of kindling on top of the two logs to allow room for air to circulate, then set another split log on top.

A Bed of Coals for Grilling

1 **Arranging charcoal.** Mound charcoal in a grill. Lay an electric fire starter on the mound, pile a layer of charcoal over the starter, and plug it in.

2 **Spreading the coals.** After about seven minutes, remove and unplug the starter. When white ash covers the coals, spread them out in a single layer.

3 **Adding the rack.** Lay the rack over the coals and let it heat for about five minutes. Use a cloth to coat the rack with oil, or tongs to grease it with pieces of fat.

Rows of Coal for Spit-roasting

1 **Starting the fire.** Mound charcoal in a rotisserie grill. Apply an electric starter (Step 1, top). As soon as the charcoal flames, remove the starter.

2 **Rearranging the coals.** When the coals are ash-covered, push them into parallel rows, making the rear row slightly higher than the front one.

3 **Adding the drip pan.** Place a foil drip pan that is both longer and wider than the food to be spitted under the space the spit will occupy.

4 **Lighting the fire.** Light a rolled newspaper and hold it up the chimney for a few seconds to start an updraft. Light the papers under the grate.

5 **Letting the fire burn down.** The kindling will blaze for about 10 minutes, igniting the surfaces of the logs. Allow the fire to burn undisturbed.

6 **Checking the coals.** When the glowing coals that fall from the logs form a thick layer—after about 30 minutes more—the fire is ready.

Marinades: Preliminary Enhancements

Almost everything that you cook over coals will benefit from being marinated beforehand. Depending on your taste, the marinade may be mild or tangy, and based on only one or two flavorings—or a myriad *(recipes, pages 159-162)*. It may be a dry blend designed chiefly to flavor food, a paste or aromatic oil to lubricate the food's surfaces or an acid-based mixture that will act as a tenderizer.

A dry marinade consists of crushed dried herbs and spices, usually—but not necessarily—mixed with salt *(top right)*. The salt combines with the juices of meat or poultry to form a brine that penetrates the flesh, carrying the flavor of the herbs and spices with it. Such a marinade is particularly useful for pork and game birds; salt attenuates the sweetness of the one and the pungency of the other.

In a paste marinade, dried or fresh spices and herbs and such aromatic elements as garlic or grated citrus peel are crushed or chopped, then combined with just enough oil to bind them together *(top, opposite)*. In an aromatic oil marinade, the proportions are reversed and the oil is combined with just enough aromatics to flavor it *(bottom, opposite)*.

An acidic marinade may be based on wine *(bottom, right)*, vinegar, soy sauce, yogurt or citrus juice. Aromatics contribute taste, and adding a little oil ensures that the food does not dry out.

Marinating time will vary not only with the intensity of flavor you desire, but also with the type of food. If your aim is only to create a savory coating, paste, liquid or saltless dry marinades can be applied almost at the last minute. But if you want these marinades to penetrate the food, allow up to two hours for vegetables, meats and poultry left at room temperature, where the exchange of flavors will be rapid, and as much as 24 hours in the refrigerator. Fish and shellfish spoil rapidly; allow 30 minutes at room temperature, two hours in the refrigerator.

The two exceptions to these rules occur when you make a dry marinade with salt and when you use an acid-based marinade to tenderize meat. Refrigerate the food and steep it for at least 24 hours, and as long as 48 hours—turning it often to keep it moistened with brine or acid.

Spices and Salt to Create a Brine

1 **Crushing flavorings.** With a mortar and pestle, crush dried spices and herbs—here, juniper berries, whole allspice, black peppercorns and thyme leaves—to make a coarse powder. Crumble bay leaves into tiny bits with your fingers; add them to the mixture.

2 **Adding salt.** Pour coarse salt into the mortar and stir it together with the crushed herbs and spices. Use the pestle to grind the ingredients until they are evenly blended.

Acid Liquid to Tenderize

1 **Preparing vegetables.** Cut an onion into thin slices and place them in a shallow dish large enough to hold the food you will marinate. Cut peeled carrots into thin rounds, and place the rounds in the dish. Add chives and sprigs of fresh parsley and dill. Grind in pepper.

2 **Adding liquids.** Moisten the ingredients with enough olive oil to coat the bottom of the dish. Pour in wine—in this case, white wine is used. Use your hand to mix the ingredients together.

Herbs and Spices in a Mixture That Clings

1 Preparing dry ingredients. With a mortar and pestle, pulverize dry spices and herbs—here, whole allspice and mace blades. Use your fingers to pry open cardamom pods; spill the seeds into the mortar and discard the pods.

2 Grinding the mixture. Crumble bay leaves and dried hot chilies and add them to the mortar. Grind the mixture with the pestle until it forms a fine powder.

3 Adding oil. Dribble olive oil into the mortar and stir it gradually into the dry ingredients. Incorporate just enough oil to moisten the mixture evenly and make it sticky enough to adhere to food.

Aromatic Oil for Moistening

1 Chopping herbs. Peel shallots and garlic cloves and set them aside. Remove the leaves from sprigs of fresh thyme and discard the stems. With a sharp, heavy knife, chop the leaves, using a rocking motion and steadying the tip of the knife blade with one hand.

2 Combining ingredients. Chop the shallots and garlic fine and mix them with the thyme in a shallow dish large enough to hold the food you will marinate. Grate the peel of an orange, being careful not to include the bitter white pith beneath the colored outside layer. Add the grated peel to the dish.

3 Incorporating oil. Pour enough olive oil into the dish to saturate the aromatics. Add a pinch of coarse salt and grind in pepper to taste. Stir to mix the ingredients well.

11

A Gallery of Accompaniments

The rich, smoky taste of foods cooked over coals is best accented and complemented by sauces, relishes and garnishes that have an assertiveness of their own. Fresh aromatic vegetables—tomatoes, peppers and shallots, for example—will supply the essential tanginess. So, too, will chilies, and herbs and spices of every kind.

These elements can be chopped, sliced, ground or puréed, cooked or left raw, and combined with other ingredients to create a spectrum of effects. As demonstrated here and on the following pages, the finished product can range from smooth barbecue sauce to chunky relish, from unctuous mayonnaise to fluid chili sauce and fluffy compound butter.

However tomatoes or peppers are used, they will have mellower flavor if their skins and seeds are removed by peeling or sieving. Tomatoes can be peeled raw after blanching (*Step 1, top right*), then halved and squeezed gently so that the seeds and excess liquid spill out, or quartered so that the seeds can be scooped out with a finger.

Sweet peppers can be peeled only if they are grilled—over coals, an open flame or in the broiler of an oven—to blister and loosen the skin. However, the skin can be removed from either raw or grilled peppers by puréeing and sieving (*page 14*). The stems and seed clusters are easily pulled out before peeling or puréeing.

Chilies need only to be stemmed and seeded. Fresh chilies such as the hot jalapeños shown at bottom right can be quartered and the seeds removed with a knife. Dried chilies such as sweet and musky *anchos (page 15)* are simply torn apart and the seeds shaken free.

For both mayonnaise and compound butter, the vegetable and herb flavorings must be chopped fine or puréed so that they blend in thoroughly. To ensure that the mayonnaise emulsifies successfully, the ingredients must be at room temperature and the mixing bowl warm. By contrast, the butter used for compound butter must be chilled and firm. Pounding it with a rolling pin will soften it enough so it can be whisked into a fluffy base for flavorings.

A Classic Barbecue Sauce

1 **Peeling tomatoes.** Cut out a conical plug at the stem end of each tomato and incise a cross in the base. Blanch the tomatoes in boiling water for 10 to 30 seconds; then plunge them immediately into a bowl of water and ice cubes to cool them. To peel each tomato, slide a knife under each section of the cross and strip away the skin.

2 **Mixing the vegetables.** Seed the tomatoes, chop them coarse and place them in a nonreactive pot. Add sprigs of thyme, bay leaves, peeled whole shallots, unpeeled garlic cloves and sliced onion. Bring the mixture to a boil, reduce the heat and—stirring occasionally—simmer the mixture, uncovered, for about two hours.

A Piquant Relish with Hot Chilies

1 **Seeding the chilies.** Chop onions and garlic cloves and place them in a bowl. Peel tomatoes (*Step 1, top*) and seed them. Stem fresh hot chilies—here, jalapeños—and quarter them lengthwise; then cut away the seedy cores. Chop the chilies fine and add them to the bowl. Remove the stems from fresh coriander leaves.

2 **Blending the relish.** Chop the coriander leaves and tomatoes coarse, and add them to the bowl. Add a large pinch of coarse salt, then pour in vinegar or freshly squeezed lime juice and mix well. Stir in olive oil. Cover and set the mixture aside for 30 minutes to allow the flavors to meld.

3 **Sieving the purée.** Purée the mixture in a food processor or a food mill. Then sieve it into a bowl, using a pestle or wooden spoon to force the purée through the mesh. Discard any seeds or skin remaining in the sieve.

4 **Lightening the purée.** Transfer the strained purée to a large mixing bowl and stir in molasses, Worcestershire sauce and olive oil.

5 **Finishing the sauce.** Continue stirring the sauce until it is thoroughly blended and uniform in color. Add salt and season to taste with freshly ground pepper. The sauce is now ready to use, but can be stored safely in the refrigerator for up to three weeks.

A Zesty Combination of Tomatoes and Shallots

1 **Preparing ingredients.** Peel, seed and chop tomatoes coarse. Chop shallots fine. Remove the stems from fresh thyme leaves, chop the leaves and place them in a bowl. Add freshly ground black pepper and whisk in vinegar and olive oil.

2 **Adding the tomatoes.** When the vinegar and oil are well combined, stir in the chopped shallots with a wooden spoon. Then add the chopped tomatoes a handful at a time.

3 **Completing the relish.** Gently stir the mixture with the spoon. Add salt to taste and, if you like, more pepper. Serve at once or set the relish aside for 30 minutes to meld the flavors.

A Colorful Mayonnaise with Basil

1 **Whisking the egg yolks.** Blanch fresh basil leaves in boiling water for three seconds. Drop them into cold water, pat them dry and chop them fine. Bring eggs to room temperature and separate them, dropping the yolks into a warmed bowl; reserve the whites for another use. Add the basil to the yolks and whisk briskly for a minute; whisk in lemon juice until the mixture is smooth.

2 **Adding olive oil.** Whisking constantly, dribble in olive oil a drop at a time. When the mixture thickens—indicating that the emulsion has begun to form—increase the flow of oil to a thin, steady stream.

3 **Seasoning.** Continue whisking and adding oil until the mayonnaise becomes thick enough to coat the wire of the whisk. Stir in salt and freshly ground pepper to taste, and add a little more lemon juice if desired. Tightly covered, the mayonnaise can be refrigerated safely for several days.

A Tangy Blend of Peppers and Butter

1 **Preparing the peppers.** Apply a light coat of oil to sweet red peppers. Grill the peppers above medium-hot coals for 20 to 30 minutes, or until the skins are blistered all over (page 19, Step 3). Remove the peppers from the grill and pull out the stems and attached seed clusters.

2 **Puréeing the peppers.** Place the peppers in the bowl of a food processor. Operating the machine in short bursts, and scraping down the sides of the bowl occasionally, process the peppers until they form a fairly smooth purée. Alternatively, press the peppers through a food mill.

3 **Sieving the peppers.** With a wooden spoon or a pestle, press the purée through a sieve into a bowl. Discard the skins and any seeds that remain in the sieve.

A Mellow Ancho Chili Sauce

1 **Grinding the chilies.** Remove the stems from dried *ancho* chilies; pull the pods apart and shake out the seeds. Place the chilies in the bowl of a food processor and grind them until they are a fine powder—about 15 minutes. Sift the chilies through a fine sieve into a bowl; discard any bits left on the mesh.

2 **Combining ingredients.** Over medium heat, sauté chopped onion and garlic in olive oil for five minutes, or until they are soft but not browned. Stir the chilies into the pot and add water.

3 **Finishing the sauce.** Stirring occasionally, simmer the mixture, uncovered, for about one hour. The sauce is ready to use when it is shiny and slightly thickened. If refrigerated in a covered container, the sauce can be stored for three weeks or more.

4 **Creaming the butter.** Soften chilled butter by pounding it with a rolling pin. Place the butter in a heavy bowl, and beat it with a whisk or a wooden spoon until it is light in color and fluffy.

5 **Finishing the butter.** Add the sieved peppers to the butter and beat vigorously until the mixture is well blended. Season with salt and pepper to taste. Serve the butter at once or refrigerate it, tightly covered, until you are ready to use it. The butter can be safely kept for seven to 10 days.

1
Vegetables
A Cornucopia
from the Garden

What better way to introduce or complement an outdoor meal than with vegetables piping hot from the coals? Every vegetable—large or small, tender or tough—is potentially a candidate for either grilling on a rack, roasting in embers or steaming in a wrapper. Which method to adopt depends on the effect desired as well as on the nature of the vegetable.

In grilling, for example, the vegetables cook 4 to 6 inches [10 to 15 cm.] above a fire that has burned down until it is still hot but not scorching. Periodic turning ensures that they cook through at an even rate. Whole vegetables that have sturdy skins—summer squashes and eggplant among them—develop tenderness and a subtly smoky taste when treated this way. To keep their skins tender, the vegetables must be oiled liberally; fleshy types must also be pierced or scored to keep the skins from bursting when their juices expand as steam *(pages 18-19)*.

Potatoes, too, can be oiled, pierced and grilled on a rack; parboiling them first speeds the process. Slicing also shortens the time required for potatoes or for such firm, juicy vegetables as slightly underripe tomatoes *(pages 20-21)*. The oil that guarantees tenderness can be enhanced with spices or herbs. And, to make turning easy, the slices can be assembled in a hinged grill basket or threaded onto skewers *(opposite)*.

For roasting in live coals, only vegetables that are both firm and protectively sheathed—such as sweet potatoes or winter squashes—are suitable. By contrast, steaming is appropriate for a cook's entire vegetable repertoire: Corn can be steamed on a rack in its own husk, and types as diverse as green peas and cauliflower can be steamed in foil packets. Soaking corn in water provides the liquid required to create steam; foil-wrapped vegetables can be moistened with water or, for more flavor, doused with stock, wine or lemon juice.

Surprisingly, perhaps, any fruit that benefits from cooking can be treated by the same methods used for vegetables, following the same guidelines. Bananas can be grilled in their skins, apples roasted in coals. Orange slices are firm yet juicy enough to be oiled and grilled on a rack; so are pineapple and papaya slices. Pears, mangoes and cherries might be skewered. And everything from peaches to grapes can be packeted in foil, sugared and splashed with rum or brandy, then steamed to create the perfect finale for a meal cooked over coals.

Kebabs brightly striped by alternating pieces of red pepper, eggplant, yellow squash and zucchini brown and crisp on a grill. Before grilling, the vegetables were first parboiled so that they would cook through quickly, then tossed while still hot and absorbent with an oil-and-oregano marinade to complement their flavors (pages 20-21).

Tactics for Whole Vegetables

Whole vegetables retain their natural moistness and develop mellow yet concentrated flavors when properly grilled on a rack or roasted in coals. Almost every vegetable with a protective skin or firm outer flesh lends itself to one of these methods; some can be cooked both ways.

New potatoes and mature boiling potatoes, for example, can be grilled (right, top), whereas baking potatoes and sweet potatoes or yams—which possess thicker skins—are also suitable for roasting (opposite, top). Here the new potatoes are boiled until almost tender, oiled and seasoned, then cooked over coals to crisp their skins. The boiling is optional, but shortens the grilling time and ensures even cooking. To facilitate turning, the potatoes are skewered; otherwise the potatoes should be pierced to keep them from bursting when their moisture turns to steam and expands.

All potatoes to be roasted must be scrubbed, and the baking variety needs to be pricked. Sweet potatoes or yams do not: Their porous skins will allow steam to escape. Onions and winter squashes can be roasted like potatoes. So can garlic bulbs and beets, if wrapped in foil to keep them from losing their juices. Candidates for grilling on skewers include parboiled radishes or small onions, and raw cherry tomatoes or mushroom caps.

Permeated with oil, mushroom caps also can be grilled on the rack, and they form natural containers for a stuffing (right, bottom; recipe, page 166). Because stuffed caps cannot be turned, the best filling is a blend of bread crumbs and vegetables that only needs heating.

Other large whole vegetables that can be simply set on the rack for grilling are zucchini, pattypan and yellow squashes, cucumbers, eggplants, sweet peppers and scallions (opposite, bottom). Incising long grooves in squashes, cucumbers or eggplants prevents bursting and allows the piquant aroma of the coals to penetrate their flesh. Otherwise, the vegetables merely need to be well oiled. The only caveat is that when different vegetables are grilled together the timing must be orchestrated. Slow-cooking types should be started first and fast-cooking ones added last so that all of them will be done at the same time.

Potatoes Impaled on Skewers

1 **Skewering.** Boil unpeeled new potatoes until barely tender—12 to 15 minutes. Drain them and toss them in oil seasoned with salt and crushed dried chilies. Thread each skewer with five or six potatoes. Pour the remaining oil over the potatoes and lay the skewers on an oiled rack 4 to 6 inches [10 to 15 cm.] above medium-hot coals.

2 **Grilling.** With long-handled tongs or a flame-resistant mitt, turn the skewers at one-minute intervals. Grill the potatoes for three or four minutes in all, until the skins are crisped evenly. To serve, place the tip of each skewer on a plate or platter and use a large fork to push off the potatoes two or three at a time.

Mushroom Caps with Stuffing

1 **Stuffing mushrooms.** Remove the stems from large mushrooms; wash and dry the caps. Marinate them for up to two hours in olive oil and lemon juice. Then drain them, reserving the marinade. For the stuffing, combine sautéed chopped red pepper, shallots and garlic with parsley and the remaining marinade. Add fresh bread crumbs, and season the mixture. Stuff the caps.

2 **Grilling mushrooms.** With a long-handled spatula or tongs, place the mushroom caps stuffing side upward on an oiled rack 4 to 6 inches [10 to 15 cm.] above medium-hot coals. Grill them for eight to 10 minutes. The mushrooms are done when the caps feel slightly soft to the touch and the stuffing is heated through.

Potatoes Roasted in Coals

1 **Embedding the potatoes.** Thoroughly scrub potatoes—a combination of russet baking potatoes and sweet potatoes is shown here. Pierce each baking potato in several places with a fork or skewer. Using long-handled tongs, lay the potatoes in coals—in this case, at the side of a fireplace; a heap of coals in a grill would do as well. With a shovel, scoop more coals over the potatoes. Avoid ashes, lest they suffocate the coals.

2 **Serving.** Roast the potatoes until they feel soft when pierced with a long-handled fork—about 45 minutes. Remove them from the coals with tongs. Wearing a mitt to protect your hand, brush the skins clean of clinging ash and gently roll each potato on a flat surface to crumble the flesh inside. Cut a cross into one side of each potato and squeeze its ends together until the flesh pops out at the cross. Serve with butter or sour cream.

A Mélange of Eggplant, Peppers and Scallions

1 **Oiling.** Place sweet red peppers in a dish filmed with olive oil and turn them about to coat them evenly. In an eggplant, cut four lengthwise and equidistant grooves, each ¼ inch [6 mm.] deep and ⅛ inch [3 mm.] wide. Rub olive oil into the eggplant. Trim scallions; oil and season them.

2 **Grilling.** Place the peppers and eggplant on an oiled rack 4 to 6 inches [10 to 15 cm.] above medium-hot coals. Turning them often, grill until the peppers are blistered all over and the eggplant is puckered—20 to 30 minutes. During the last five minutes, add the scallions and grill them until the green tops wilt.

3 **Serving.** Working quickly, transfer the scallions to a platter. Quarter the eggplant by cutting through the grooves; divide the quarters in half crosswise, then arrange them on the platter. Halve the peppers, scoop out the seedy cores, peel off the skin and add the peppers to the platter. Serve at once.

Tidy Slices That Grill Speedily

Vegetables that have been cut into slices, chunks or segments cook fast over coals and acquire an appetizing brown finish. Because they are exposed to direct heat, the pieces must be well slathered with oil to remain moist. However, necessity can be turned to advantage by adding seasonings and herbs to the oil to endow the vegetables with extra flavor.

The best candidates for such treatment are vegetables with firm, moist flesh—among them, eggplants, summer squashes, sweet peppers, onions, and underripe or green tomatoes. Root vegetables, such as potatoes and turnips, and fibrous fennel or celery ribs are also suitable, but they must be parboiled until about half-cooked lest they char outside before they become tender inside.

If, like the potatoes at top right, the pieces are large enough for easy turning with tongs or a spatula, they can go individually onto the grill rack. If the pieces are small or fragile—or if there are so many pieces that turning them one at a time would be tedious—you can safeguard their structure and lighten your task in two ways: Impale the pieces on a skewer to form kebabs, as demonstrated at top, opposite; or assemble them in a hinged grill basket, as is done with the tomato and onion slices at bottom right.

For grilling on a rack or in a basket, vegetables should be cut into slices that are thick enough to tolerate handling yet thin enough to cook through evenly in the time they take to brown. As a rule, a thickness of about ⅓ inch [8 mm.] is appropriate, although any especially juicy specimens might be cut ½ inch [1 cm.] thick. In either case, be sure that all of the pieces are the same thickness so that they will be done simultaneously.

For skewering, the slices can be somewhat thinner or thicker, but they should be similar in diameter—1½ to 2 inches [4 to 5 cm.]. Parboiling the slices for a minute or two will guarantee they all cook uniformly. When assembling a kebab—or a brochette, as it is sometimes called—begin and end the skewer with a firm-fleshed specimen, such as the sweet red pepper shown here, that will provide an anchor for juicier vegetables such as zucchini. Otherwise, the vegetables can be arranged in any sequence you like.

Potatoes with a Lattice Design

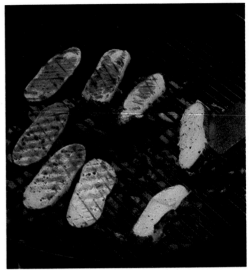

1 **Slicing.** Pour olive oil onto a platter and add salt and pepper. Parboil unpeeled potatoes—here, baking potatoes—for seven minutes, or until a fork can penetrate partway but meets firm resistance toward the center. Drain, then slice the potatoes about ⅓ inch [8 mm.] thick. Place the slices in the oil and turn them to coat both sides.

2 **Grilling.** Arrange the potato slices diagonally on an oiled rack 4 to 6 inches [10 to 15 cm.] above medium-hot coals. After three minutes, rotate the potatoes 90 degrees so that the wires of the rack sear a crosshatch pattern into the slices as they brown. Cook for two minutes. Turn the slices, and grill until they are tender when pricked with a fork.

Tomatoes and Onions in a Hinged Basket

1 **Preparing slices.** Pour olive oil onto a platter and toss fresh rosemary sprigs in the oil. Slice red onions ⅓ inch [8 mm.] thick and lay them on the platter. Turn them to coat both sides. Core firm tomatoes and slice them ⅓ inch thick. Push the onions aside and oil the tomato slices.

2 **Arranging the basket.** Strew sprigs of the rosemary in the basket of an oiled hinged grill. Lay the onion and tomato slices in the basket and top them with the remaining rosemary. Season to taste. Lower the lid of the grill over the vegetables and join the two handles with the sliding clasp.

Composing Kebabs

1 **Preparing the vegetables.** Cut zucchini and yellow squash into ½- to ⅔-inch [1- to 2-cm.] rounds. Slice an eggplant into thirds lengthwise; rotate it 90 degrees and slice it into thirds again; quarter the strips crosswise. Stem, seed and derib red peppers; cut them into 1½-inch [4-cm.] pieces.

2 **Marinating.** Parboil the vegetables for two minutes, then drain them in a colander. In a bowl, combine olive oil, salt and pepper, and chopped fresh oregano. Add the vegetables and use two spoons to toss them with the oil mixture. Let the vegetables marinate for about 30 minutes.

3 **Grilling.** Thread the vegetable pieces onto skewers, beginning and ending with red pepper and adding the others alternately. Turning them often, grill the kebabs on an oiled rack 4 to 6 inches [10 to 15 cm.] above medium-hot coals for five minutes, or until tender and evenly browned.

3 **Grilling and serving.** Place the basket on a rack set 4 to 6 inches [10 to 15 cm.] above medium-hot coals. Grill the slices for about three minutes; then turn the basket and grill the other side of the slices for three minutes, or until they are delicately browned. The onions will still be slightly crisp, but the tomatoes will be soft. Remove the basket from the coals and, holding it bottom side up, detach it. Slide the slices onto the platter that was used to oil the vegetables. Serve at once.

Wrapping to Seal In Juices

When moist vegetables are enclosed in wrappers before grilling, the heat of the coals turns their juices into steam that cooks them through to perfect succulence. Furthermore, wrappers keep their contents piping hot for 10 minutes or even longer, thus simplifying the timing of an outdoor meal.

Only corn comes with its own wrapping material—its fibrous husk. The husks are drawn away so that the silk can be removed, then are pulled back into place. Soaking the reassembled ears in water ensures that they are amply moistened for steaming.

For other vegetables, heavy-duty aluminum foil can be shaped into sturdy packets, as in the bottom demonstration here. Wrapped in this manner, any vegetable—tough carrots or cabbage as well as tender squashes and mushrooms—can be safely steamed.

The vegetables should be prepared for eating: peeled, cored, shelled or stemmed according to their type, and sliced, cut up or divided into sections as desired. Whole potatoes in their jackets should be pierced or scored around the middle to prevent them from bursting.

If a single kind of vegetable is packeted on its own, all the pieces must be of similar size so that they steam at the same rate. When cooked in combination, tougher kinds should be cut into smaller pieces than tender kinds—and the tough ones placed at the bottom of the packet where the temperature will be highest.

Juicy vegetables such as squashes supply all the moisture required for steaming; drier kinds should be dipped in water before wrapping. A chunk of butter will provide enrichment. Adding a few drops of stock, citrus juice, vinegar or wine will supply flavor as well as moisture; possible embellishments include grated cheese, bits of lightly sautéed bacon or fresh or dried herbs.

Although the sizes of the packets can be adjusted to yield individual servings or a platterful, they must always be kept small and light enough to be handled with ease. Two layers of foil are essential to make the packets strong, and double folds seal their edges tightly.

Corn Encased in Its Own Husks

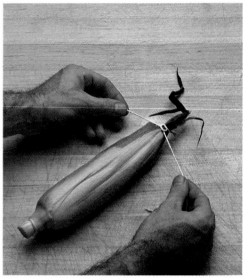

1 **Readying corn.** One section at a time, carefully peel back—but do not remove—the husk of each ear of corn. Pull off the threadlike silk inside.

2 **Tying the ears.** Return each section of husk to its original position, and secure the husk by tying a string around the tip of the ear. Soak the ears in cold water for 10 minutes; then drain but do not dry them.

Mixed Vegetables Steamed in Foil

1 **Preparing vegetables.** Cut out the core of a cauliflower and cut or break the head into small florets. Cut broccoli stems lengthwise from the bottom upward, and then pull away florets by hand. Peel carrots and cut them into ¼-inch [6-mm.] strips. Trim the ends of zucchini and yellow squashes, and slice them into ½-inch [1-cm.] strips 2 inches [5 cm.] long. Halve, stem, seed and derib sweet red peppers; cut them into ¼-inch [6-mm.] strips. Halve a cabbage, core it, then shred the leaves crosswise.

3 **Grilling the corn.** Lay the ears on an oiled grill rack 4 to 6 inches [10 to 15 cm.] above medium-hot coals *(left)*. Turning the ears often, grill them until the husks are deep brown—about 15 minutes. Remove the corn from the fire; discard the string, open the husks and butter the kernels. Reclose the husks to melt the butter and keep the corn warm.

2 **Assembling a packet.** Dip the vegetables in water to moisten them. Place them on a long, doubled sheet of heavy-duty foil, with the carrots, cabbage and cauliflower on the bottom, the other vegetables on top. Add herb sprigs—here, oregano—and a chunk of butter. Season to taste.

3 **Grilling the packets.** To seal each packet, draw the two sides together, fold them over ½ inch [1 cm.] from the top edge, then fold them again to enclose the edge. Make similar double folds at the ends of the packets. Then place them on a rack 4 to 6 inches [10 to 15 cm.] above medium-hot coals.

4 **Serving the vegetables.** Steam the vegetables for 10 minutes, or until they yield to pressure when squeezed gently with tongs. Do not open or prick the packets, lest the steam escape. To serve, unfold each packet carefully, guarding against the steam, and turn the contents out onto a dish.

23

2
Meats
Matching the Cut to the Method

Nothing so epitomizes the pleasures of cooking outdoors as the preparation of meats, their juices sizzling and their aromas blending with the scent of smoke in a medley of appeals to the senses. Proper results start with matching the meat you are using—whether beef, veal, lamb or pork—to a suitable cooking method: grilling, spit-roasting or smoking.

In grilling, meat is exposed one surface at a time to direct heat ranging from 350° to 500° F. [180° to 260° C.]. These high temperatures dictate that the cut should be thick enough to resist drying, but not so thick that it blackens by the time it cooks through: Anywhere from 1 to 3 inches [2½ to 8 cm.] will do. To brown evenly on a rack, the meat also should be reasonably flat—a qualification that makes steaks and chops unmistakable candidates for grilling. Less obvious choices, but as suitable, are small boneless loins and boned legs of lamb or fresh ham. And cuts of every description become appropriate when reduced to small pieces for skewering or when ground for hamburgers or sausages.

By contrast, large roasts including those with irregular shapes are the best choices for spit-roasting. The heat is indirect and its temperature is only about 250° to 300° F. [120° to 150° C.]; the constant turning of the spit exposes the meat evenly to the coals. The lowest heat is found in a charcoal-water smoker, where the temperature fluctuates from 180° to 220° F. [85° to 110° C.] to cook meats gently while the moisture rising from the water pan above the coals mingles with the smoke to tenderize tough cuts. Meat of any size or shape can be finished by smoking.

The diversity of cooking temperatures is mirrored in the time each method requires. A 1-inch [2½-cm.] pork chop can be grilled to perfection in 15 minutes but requires three to four hours of smoking. In grilling, where every minute counts, the initial temperature of the meat becomes important too. In order to heat quickly and cook evenly, the meat should be removed from the refrigerator and allowed to stand at room temperature for an hour or so before it is set over coals. Regardless of method, frozen meats must first be defrosted thoroughly in the refrigerator: a process that requires about five hours for each pound [½ kg.] of meat.

In the demonstrations on the following pages, the timings suggested are minimal, on the theory that you can cook meat longer if the first tests indicate that it has not reached the right degree of doneness.

Long-handled tongs are used to turn one of four thick loin lamb chops—each with its apron wrapped around a halved kidney—that are grilling over hot coals (pages 28-29). After being seared quickly on both their flat sides and curved edges, the chops will be cooked through more slowly at lower heat, achieved by shifting the meat to the edge of the rack, raising the rack or closing the vents of the grill.

A Two-Stage Strategy for Steak

The paradigm of grilled meats is beef steak, crisp and mahogany-colored outside but juicy and pink within. Achieving that effect takes practice, but the two-stage method demonstrated here is basic: First the steak is seared over intense heat to firm its surfaces, then it is cooked to doneness over reduced heat.

The tenderest steaks come from premium cuts—ribs, tenderloin, top loin, T-bone, porterhouse and sirloin. However, less expensive top-round, rump and flank steaks also are suitable candidates for the grill, providing they have been tenderized in a marinade *(pages 10-11)*.

With any cut, the best beef is fine-textured and streaked with internal fat, or marbling, that melts during grilling to keep the meat moist. To cook through without drying and toughening or becoming charred, the steak must be at least 1 inch [2½ cm.] thick, but no more than 3 inches [8 cm.].

The border of fat on most steaks protects the edges, but may cause flare-ups in the firebox unless trimmed to about ¼ to ½ inch [6 mm. to 1 cm.]. Even then the fat will cook faster than the meat and shrink in the process, thus making steaks buckle if they are less than 2 inches [5 cm.] thick. To prevent this, nick the border at ¾-inch [2-cm.] intervals.

A porterhouse such as the one shown here contains sections of tenderloin and top loin at either side of the bone. To keep the tenderloin juicy, ask the butcher to leave on the long tail, or strip of meat, at the steak's narrow end. Wrap the tail around the tenderloin and attach it with picks. To prevent sticking, grease the rack with scraps of steak fat or a piece of fatback or bacon and—unless the meat has marinated—oil the steak itself.

Grilling time depends on the thickness of the steak and the degree of doneness desired. Including searing, which should take no more than five or six minutes in all, allow eight to 10 minutes for each inch of thickness to produce rare steak, about 12 minutes for medium steak and 15 minutes for well done. Before removing the steak from the grill, test for doneness by pressing the surface with the back of a fork or tongs to feel its resilience *(Step 6)*, or make a small cut alongside the bone to check for color.

1 Trimming the steak. Place the steak—here, a porterhouse 2½ inches [6 cm.] thick—on a cutting board. With a sharp knife, slice off the excess fat from the edges, leaving a border about ¼ to ½ inch [6 mm. to 1 cm.] wide. If there is a large deposit of solid fat between the tenderloin and the tail, cut it out. Reserve the pieces of fat.

2 Seasoning the steak. Spread a few drops of oil on both sides of the steak, then sprinkle them with salt and freshly ground pepper, and rub the seasonings into the flesh with your hand. Wrap the tail of the steak around the tenderloin and secure it with two or three wooden picks that have been soaked in water for 10 minutes.

6 Cooking the steak. Move the steak to one side, where the heat will be less intense, or reduce the heat by closing the grill vents or by raising the rack 1 or 2 inches [2½ or 5 cm.]. Grill the steak until it is done to your taste, turning it once midway through the cooking. Test for doneness by pressing the back of a fork against the meat. If it is soft, the meat is rare; if springy, it is medium; if stiff, it is well done.

7 Removing the bone. Transfer the steak to a carving board and let it rest for 10 minutes. Pull out the wooden picks, then cut off the tail. Steadying the steak with the back of the fork, cut around one side of the T-shaped bone to free the tenderloin and around the other side of the bone to free the top-loin section.

3 **Greasing the grill.** About five minutes before you plan to grill the steak, set the rack 4 to 6 inches [10 to 15 cm.] above the hot coals to preheat it. Grip a piece of reserved fat in long-handled tongs and push the fat along the wires of the hot rack to grease it. Work quickly, lest fat drip into the coals and cause the fire to flare up.

4 **Searing the steak.** Place the steak on the center of the rack where the fire is hottest, and sear the steak for a minute or two. When small red beads of juice appear on the top surface, turn the steak over and sear the second side for about a minute until juices rise to the top again.

5 **Searing the fat.** Using the tongs to hold the steak upright, stand it on edge and sear the fat for a minute to brown it. Turn the steak and sear the fat bordering the opposite edge.

8 **Slicing the steak.** Cut across the grain to carve the top loin, the tail and the tenderloin, section by section, into slices ¼ inch [6 mm.] thick *(above)*. Overlapping them slightly, arrange the slices in separate rows so that every diner can take some of each kind of meat. Garnish with sprigs of fresh watercress and serve at once *(right)*.

Wrapping a Lamb Chop in Its Apron

Like beef steaks, lamb and pork chops reach perfect succulence if grilled in two stages—fast searing and slow cooking. To ensure that the chops will stay juicy inside, they ought to be no less than 1 inch [2½ cm.] but no more than 3 inches [8 cm.] thick.

With both lamb and pork, the best candidates for grilling are tender rib and loin chops. Steeping them in an oil-based marinade *(pages 10-11)* will enrich their taste and lubricate their surfaces. Less costly blade chops should be marinated in an acidic mixture to tenderize them as well. Chops that are not marinated should be rubbed with oil.

Loin lamb chops such as those in this demonstration can be further safeguarded and flavored if the butcher leaves the tails, or aprons, of flank meat attached. Each apron can then be wrapped around the loin to protect it from overcooking, and the space between the apron and the loin can be filled with mushroom caps, blanched pieces of bacon or salt pork, or the lamb kidneys shown here.

To eliminate the risk of fires from dripping fat, the borders of fat around the chops should be cut back to about ¼ inch [6 mm.]. In the case of loin lamb chops, the aprons also need trimming.

Lamb chops can be grilled to any degree of doneness you like. Allow eight to 10 minutes of total searing and cooking time for each inch of thickness—about 12 minutes an inch for medium and 15 minutes an inch for well done. Pork chops, on the other hand, must always be cooked until well done. Including searing time, grill them for at least 15 minutes an inch.

As with beef, you can test lamb for doneness by pressing it with the back of a fork or tongs. The meat will feel slightly soft at the rare state, slightly firm at medium, very firm at well done. Pork chops should be tested by inserting the tip of a knife near a bone to check the color of the meat: It will appear creamy white when the pork is done.

Grilled vegetables make perfect accompaniments for chops. In this demonstration, cherry tomatoes and mushroom caps, well oiled to keep them from drying out, share the space on the rack with the chops during the last minutes of grilling.

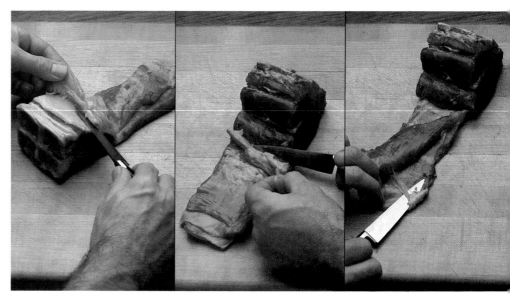

1 **Trimming a chop.** With a knife, loosen the layer of fat surrounding the chop—here, a loin lamb chop 2½ inches [6 cm.] thick—and use your fingers to pull the fat away, leaving a border only ⅛ to ¼ inch [3 to 6 mm.] thick *(above, left)*. Turn the chop over and cut out the wedge of fat lodged between the loin and the apron *(center)*. Cut into the apron, separate the layers of lean from fat, and remove the fat *(right)* and reserve it.

5 **Marinating the chops.** Place the chops in the dish with the marinade and rub their surfaces with the mixture. Set the chops aside at room temperature for up to two hours, periodically turning them over and brushing them with the marinade. At the last minute, rub salt and pepper into both sides of each chop.

6 **Searing the chops.** Set the rack 4 to 6 inches [10 to 15 cm.] above hot coals and grease it with pieces of fat *(page 27, Step 3)*. Place the chops on the center of the rack and sear them for one or two minutes on each flat side. Stand each chop on edge and sear the apron surfaces, rolling the chop to crisp it all around.

2 **Preparing a lamb kidney.** Make a slit about ⅛ inch [3 mm.] deep along the rounded side of a kidney to split the membrane. Pull the membrane away, then cut through the rounded side to open the kidney out into a butterfly-like shape. With the tip of the knife, remove the fatty core of the kidney.

3 **Stuffing a chop.** In a flat dish, prepare a marinade—here, finely chopped rosemary, spearmint and parsley leaves combined with a little olive oil. Rub the marinade over all of the surfaces of the loin and apron. Stand the chop on its edge and place an opened kidney, cut side down, at the juncture of the loin and apron.

4 **Securing the kidney.** Pull the apron tightly around the kidney and the loin, and fasten it with a skewer—in this case, a bamboo skewer that has been soaked in water for 10 minutes to prevent it from burning on the grill. Push the skewer into the end of the apron, through the loin and kidney, and out the base of the apron.

7 **Serving.** Move the chops to the side of the rack, or reduce the heat by closing the grill vents or by raising the rack 1 or 2 inches [2½ or 5 cm.]. Grill the chops until done to your taste, turning them once. Meanwhile, skewer oiled cherry tomatoes and mushroom caps *(above)* and grill them for five minutes, or until delicately browned. Arrange the chops and vegetables on a platter, and garnish with watercress *(right)*.

Ensuring Juiciness in a Boneless Loin

Pork and lamb loins and beef tender-loins yield boneless roasts that are small enough in diameter—usually from 2 to 3 inches [5 to 8 cm.]—to be grilled flat on a rack like steaks or chops. Because such roasts are made up of solid lean meat, they are easily carved for serving and the slices can be made generously broad by merely holding the knife at an angle and cutting the meat diagonally across the grain as demonstrated in Step 6.

The number of servings depends on the length of the roast and the thickness of the slices. The pork roast shown here consists of a whole center loin plus a section of sïrloin: It measures nearly 12 inches [30 cm.] from end to end and yields three dozen ⅓-inch [8-mm.] slices. A whole beef tenderloin can range from 10 to 14 inches [25 to 35 cm.]; a similarly long lamb roast can be made by leaving part of the rib section attached to the loin.

Butchers can supply the roasts already trimmed for grilling, but preparing them yourself may save you money. The beef only needs to be ridded of its fatty covering and the membrane, or silver skin, that runs the length of the tenderloin. A pork or lamb roast is boned by cutting down the inside edge of the ribs along the length of the loin, then across the chine bone to free the meat. After that, the fat is trimmed down.

Loins and tenderloins all should be oil-coated ahead of time. To introduce flavor as well as lubrication, the roasts can be marinated in an oil-based blend of seasonings such as the orange peel, ginger, garlic and sage used here.

As with steaks, boneless roasts are first seared, then cooked. The fat bordering loins will baste the meat during grilling; tenderloins should be basted regularly with plain or flavored oil. Figure a total grilling time of eight to 10 minutes per inch [2½ cm.] if you like beef or lamb rare, 12 minutes if you prefer it medium and about 15 minutes for well-done meat. The pork requires 15 minutes per inch to reach a safe internal temperature of 165° to 170° F. [75° C.]. After they are grilled, the roasts should be allowed to rest for about 10 minutes—a process that firms the meat and helps preserve its juices when it is carved.

1 **Trimming the loin.** With a sharp knife and your fingers, remove all but a ¼-inch [6-mm.] layer of fat from a boned loin. Use the knife to cut into the fatty border parallel to its top surface and pull away the fat and membrane strip by strip. Reserve the fat.

2 **Rubbing with marinade.** In a shallow dish, prepare a marinade— here, grated orange peel, chopped garlic and fresh ginger, and a bit of sage leaves are combined with just enough olive oil to bind the mixture into a soft paste. Place the loin in the dish and rub the marinade into all its surfaces. Set the meat aside for up to two hours.

4 **Grilling the loin.** Move the loin to the side of the rack, or reduce the heat by closing the grill vents or by raising the rack 1 or 2 inches [2½ or 5 cm.]. Grill the loin for about 20 minutes, turning it after 10 minutes. The loin is done if the juices run clear when a skewer is inserted into it or a meat thermometer registers 165° to 170° F. [75° C.].

5 **Grilling potatoes.** During the last minutes of cooking, push the loin aside to make room for skewered parboiled potatoes *(page 18)*. Turning them often, grill the potatoes for about three minutes or until the skins are crisp. Move the potatoes to the edge of the grill to keep them warm. Transfer the loin to a carving board and let it rest for 10 minutes.

3 **Searing the loin.** Use the reserved fat to grease a preheated grill rack set 4 to 6 inches [10 to 15 cm.] above hot coals. Place the loin in the center of the rack and sear it for about two minutes on each of its four long sides. Use the tongs to scrape off charred bits of marinade seasonings, lest they give the meat a burned taste.

6 **Serving.** Holding the knife at an angle, slice the loin crosswise into slices about ⅓ inch [8 mm.] thick. Arrange the slices on a serving platter. Push the potatoes off the skewers and place them around the sliced pork; garnish with watercress. Serve the pork accompanied, if you like, by olive-and-anchovy compound butter (recipe, page 165).

Butterflied Lamb with a Minty Fragrance

When boned and butterflied, a leg of lamb or a fresh ham forms a thick slab of solid meat that grills evenly with delectable results. Because the boneless meat is so easy to carve, no morsel is wasted by being inaccessible.

You can, of course, ask the butcher to bone and butterfly the leg. However, preparing the meat for yourself ensures that it will be as nearly uniform in thickness as possible. All you need is a sharp knife, patience and a little understanding of the leg's structure. The leg contains three bones: the large pelvic bone in the broad sirloin or butt section, the leg bone in the tapered middle section and the small hindshank bone in the narrow shank section. Each bone is removed in turn, from the largest to the smallest. During the process, the leg is slit open so that it can be spread out into a butterfly shape. The thicker parts are then split and folded outward to equalize the thickness of the meat.

Boning a leg sacrifices some of its natural juiciness, but the loss is readily balanced by marinating the meat. Here the butterflied leg of lamb is steeped in a tangy combination of yogurt—an acidic tenderizer—olive oil, mint and garlic (recipe, page 162). Wine or cider might replace the yogurt, and any desired aromatic herbs and vegetables could be substituted for the mint and garlic.

Depending on its thickness, which can range from 2 to 3 inches [5 to 8 cm.], a butterflied leg of lamb will need 20 to 30 minutes of grilling time if you want the meat rare, 25 to 35 minutes for medium and up to 45 minutes for well done. Like other cuts of pork, a butterflied fresh ham should be grilled until it is thoroughly cooked—about 45 minutes. The meat will be done when its internal temperature registers 165° to 170° F. [75° C.] on a meat thermometer.

1 Loosening the pelvic bone. Place the leg—in this case, lamb—on a cutting board, and with a sharp knife cut around the exposed edges of the pelvic bone that are visible at the sirloin end of the leg. Gradually work the knife deeper into the flesh, following the contours of the bone.

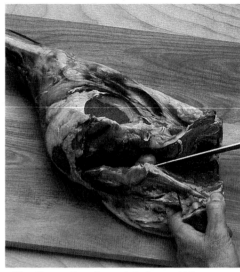

2 Removing the pelvic bone. When you have penetrated as far as the ball-and-socket joint between the pelvic bone and leg bone, sever the ligaments that connect the joint. Then grasp the pelvic bone and pull it out.

6 Marinating the meat. Prepare a marinade—here, yogurt and a few spoonfuls of olive oil flavored with chopped mint and garlic and freshly ground pepper—and rub it onto the surfaces of the lamb. Marinate at room temperature for up to two hours. At the last minute wipe off the excess marinade with a paper towel.

7 Searing the lamb. Place the lamb on the center of a greased grill rack set 4 to 6 inches [10 to 15 cm.] above hot coals, and sear it for one or two minutes on each side. Move the lamb to the side of the rack, where the heat is less intense. Turning it once, grill the lamb until it reaches the desired doneness.

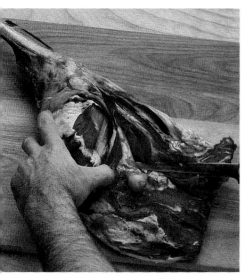

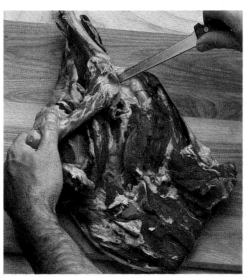

3 **Loosening the leg bone.** Slice the leg open lengthwise along the center, cutting from the sirloin end toward the shank end, to expose the leg bone. Cut the flesh away from the leg bone.

4 **Removing the leg bone.** Cut around the joint between the leg and hindshank bones to expose it. With one hand, hold the loosened end of the leg bone steady. Then sever the ligaments at the joint and lift out the leg bone. Cut around the hindshank bone and pull it free.

5 **Butterflying the meat.** Spread the leg flat. Cut out the membranes and tendons and discard them. Slice horizontally into—but not completely through—the thick section of flesh at one side of the leg and open out the resulting flap as if turning over the page of a book. Then slice and open out the opposite side similarly.

8 **Serving the lamb.** Transfer the lamb to a carving board and let it rest for 10 minutes. Meanwhile, make a garnish—in this case, a cucumber sauce *(recipe, page 166)*. Carve the lamb crosswise to separate the sirloin, round and shank sections. Cut each section across the grain into slices ¼ inch [6 mm.] thick.

A Trio of Techniques for Kebabs

When you want meat to cut into pieces for skewering, as demonstrated here, you can take your pick of beef, veal, lamb or pork. Virtually any cut—from rib and sirloin to shoulder and chuck—can be boned and trimmed of fat, membranes and connective tissue to yield lean meat. And initial tenderness need not matter, since an acidic marinade (pages 10-11) will soften tough meat fibers.

For kebabs, pieces should be roughly equal in size, whether they are shaped as cubes or as bars. Dimensions can vary from 1 to 2½ inches [2½ to 6 cm.]: small enough to grill quickly, but large enough to hold in the meat's juices. To brown and cook evenly on all four sides, kebabs should be grilled over medium-hot coals and turned and basted with regularity.

If the meat is interspersed on the skewers with vegetables, as shown at right, firm types of vegetables should be parboiled briefly to ensure that they will be fully cooked when the meat is done. Here, pieces of parboiled onion, sweet pepper,

yellow squash and zucchini are used; parboiled pearl onions or cucumber chunks or raw scallions, mushroom caps or cherry tomatoes could replace them.

In the demonstration below, the meat pieces are alternated with bay leaves and bread cubes as well as bacon cubes, which help baste the kebabs as they cook. Salt pork or fresh pork belly could be used instead of bacon, but would not lend as much flavor to the assembly.

For quicker effects, meat also can be cut into thin strips as shown bottom right. Threaded lengthwise onto skewers, these strips will cook through in a few minutes over hot coals and do not require basting.

Skewered meats can be cooked on any grill—even a small hibachi such as the one shown here. Kebabs of beef and lamb will require about eight to 10 minutes per inch of thickness for rare meat, 12 minutes for medium, 15 minutes for well-done. Pork or veal kebabs need 15 minutes per inch to become safely well done.

Vegetables to Add Color

1 **Preparing meat.** Remove the fat and membranes from the meat—here, pork loin. Slice the meat 1½ inches [4 cm.] thick and cut the slices into bars 2 inches [5 cm.] long and 1½ inches wide. In a shallow dish, assemble grated lemon peel, paprika and olive oil. Rub the meat with this marinade and let it stand for up to two hours.

Bacon and Cubed Bread for Textural Contrast

1 **Skewering.** Slice trimmed pork loin 1 inch [2½ cm.] thick, and cut it into bars 1½ inches [4 cm.] long and 1 inch wide. Cut rye bread and slab bacon into ½-inch [1-cm.] cubes. Marinate the meats in olive oil, rosemary and pepper. Thread the meats and bread onto skewers alternately with bay leaves that have soaked in water for 10 minutes.

2 **Grilling.** Season the kebabs, then dribble olive oil over them to moisten the surfaces. Place the skewers on an oiled rack 4 to 6 inches [10 to 15 cm.] above medium-hot coals. Turning them often, grill the kebabs until the meat is done and the bacon crisped.

3 **Serving.** Place the kebabs on a serving platter and remove the meats, bread cubes and bay leaves from the skewers (Step 4, above). Here the platter is lined with shredded lettuce leaves and garnished with lemon wedges.

2 **Assembling.** Slice yellow squash and zucchini ⅓ inch [8 mm.] thick and cut red pepper into 1½-inch [4-cm.] squares; parboil them for one minute. Cut an onion into six wedges and parboil for two minutes. In a bowl, toss the vegetables with olive oil, thyme and seasonings. Thread the pork and vegetables alternately onto skewers.

3 **Grilling.** Lay the skewered meat and vegetables on the oiled rack of a grill—in this case, a hibachi—and cook them 4 to 6 inches [10 to 15 cm.] above medium-hot coals. Turning the skewers frequently and basting the kebabs with the remaining marinade, grill them until the meat is a rich brown color and done to your taste.

4 **Serving.** Place the kebabs on a platter. Grasp the handle of each skewer with a cloth napkin and use the back of a fork to push the meat and vegetables off the skewer, a few pieces at a time. Accompany the kebabs, if you like, with a sauce of chopped tomatoes and yogurt, garnished with sprigs of fresh dill.

A Spicy Marinade for Slender Strips

1 **Preparing the meat.** Trim pork sirloin by first removing the fatty border. Trim away the remaining fat and membranes. Place the trimmed meat in the freezer for 20 minutes to firm it and make it easier to slice thin. Cut the meat across the grain into slices ⅛ inch [3 mm.] thick. Cut the slices into strips about 1 inch [2½ cm.] wide.

2 **Threading the strips.** Soak small wooden skewers in water for 10 minutes. Insert each skewer into one end of a pork strip and push the skewer through the meat, threading it in and out at ½-inch [1-cm.] intervals. Roll the strips in soy-sauce marinade (recipe, page 162) to coat them evenly, then marinate them for up to two hours.

3 **Grilling.** Place the skewers on an oiled rack 4 to 6 inches [10 to 15 cm.] above hot coals. Turning them once, grill the strips until evenly browned—about two minutes. Arrange the skewers on a platter. Here they radiate from a mound of sliced red onions that have soaked for an hour in lemon juice; lime wedges provide a garnish.

Grinding Meat for the Freshest Hamburgers

Few meats are as popular as hamburgers—and for excellent reasons. Ground meat is easy to prepare, quick to cook, and congenial with endlessly varied garnishes. Beef is classic, but lamb, veal or pork can be substituted or mixed together with the beef. You can be lavish and choose premium cuts—or be more frugal with cuts such as the beef sirloin tip shown in this demonstration. Because grinding meat tenderizes it, less expensive cuts make excellent hamburgers.

If you use a lean cut, you may need to add suet, or beef kidney fat. Fat protects the meat from the drying heat of the grill, and one part fat to four parts lean is just right for producing hamburgers that are pleasantly moist without being greasy.

Hamburgers should be about 1 inch [2½ cm.] thick to cook through without charring. Their diameter will depend to some extent on how you plan to cook them. If grilled on a rack, hamburgers can be 2 to 4 inches [5 to 10 cm.] across—providing they are not much wider than the blade of the spatula used to turn them. If grilled in a hinged basket, the patties can be as diminutive as 1 inch.

Any conventional grill can be used for cooking hamburgers, and—as the demonstration opposite, top shows—so can a fireplace. All you need to do is to stack two parallel columns of bricks on the hearth at right angles to the firebox and set a rack or basket grill between them. Build the columns 7 or 8 inches [18 or 20 cm.] high so that the rack or grill will be 4 to 6 inches [10 to 15 cm.] above the heat when you rake out coals from the fire to do the cooking.

On a rack, the hamburgers are too fragile to be turned until the undersides are browned and firmed. For this reason, they are not separately seared but instead are cooked through over medium-hot coals—and turned only once. Grill them for four or five minutes on the first side, then for about five minutes on the second side if you want the meat rare, seven minutes for medium and 10 minutes for well-done.

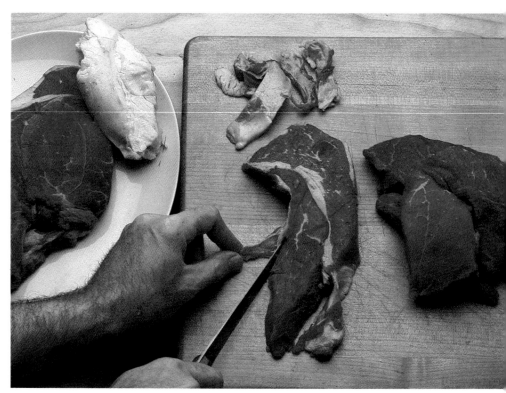

1 **Trimming the meat.** With a sharp knife, trim all fat from meat—here, beef sirloin tip. Reserve the fat. Trim off and discard all membranes and connective tissue. Cut the meat into strips that will be easy to feed into a grinder: Chop the beef fat and the suet, if you are using it, into chunks.

2 **Grinding the meat and fat.** Attach a medium disk to a food grinder, and set a plate in front of the disk. Turning the handle of the grinder slowly but steadily, feed the strips of meat into the bowl of the grinder alternately with the chunks of fat and suet.

3 **Forming patties.** Transfer the meat to a mixing bowl, season it with salt and pepper and toss it lightly. For each patty, shape a handful of the meat into a thick disk. Flatten the top and bottom surfaces, then even the edges by rotating the patty between two cupped hands.

Grilling at the Hearth

1 **Preparing the fire.** Build two columns of bricks on the hearth in front of a fireplace. Rake out enough coals to form a layer about 2 inches [5 cm.] deep between the bricks. Prepare hamburgers (*Steps 1-3, left*) and place them side by side in an oiled hinged grill basket. Cover the grill with its lid, clamp the handle and set the grill—basket side down—on the bricks.

2 **Grilling the hamburgers.** Cook the hamburgers for about five minutes, or until the undersides brown. Then turn the grill over and brown the hamburgers for five to 10 minutes longer, until they are done to your taste. To serve, turn the grill with its basket side upward, undo the clamp and lift up the basket. Slide the hamburgers off the lid onto a platter

4 **Grilling.** With a long-handled, broad spatula, slide one patty at a time onto an oiled rack 4 to 6 inches [10 to 15 cm.] above medium-hot coals. Grill the hamburgers until they are brown on the underside and the spatula slips easily beneath them—about five minutes. Turn them over and grill for five to 10 minutes more.

5 **Serving.** Arrange the hamburgers on a platter and present them with garnishes. Here, grilled tomato slices (*pages 20-21*) are placed around the platter and parsley sprigs are used as decoration. Each hamburger is topped with spoonfuls of avocado sauce and raw vegetable relish (*recpes, pages 165 and 164*).

Sausage Spirals Crisped in a Basket

From mild frankfurters to spicy *chorizos*, sausages are never better than when grilled. The dry heat of the coals crisps and browns the casing, which keeps the meat inside it soft and moist.

To suit your own taste to a T, you can buy sausage casing from a butcher and stuff it with the kind of meat you choose, flavored as you like. In this demonstration, pork is spiked with sage and garlic *(recipe, page 167)*.

For pork or veal sausages, which need long cooking, the stuffing should contain 35 to 45 per cent fat. For beef or lamb, a fat content of 25 per cent is ample. You can add fatback or suet to lean meat—or combine a fatty cut with a lean one.

Before grilling, prick all sausages lest they burst when their moisture turns to steam. They then can be laid on the grill rack, impaled on skewers or enclosed in a hinged grill basket. Allow 15 minutes per inch [2½ cm.] of thickness for pork or veal sausages, 10 minutes for others. Precooked kinds, including frankfurters, need only five minutes to heat through.

1 Grinding the meat. Cut meat—here, pork shoulder and loin—into manageable strips. Leave the fat intact, but remove and discard membranes and connective tissue. Attach a medium disk to a food grinder and drop the strips of meat into the grinder one by one. For a smooth texture, grind the meat a second time.

2 Adding flavorings. Transfer the meat to a large bowl, and season it with salt and pepper. Chop and add garlic and fresh sage leaves. Mix the ingredients well. Fry a spoonful of the stuffing mixture until all traces of pink disappear—about three minutes. Taste the cooked mixture, and correct the seasoning of the raw stuffing.

A Sausage Chain

Forming links. With your hands, roll the sausage on a table to distribute the filling evenly. Form links by twisting the sausage at regular intervals, here every 4 inches [10 cm.]. To prevent unwinding, twist successive links in opposite directions.

6 Making sausage spirals. Roll the sausages on a work surface to smooth them. Coil the sausages into tight spirals. Place them in the basket section of an oiled hinged grill or—if you prefer to cook the sausages on the grill rack—secure each spiral by inserting a skewer horizontally across it. Then, with a skewer or knife tip, prick each sausage in several places.

7 Grilling the sausages. Cover the grill basket with its lid, and clamp the handle tightly. Place the basket on a rack 4 to 6 inches [10 to 15 cm.] above medium-hot coals and cook for eight to 10 minutes on each side, or until the sausages are golden brown.

3 **Preparing casing.** Soak sausage casing—here, hog—in a bowl of tepid acidulated water until the casing becomes soft and elastic—about 30 minutes. Using a funnel, run cold tap water into each piece of casing to rinse and open it. Examine the casing for holes; if you find any, cut out the torn segments and discard them.

4 **Attaching the casing.** Slide one end of casing—here a 6-foot [180-cm.] length—onto the tube of the sausage-stuffing attachment of a food grinder. Gather the casing over the tube until only the final 6 inches [15 cm.] hang free. Make a knot in the casing about 3 inches [8 cm.] from the end.

5 **Filling the casing.** Press the stuffing into the grinder bowl a handful at a time and turn the handle at a steady pace. Smooth the casing as it fills. When the sausage is about 30 inches [75 cm.] long, pull 6 inches [15 cm.] of empty casing from the tube, cut it in the middle and knot it. Tie off the remaining casing and stuff a second sausage.

8 **Serving the sausages.** Turn the grill over so that the lid is on the bottom, unclamp the handle and lift the basket section away. Slide the sausages from the lid onto a cutting board. Slice across the spiral of each sausage at 1-inch [2½-cm.] intervals; then slice it at right angles to the first cuts, to produce bite-sized pieces. Serve the sausages accompanied by wedges of fresh lime.

Barbecued Spareribs with a Crunchy Glaze

Glazed with a tangy sauce, spareribs are the quintessential finger food and welcome as either an hors d'oeuvre or a main course for dinner outdoors. Although ribs are easiest to eat when cut into individual pieces, their meat will be juiciest if the rack, or side, is kept intact for cooking. Even so, the layer of meat is thin and will tend to become dry and stringy unless the rack is cooked slowly over relatively gentle heat.

A rack of spareribs can be grilled safely, but this method requires constant attention to prevent the meat and sauce from burning. A simpler approach is to thread the rack onto the spit of a rotisserie and roast it as demonstrated here.

Because fat is the bane of spareribs, the first step in preparing them is to trim off the excess surface fat and membrane. For grilling, the spareribs then should be parboiled for 10 minutes or so. For roasting, they can be threaded onto the spit immediately. In either case, though, marinating the rack for up to two hours will give the ribs extra tang.

Grilling or roasting will draw out the internal fat from the spareribs, so they must always be cooked over a drip pan. To ensure ribs that are crisp, not greasy, the rack must be grilled or roasted for 20 minutes or so before basting begins. Here the ribs are glazed with tomato barbecue sauce (demonstration, pages 12-13; recipe, page 163), but leftover marinade or other sauce mixtures (recipes, pages 159-161) could be used instead. To coat the ribs well, the sauce or marinade should be applied generously and frequently.

Like all pork, spareribs must be cooked thoroughly. Depending on the size of the ribs, allow 35 to 45 minutes for grilling, 50 to 70 minutes for roasting. To test for doneness, prick the meat with a skewer or the tip of a knife. When the juices run clear, the spareribs are ready to serve.

1 **Trimming the spareribs.** Place the rack of ribs with its meaty side up on a cutting board. Using a sharp knife, trim away excess surface fat and as much of the thick, whitish connective tissue as possible without cutting into the flesh.

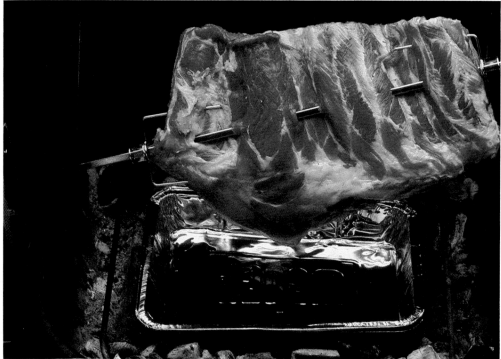

4 **Securing the spit.** With long-handled tongs, push the hot coals from the center of the firebox (pages 8-9). Set a drip pan in the cleared space. Place the tip of the spit into the receptacle on the motor and set the handle in its bracket. Turn on the rotisserie.

5 **Roasting.** Let the spareribs roast for 20 minutes, then use a long-handled brush to baste them on both sides with barbecue sauce. When the coating of sauce has dried—after about 10 minutes—baste the rack again. Continue to baste the spareribs at 10-minute intervals for 30 to 45 minutes, or until they no longer exude fat, the surfaces look crisp and the juices run clear when the meat is pricked.

2 **Removing the membrane.** Turn the rack over and use your fingers to loosen the sheet of thin, papery membrane that covers the bones. Pull off the membrane and discard it.

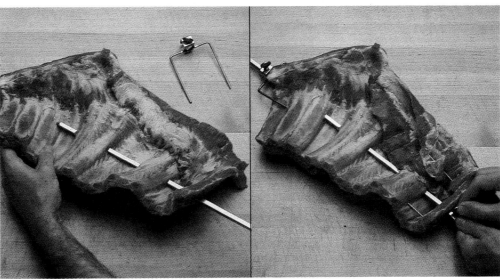

3 **Spitting.** Slide a holding fork onto the spit rod with the prongs pointing away from the handle. Starting near the middle of the rack at the narrow end, push the tip of the spit into the meaty side between the first and second ribs. Then push the tip into the bony side between the fourth and fifth ribs. Continue threading the rod over and under alternate pairs of ribs to the wide end of the rack (above, left). Slide the second fork onto the spit. Push the prongs of both forks into the rack, using one prong at the narrow end to secure the loose flap of meat there (right). Tighten the forks.

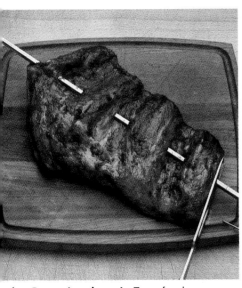

6 **Removing the spit.** Transfer the spareribs to a carving board and remove the holding fork nearest the tip of the spit. Pull out the prongs of the other holding fork, grasp the spit handle in one hand, and slip the tines of a carving fork over the spit. Pulling the handle of the spit while simultaneously pressing the spareribs with the fork tines, push the spareribs off the spit.

7 **Separating the ribs.** Slice the rack of ribs crosswise into two pieces for easy handling. Slide the carving fork's tines over the narrow end of one piece at a time and lift the piece upright. Slice down between the ribs to separate them.

8 **Serving.** Pile the ribs onto a large plate and serve them at once, garnished with fresh parsley. Accompany the ribs, if you like, with a spicy sauce such as a raw vegetable relish (demonstration, page 13; recipe, page 164).

Balancing a Leg of Lamb on a Spit

Smoke scents a large roast that is cooked gently on a spit rotating over coals. Leaving the bones in place helps to keep the meat moist and compensate for juices lost where the spit and holding-fork prongs penetrate the roast.

To rotate smoothly and thus cook evenly, the roast must be balanced well on the spit rod. With a fresh ham or a leg of lamb, shown in this demonstration, balance is achieved by cutting out the pelvic bone and inserting the spit alongside the leg and shank bones. With a rib, loin or shoulder roast of pork, lamb or beef, the spit is inserted into the side of the roast near the bones at one corner and pushed diagonally through the meat to emerge close to the opposite corner. The balance then can be checked as described in Step 6, page 44.

The fat covering the roast will melt to help baste it, but should be trimmed to about ¼ inch [6 mm.]. For flavor, the roast can be marinated in an aromatic oil (pages 10-11).

Unless the roast has been marinated, it should be liberally oiled after it is spitted. In either case, it will need frequent basting with pan drippings, leftover marinade or both to keep the meat moist and give the roast a golden glaze. Here, the drip pan holds stock, lemon wedges, garlic and rosemary—a mixture that blends with fat and juices released by the meat to create a savory basting liquid.

Roasting time varies with the kind and size of the roast, and the degree of doneness you like. Allow 15 minutes a pound [½ kg.] for rare, 20 minutes for medium and 25 minutes for well-done meat.

To be certain the roast is cooked perfectly, test its internal temperature with a meat thermometer before removing it from the spit. The temperature should reach 120° to 125° F. [50° C.] for rare beef, 135° F. [55° C.] for medium and 150° F. [65° C.] for well-done. Roast lamb to 140° F. [60° C.] for rare, 150° F. for medium and 160° F. [70° C.] for well-done. Pork must always cook to 165° to 170° F. [75° C.]; veal is properly cooked at 150° F.

After roasting, the meat should be left to rest for 10 minutes or so to facilitate carving. During this period, the meat will continue to cook and its internal temperature will rise five to 10 degrees.

1 Trimming off fat. Remove the pelvic bone from the sirloin end of a leg of lamb (page 32, Steps 1 and 2); discard it. With a small knife, trim any large chunks of fat from the inner, flatter side of the leg, but avoid cutting the flesh.

2 Peeling off fell. Turn the leg over so the rounded side faces up. Grasp the leg at the sirloin end in one hand and, with your other hand, peel back the edge of the papery fell that covers the fat. Pull the fell off at the shank end of the leg, using a small knife to free the fell where it resists. With the knife, trim the fat to a thickness of about ¼ inch [6 mm.].

6 Roasting. Push the hot coals from the center of the grill's firebox and set a drip pan in the cleared space (page 9). Pour a ½-inch [1-cm.] layer of liquid into the drip pan and add aromatics—in this case, stock is flavored with lemon wedges, garlic cloves and rosemary sprigs. Place the spitted roast over the pan and turn on the rotisserie.

7 Testing. Baste the leg at 10-minute intervals with the liquid from the drip pan until the lamb is done to your liking. To test it, insert a meat thermometer into the thickest part of the leg. Transfer the leg to a carving board. Remove the spit forks. Grasping the spit handle in one hand, press a carving fork against the sirloin end of the leg and pull the spit out. Cut off the trussing strings.

3 **Seasoning.** Slide a holding fork onto the spit rod, prongs pointing away from the spit handle. Insert the spit into the leg at the sirloin end, next to the knob of the leg bone. Carefully push the spit through the leg, parallel to the bone. Salt and pepper the exposed flesh and place rosemary sprigs and garlic cloves around the knobby bone.

4 **Inserting holding forks.** Fold the flap of flesh over the seasonings. Holding the flap in place with one hand, push the prongs of the spit fork through it into the leg. Push one of the prongs of the second spit fork into the narrow shank end of the leg parallel to the bone. Secure the forks to the spit.

5 **Trussing.** To keep the sirloin end compact during roasting, loop four or five pieces of kitchen string around the sirloin area, knotting each loop firmly and cutting off the excess string. Rub the leg with salt and pepper.

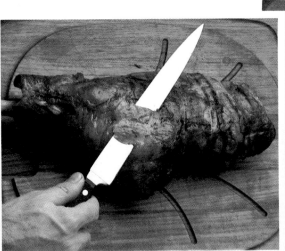

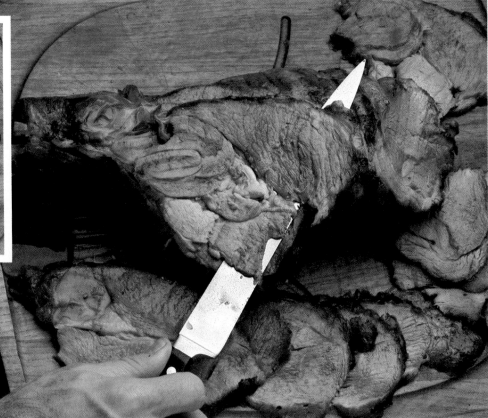

8 **Carving the leg.** Let the roast rest for 10 minutes. Then wrap a cloth towel around the shank bone and grasp it firmly as you cut thin slices from the rounded side of the leg (above). Always cut away from yourself and keep the blade of the knife nearly parallel to the bone (right). When all the meat is sliced from the first side, carve the inner, flatter side. Finally, slice the meat from the shank. Serve at once; no meat cools faster after carving than lamb.

A Self-basting Veal Roast

Because it is boneless and cylindrical, a rolled roast balances neatly on the spit rod of a rotisserie and cooks through at a steady rate. To conserve the juices of the meat and protect its surfaces from parching, the roast needs to be wrapped in a thin sheet, or bard, of fat that will baste it continuously. Thus sheathed, inexpensive cuts such as beef round or pork shoulder turn into delectable roasts with the gentle heat used in spit-roasting. Even veal, which is usually considered too lean to be cooked over coals, emerges moist and tender.

Like the boning of the roast, its rolling and barding can be left to the butcher. But there is a bonus in doing these jobs yourself: You can introduce flavorings inside the roll to make them an integral part of the roast. For barding, the roast's own fat can be peeled off in layers and pounded into a flat cohesive sheet about ¼ inch [6 mm.] thick. Or you can buy ¼-inch slices of fresh pork fatback; these too should be pounded together to form a uniform wrapping for the roast.

Before rolling the roast in the bard, marinate it—choosing an oil-and-acid mixture for tougher cuts—or oil it thoroughly and season it with salt and pepper. Here, the inside of the roast is flavored simply with a mixture of chopped fresh herbs. Other appropriate flavorings include grated lemon or orange peel, raisins, slivered garlic or anchovy fillets that have been soaked in cold water for 30 minutes to decrease their saltiness.

The timing guidelines for rolled roasts are based on weight. For rare beef or lamb, allow 15 minutes a pound [½ kg.]; for medium, 20 minutes; for well-done meat, 25 minutes. Like pork, veal is always roasted to the well-done stage; both should cook for 25 minutes a pound.

During the final hour or so of roasting time, you can make the coals of the fire do double duty by laying foil-wrapped packets of vegetables among them. Small whole beets, onions or sweet potatoes are all options, but here the choice is new potatoes and garlic bulbs. When garlic bulbs are cooked this way, the flesh of each clove becomes a mild-tasting paste that can be squeezed out of the papery skin onto a slice of meat.

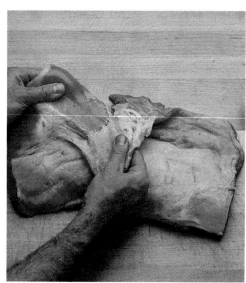

1 **Removing the fat.** Lay the boned roast—here, the loin and sirloin of veal—fatty side up on a work surface. Pull off the fat in large pieces, leaving a layer of no more than ¼ inch [6 mm.]. Use the tip of a small knife to loosen the fat where it resists, cutting parallel to the surface of the roast to avoid piercing the flesh. Set the fat aside.

2 **Flavoring.** Turn the roast over and use the knife to cut out any pieces of fat and trim off the membranes. Rub a few spoonfuls of olive oil into the roast and sprinkle it with salt and pepper. Scatter herbs over the meat—chopped fresh parsley and coriander are shown—and press them into the surface.

6 **Balancing the roast.** Slide a holding fork onto the spit rod. Push the spit lengthwise through the middle of the roast; secure the prongs of the fork in the meat. Slide the second fork onto the spit, push in its prongs and center the roast on the spit. Tighten both forks. Roll the spit across your hands. If it does not rotate smoothly, reinsert the spit.

7 **Preparing the garnishes.** Place whole garlic bulbs, one for each diner, on a large square of heavy-duty foil two layers thick. Dribble olive oil over the bulbs and season with salt and pepper. Wrap the foil around the garlic bulbs and seal the edges securely (page 23). Prepare small whole potatoes in the same manner.

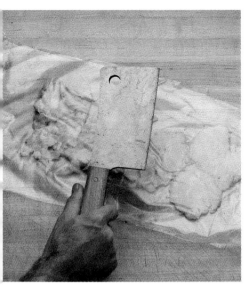

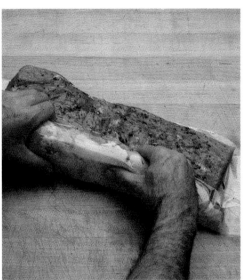

3 **Pounding the fat.** Place the reserved pieces of fat side by side on a large sheet of strong plastic wrap to form a roughly rectangular layer. Cover the fat with more plastic. Use the side of a cleaver to pound the fat until the pieces cohere and form a bard about ¼ inch [6 mm.] thick.

4 **Barding the roast.** Refrigerate the wrapped bard for 10 minutes to firm the fat slightly. Return the bard to the work surface and peel off the top piece of plastic. Center the roast meaty side up on the barding sheet and, starting at the thinnest long side of the roast, roll the fat and meat into a cylinder. Then peel off the rest of the plastic.

5 **Trussing.** Turn the cylinder seam side down. Using 10 feet [300 cm.] of kitchen string, loop one end around the narrow end of the roast and knot it. Form another loop, slide it onto the roast and pull it tight about 2 inches [5 cm.] from the first loop. Repeat at 2-inch intervals, then draw the string lengthwise under the roast and tie it to the first knot.

8 **Adding the garnishes.** Build a fire in the grill and, when the coals are covered with white ash, set a drip pan in the firebox (pages 8-9). Position the spitted roast above the pan, and turn on the motor of the rotisserie. About an hour before you expect the roast to be done, place the vegetable packets among the coals at the edge of the firebox. Roast the meat until it reaches the degree of doneness you desire.

9 **Garnishing the meat.** Transfer the roast to a carving board and remove it from the spit. Let the roast rest for 10 minutes. Cut off the trussing strings and carve the meat crosswise into ¼-inch [6-mm.] slices. Arrange the slices on a platter, surrounded by the garlic bulbs and potatoes, and garnish with watercress.

A Medley of Meats Perfumed with Smoke

In a charcoal-water smoker, the aroma of the smoldering embers penetrates meat to give it a marvelous flavor. Although charcoal is the primary fuel, most of the smoke is produced by small logs or wood chips that are placed on the coals when they have reached the white-ash stage.

The logs or chips should be of hardwood, which burns evenly and releases pleasant aromas. Such logs or chips are obtainable where firewood is sold; some of the types available are apple, beech, hickory, mesquite, oak and pecan. To keep the wood smoldering as long as the coals do, look for freshly cut green logs or chips, or soak dried ones in water for at least half an hour before adding them to the smoker. Corncobs may be substituted—their aroma resembles hickory—but do not attempt to use softwood, which would give meats a resinous taste.

The liquid in the water pan above the fire can also impart aroma as it steams if it contains flavorings such as the garlic and chilies used in this demonstration. For even richer effect, the water itself can be replaced or augmented by stock, beer, wine or citrus juice.

Because the steam rising from the water pan provides moisture that will tenderize meats, almost any cut—including sausages and such firm innards as heart or tongue—can be smoked. All you must do in advance is trim undesirable fat. You may, however, marinate the meat or coat it with sauce beforehand.

Depending on the time you want to spend, the meats can be cooked or simply flavored in the smoker. At the prevailing temperature of 200° F. [100° C.], 1-inch [2½-cm.] steaks or chops will take a minimum of three hours to cook; for larger cuts, allow an hour per pound [½ kg.].

To speed the process, either precook meats and use the smoker as a way of flavoring them, or smoke meats for two or three hours and then finish their cooking in the oven or on a spit or grill. Here, beef tongue, brisket and short ribs are poached before smoking. The rice-stuffed red peppers that accompany them cook quickly; and the sausages—mild German knockwurst and bratwurst, spicy Spanish *chorizo* and blood sausage, and garlicky Portuguese *linguiça*—require only to be heated through.

1 Preparing beef tongue. Soak a fresh beef tongue in cold water for several hours. Put it in a pan of fresh water and bring the water to a boil; skim the surface and add carrots, onions and seasonings. Simmer for one and a half hours; then let the tongue cool in the pan before draining it. Trim away fat, gristle and bone; slit the skin lengthwise and peel it off.

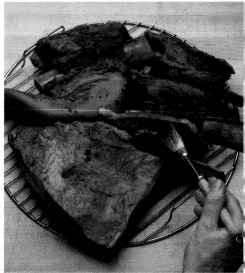

2 Saucing the meats. Immerse a beef brisket and beef short ribs in cold water and bring to a boil. Skim off the scum, reduce the heat and add aromatics and seasonings. Simmer for one and a half hours. Drain the meats and place them along with the tongue on a rack of the smoker. Brush them with *ancho* chili sauce (demonstration, page 15; recipe, page 164).

6 Inserting the water pan. Place aromatics—here, whole dried chilies and unpeeled garlic cloves—in the water pan. Still wearing a protective mitt, set the pan in the smoker.

7 Adding the water. Fill the water pan to its brim with hot water. Do not try to fill the pan before putting it into the smoker lest the water spill out onto the hot coals and extinguish the fire.

3 **Stuffing peppers.** Slice the tops off red peppers, cut out the stems and set the tops aside. Remove the ribs and seeds and fill the peppers with a stuffing—here, cooked rice, chopped scallions, salt and pepper. Set the tops on the peppers. Place the peppers on a rack together with sausages—knockwurst, bratwurst, blood sausage, *chorizo* and *linguiça* in this demonstration.

4 **Preparing the fire.** Build a small mound of charcoal in the charcoal pan of the smoker. Place an electric starter on the mound, then heap a layer of charcoal 8 inches [20 cm.] deep over the starter. When the charcoal begins to flame—in about seven minutes—unplug the starter and remove it, using a flame-resistant mitt to protect your hands.

5 **Adding the wood.** When the coals are covered with white ash—after about 20 minutes—top them with a small moistened or freshly cut log, such as the green, 1-foot [30-cm.] hickory logs shown here. Or top the coals with two handfuls of moistened wood chips.

8 **Adding the food.** Set the rack containing the tongue, brisket and short ribs on the brackets just above the water pan. Set the rack containing the stuffed peppers and the sausages on the upper brackets; place the lid on the smoker.

9 **Removing the foods.** Let the meats and peppers smoke undisturbed for three hours. Use tongs to transfer the sausages and peppers to a platter, then lift out the upper rack. Remove the lower rack from the smoker and add the short ribs to the platter.

10 **Carving the tongue.** Transfer the brisket and tongue to a cutting board. Slice the brisket crosswise and arrange the slices in a row on the platter. To slice the tongue, turn it on its side and steady it with a carving fork. Cut the tongue crosswise into thin slices. Add the slices to the platter.

3
Poultry
Dealing with Diversity

Opening out birds for tidy parcels
Basting birds whether fatty or lean
Supports for a fireplace rotisserie
How to truss birds for roasting

Every kind of poultry—from Rock Cornish game hens, chickens and capons to ducks, geese and turkeys—becomes a treat when cooked over glowing embers. So, too, do those domesticated fowl rarely found except at specialty butchers—the fledgling pigeons called squabs, and guinea hens, which are the size of small chickens but more assertive in taste. Even game birds such as quail and pheasant are suitable, providing they are young and tender.

Birds can be grilled, spit-roasted or smoked; the cooking method dictates the appropriate type of bird and the advance preparation it requires. To cook and brown evenly on a grill rack, the bird should be small and can be flattened by slitting it lengthwise, spreading it open and crushing its breastbone *(pages 50-51),* or it can be cut apart to form easily maneuvered pieces *(pages 54-55).* To balance on a spit, a whole bird of any size must be securely trussed into a compact shape *(pages 58-59),* but to smoke uniformly the bird's cavity must be left agape and its legs allowed to project naturally from the body *(page 63).*

Because the ambient temperatures in spit-roasting and smoking are relatively low—and the cavity of a bird is broad and deep—a stuffing will not heat through in the time required to cook the meat. However, a whole bird can be flavored by tucking aromatic vegetables, fruits or herbs into its cavity beforehand, and rubbing its skin with seasoned oil. For flattened or cut-up birds, marinades offer another way to introduce flavor. If they incorporate oil, marinades also will lubricate lean birds.

Basting during grilling or roasting further nourishes the meat and crisps the skin. For lean birds, the basting liquid can be leftover marinade, seasoned butter or oil, barbecue sauce *(pages 10-15)* or—in spit-roasting—juices from the drip pan. For ducks and geese, basting with acidic cider or wine will help draw off excess fat *(pages 60-61).*

Being naturally tender, young poultry and game birds should be grilled or spit-roasted just long enough to fully develop their flavor: Test them as soon as they have cooked the requisite number of minutes. The meat is done when a skewer, inserted in the thigh, releases clear juices or a cooking thermometer registers 170° F. [75° C.]. To firm the meat for carving, let whole birds rest for 10 minutes; they will continue to cook and their internal temperatures will rise five or 10 degrees.

Secured to a spit and suspended above a drip pan that is surrounded by hot coals, a duck is basted with cider and pan juices as it roasts. Apple slices are added to the pan to intensify the tanginess of the cider and counterpoint the rich flavor of the duck.

Flattening Whole Squabs for Grilling

A whole bird that has been opened out flat for grilling makes a handsome single serving if it is as tiny as the squabs in this demonstration—and proves easy to carve if its proportions are somewhat larger *(pages 52-53)*. Flattening transforms the bird into a neat parcel whose relatively uniform surfaces ensure that the meat cooks through evenly. However, the parcel must not be too thick, lest the meat dry out in the time it takes for the surfaces to brown. Thus, only small birds will do: squabs, quail, partridges, grouse, pheasant, Rock Cornish game hens, guinea hens and chickens weighing no more than 3 pounds [1½ kg.].

To keep the delicate breast meat enclosed in its protective skin, the bird is opened by being cut down the back. The bone there is then removed with a knife for a small bird *(Step 1, right)*, kitchen shears for a larger one *(page 52, Step 1)*, to make the parcel symmetrical. After the bird is spread flat and the breastbone crushed, tucking in the wings and drumsticks compacts the parcel.

For extra flavor, the flattened bird can be marinated for up to two hours at room temperature, or up to 24 hours in the refrigerator. Any paste, oil or acidic marinade will serve *(pages 10-11)*. Here the marinade is based on puréed raspberries—strawberries, blueberries, blackberries or gooseberries could be substituted—whose acids can help tenderize the meat of poultry and game birds.

Grilling the parcels is a straightforward process, and their shape facilitates handling them. The birds are initially browned skin side down, then turned bone side down and grilled until they are cooked through. Regardless of size, the browning will take four or five minutes. After that, birds weighing up to 1 pound [½ kg.] will require eight to 10 minutes of cooking, those up to 2 pounds [1 kg.] require 15 to 20 minutes, and 3-pound [1½-kg.] birds as much as 30 minutes.

The standard test for doneness is to pierce a thigh of each bird with a skewer: When the juices run clear, the bird is fully cooked. In this case, however, the berry marinade reddens the skin, so the juices appear colored; the best way to gauge doneness is to press the breast with tongs to feel if the meat is firm.

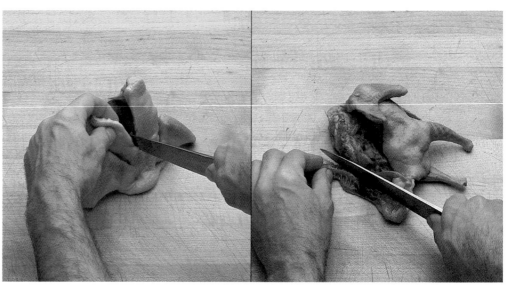

1 **Removing the backbone.** Holding each bird—in this case, a squab—upright on its neck with the vent cavity facing away from you, slit it open lengthwise by cutting down one side of its backbone, from tail to neck, with a heavy knife *(above, left)*. Lay the bird on its side and cut the backbone off *(right)*. Discard the bone, or set it aside for use in making stock.

4 **Marinating the birds.** Place the squabs in a dish and pour the raspberry mixture over them. Add sprigs of a fresh herb—here, thyme—and turn the birds over to coat them evenly with the marinade. Cover the dish with foil or plastic wrap, and let the birds marinate for up to two hours, turning them from time to time.

5 **Browning the birds.** Lay the squabs, skin side down, on an oiled rack set 4 to 6 inches [10 to 15 cm.] above medium-hot coals. Place the thyme sprigs around the birds: The thyme will smoke and impart aroma to the birds. When the skin is browned—after four or five minutes—turn the squabs over.

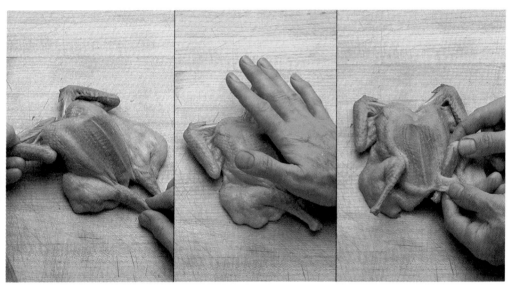

2 **Flattening the bird.** Spread each squab open and lay it breast side up. Tuck the tips of the wings behind the back *(above, left)*. Using the heel of your hand or the flat side of a cleaver, strike the breast with a blow hard enough to break the breastbone, collarbones, rib cage and wishbone. Then press the bird flat *(center)*. With a small knife, make a horizontal slit in the skin between the thigh and breast. Push the end of the leg through the slit *(right)*. Secure the other leg in the same way.

3 **Puréeing raspberries.** With a wooden spoon or pestle, press raspberries through a fine-meshed strainer. Set aside enough of the raspberry purée to make a compound butter *(recipe, page 165)* to garnish the bird. Taste the remaining purée and, if it is very sweet, add some red wine vinegar. Stir in a little oil.

6 **Finishing the birds.** Grill the squabs, bone side down, for eight to 10 minutes, or until the breast meat feels firm when prodded with tongs. Meanwhile, spread orange slices on the rack and grill them for about two minutes—rotating the slices 90 degrees after one minute to brand them with a crosshatch pattern. Turn the slices over and grill them similarly on the other side.

7 **Serving the birds.** Arrange the squabs and orange slices on a serving platter. Garnish the platter with sprigs of watercress and present the squabs accompanied by raspberry compound butter. Spoon a dollop of the butter onto each squab, then serve them immediately.

Flavorings Inserted under the Skin

An imaginative way to suffuse a flattened bird with flavor is to spread seasoned fat beneath the skin of the breast, thighs and drumsticks. Over the coals, the fat will melt slowly, basting the bird internally to keep it moist. When the bird is done, it will have absorbed most of the fat; only cracklings and morsels of seasonings will remain as textural counterpoints to the tender meat and crisp skin.

Unusual though the idea of inserting a fatty coating under the skin of a bird may seem, the process is simplicity itself. The skin is strong but supple, and only attached tightly at the backbone, drumstick tips and crest of the breastbone. Flattening the bird before adding the coating crushes the breastbone, loosening it from the skin. Elsewhere, the thin membranes joining the skin and flesh are easily parted so that you can work your fingers between them.

Squabs, quail, partridges, pheasant, Rock Cornish game hens, guinea hens and chickens of up to 3 pounds [1½ kg.] all can be flavored and basted this way. In the demonstration at right, the inside of a chicken is coated with finely chopped bacon, sage and rosemary. Fatback or blanched salt pork can replace the bacon; so can butter, although it will not provide bits of rendered fat. Dill, parsley, savory or thyme can replace the sage and rosemary, and any herbs can be supplemented by chopped mushrooms, celery, shallots or garlic. Whatever its ingredients, the coating should be ample enough to form a layer ⅛ to ¼ inch [3 to 6 mm.] thick. In this case about 2 cups [½ liter] of chopped bacon and 2 tablespoons [30 ml.] of chopped herbs are used.

Even with the coating of fat inside, the outer surfaces of the bird need to be rubbed with oil before it is placed on the grill rack, and the surfaces should be basted frequently while it cooks. If you wish to marinate the bird, choose an oil mixture (pages 10-11) and season it to complement the coating.

After the bird is grilled, it will be too rich and assertive in taste to benefit from a sauce. It can be garnished with grilled vegetables or fruits or, as shown here, with fresh herb sprigs and chicken-liver kebabs that are grilled while the bird rests to firm its meat for carving.

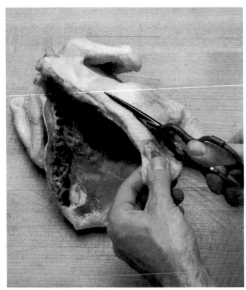

1 **Loosening skin.** Lay the bird—here, a 3-pound [1½-kg.] chicken—on its breast and cut out the backbone with kitchen shears. Chop off the ends of the legs. Turn the bird over and break the breastbone (page 51, Step 2). Slip your fingers under the skin at the neck and work down to loosen the skin over the breast, then over each leg.

2 **Seasoning the fat.** Remove the rind from slab bacon and slice the bacon thin. Gather the slices together and cut them into narrow strips. Pull the leaves from sprigs of fresh sage and rosemary, and chop the leaves coarse. Then mix all of the ingredients together and chop them fine.

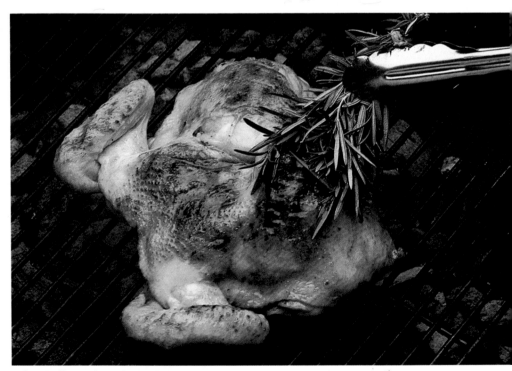

6 **Grilling.** Place the bird, skin side down, on an oiled rack 4 to 6 inches [10 to 15 cm.] above medium-hot coals. Brown it for four to five minutes, turn it over and baste it with oil and lemon juice, using rosemary as a brush. Basting often, grill the bird for 30 minutes, until the juices run clear when the thigh is pricked. Let it rest on a cutting board for 10 minutes.

3 **Coating the chicken.** Lift the skin at the neck and push the seasoned fat down around the bird's thighs and drumsticks. With your other hand, smooth the coating from outside. Then coat both sides of the breast. Slit the skin where each thigh meets the breast and secure the legs *(page 51, Step 2)*. Rub the bird with olive oil.

4 **Preparing livers.** Remove all bits of fat and loose membrane from chicken livers. Cut the livers into halves or thirds, depending on their size.

5 **Skewering the livers.** Slice fatty bacon ¼ inch [6 mm.] thick and cut the slices into pieces about ¼ inch wide and ½ inch [1 cm.] long. Roll the bacon in chopped rosemary. Thread the chicken livers and bacon pieces alternately onto skewers. Pour oil into a shallow dish and roll the skewers in the oil to coat the livers evenly. Set aside.

7 **Serving.** Grill the liver kebabs *(above)* until they are firm and browned on all sides—about five minutes. Meanwhile, carve the chicken by first cutting off the legs at the joint where the thigh meets the body. Separate the thighs and drumsticks. Cut off the wings at the shoulder joints and divide the breast in half lengthwise. Reassemble the pieces on a platter and, if desired, garnish with black olives and rosemary sprigs. Push the livers off the skewers onto the platter.

Smaller Pieces for Quick Cooking

Cutting a bird into pieces shortens the grilling time it requires and simplifies serving it. However, cutting releases the juices, so only plump poultry is suitable: chicken, capon, turkey, duck or goose. To yield pieces that will cook through evenly without charring, the bird should weigh at least 2 pounds [1 kg.] but no more than 6 pounds [3 kg.].

You can, of course, buy a bird that is already cut up or, in the case of chicken and turkey, buy only particular pieces, such as chicken wings (opposite, below). Nonetheless, dissecting the bird yourself helps ensure neat pieces and usually saves money. The technique shown here with a chicken applies to every species, but some cooks leave the thin wings of duck or goose attached to the breast and others quarter these birds.

Steeping the pieces in an oil-based marinade will contribute flavor as well as lubrication. Here the chicken is marinated in an herb-and-lemon mixture, the wings in a tangy soy-sauce blend.

How the grilling is accomplished will vary with the type of bird or pieces and the result desired. For example, duck and goose must be grilled above a drip pan (page 60); other birds are cooked directly over coals. A collection of wings or thighs can be handled efficiently if impaled on skewers; for drumsticks, run two skewers through the ends and alternate the direction in which the tips point so that the pieces fit closely together.

Usually, the pieces are browned well on one side, then turned over and cooked through. If you use a barbecue sauce, however, brown the pieces lightly, coat them with sauce, turn them, then continue coating and turning them frequently.

The grilling time will depend mainly on the size of pieces except in chicken, capon and turkey, where the white meat of wings and breast halves, being relatively dry, will cook more quickly than the moister dark meat of thighs, drumsticks and backs. Remove white-meat pieces from the grill as soon as their juices run clear, or set them atop the dark-meat pieces to keep them warm.

Disjointing a Bird

1 **Removing the legs.** Place the bird on its back and slit the skin where one leg is attached. Bend the leg out until the thighbone pops from the hip joint; sever the leg at the joint. Separate the thigh and drumstick. Repeat with the other leg. Cut off the wing tips. Pull each wing outward, and sever it at the joint where it meets the breast.

5 **Grilling.** Place the chicken on an oiled rack 4 to 6 inches [10 to 15 cm.] above medium-hot coals, setting the breast and back with the skin side down. Brown for four or five minutes, turn, and baste with marinade. After eight to 10 minutes, prick the wings and breast; if the juice runs clear they are done. Lay them on the dark meat. Meanwhile, grill potato slices (page 20).

6 **Serving.** After two or three minutes, test the legs, thighs and back halves for doneness. Arrange all of the chicken pieces on a platter using the grilled potato slices as little rafts. Garnish the platter with parsley and scoop a little red-pepper compound butter (pages 14-15) onto each chicken piece. Serve at once.

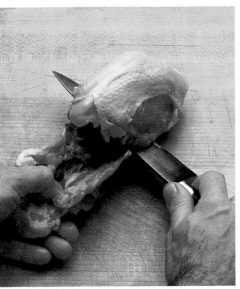

2 **Cutting off the breast.** Hold the bird by the tail and insert the knife crosswise at the base of the spine. Slide the knife in the direction of the neck, lifting the breast as you go to remove it from the back. At the lower end of the rib cage, halve the back crosswise.

3 **Halving the breast.** Grasp the side of the breast to steady it. Then cut through the skin and flesh just to one side of the breastbone in order to split the breast lengthwise.

4 **Marinating the chicken.** Put the chicken pieces in a shallow dish and sprinkle them with pepper, grated lemon peel, and chopped parsley, thyme and savory. Pour oil over the pieces, then turn them to coat them evenly with the oil and flavorings. Marinate the pieces at room temperature for up to two hours, turning them occasionally.

Arranging Wings on Skewers

1 **Skewering the wings.** Steep chicken wings for up to two hours in marinade—here, a combination of soy sauce, oil, chopped onion, grated orange peel and pepper is used. To thread the wings onto skewers, pierce each wing first through the center of the middle joint and then through the centers of the tip and base joints.

2 **Grilling the wings.** Place the skewered wings on an oiled rack 4 to 6 inches [10 to 15 cm.] above medium-hot coals. Brushing the wings often with the remaining marinade, grill them for five or six minutes on each side, or until the juices run clear when the wings are pricked with a skewer or trussing needle.

3 **Serving the wings.** Push the tines of a large fork onto the handle end of one skewer at a time. Shove the fork down the length of the skewer to push the wings off onto a serving platter. Garnish them, if desired, with lemon and orange wedges and fresh coriander leaves. Serve the wings immediately.

Tender Scallops Enlivened with Spices

Chicken breasts that are boned and then halved can be pounded flat to form pairs of delicate scallops only ⅓ inch [8 mm.] thick and twice the breadth and length of the original pieces. Capon or turkey breast can be used instead, if the halves are first cut horizontally into slices ½ inch [1 cm.] thick. Because pounding breaks down muscle fibers and thus further softens the tender breast meat, the scallops will be ready to eat as soon as they are browned on both sides—after no more than five minutes of grilling.

Any smooth, heavy instrument will serve for pounding the breast meat: a kitchen mallet, the bottom of a skillet or—as demonstrated here—the side of a cleaver. To prevent tearing the meat, enclose each half in strong plastic wrap.

Flattened meat is especially susceptible to parching, so the scallops should be liberally oiled before and during grilling. Here, they are marinated and basted with a pungent blend of oil, cardamom, cayenne and black pepper. For milder flavor, herbs could replace the spices.

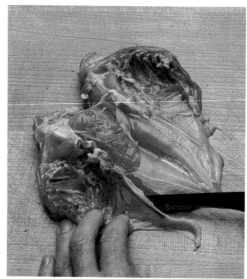

1 **Removing the breastbone.** Peel the skin from each breast—in this case, chicken—and place the breast with its skin side down. Grasp it at the midpoint of the breastbone with both hands and bend the sides away from you until the breastbone pops up. Then pull out the bone. Use the tip of a knife to free any remaining ribs.

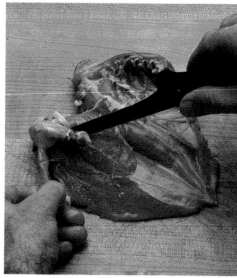

2 **Removing collarbones.** With your fingers, pry out the cartilage that is attached to the narrow end of the breast. With the tip of the knife, cut through the flesh that covers the collarbones; draw the bones out.

6 **Grilling the scallops.** Place the scallops on an oiled rack set 4 to 6 inches [10 to 15 cm.] above medium-hot coals, and grill them for about one minute. Turn the breasts over and brush them with the remaining marinade. Turning and basting them often, grill the scallops for five minutes, or until they are firm, opaque and pale gold.

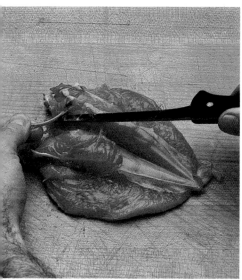

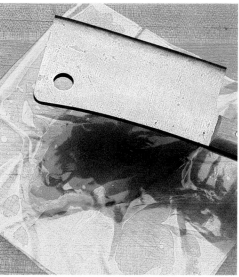

3 **Removing the wishbone.** Scrape away the flesh that surrounds the wishbone. When the entire wishbone is visible, grasp it by both prongs and pull it out. Then cut the breast in half along the cleft that contained the breastbone. Trim off fat and membrane.

4 **Flattening the breast.** Oil a large piece of strong plastic wrap. Lay one breast half on it, and fold the plastic over to cover the flesh. With the flat side of a cleaver, beat the flesh firmly—moving from the center outward—until the breast is about ⅓ inch [8 mm.] thick and twice its original size. Flatten the other half similarly.

5 **Marinating the scallops.** Pour olive oil into a shallow dish and add ground cardamom, cayenne pepper and black pepper. Coat both sides of each scallop with this marinade. Then marinate the scallops in the dish for up to two hours, turning them from time to time. Prepare lemon compound butter (recipe, page 165).

7 **Serving the scallops.** Arrange the grilled scallops attractively on a warmed platter. Here they are garnished with sprigs of watercress and halved slices of red onion. Spoon a little of the compound butter onto the scallops and serve them at once, accompanied by the remaining butter.

An Herb-scented Chicken Roasted on the Hearth

With periodic basting to keep their meat moistened, chickens, capons and small turkeys all can be roasted to golden perfection on a spit rotating above a grill or, as shown here, in front of a fireplace. The drip pan beneath the spit will conserve the bird's juices for the basting, which should stop about 20 minutes before the bird is done to ensure crisp skin. For even cooking, the spit itself should be stopped—with the bird's legs facing the fire—during the last five minutes.

Before roasting, the bird must be oiled inside and out and trussed into a compact form that will balance well on the spit. Its cavity can be filled with flavoring elements such as herbs; conventional stuffing would not heat through.

Over a grill, the embers around the drip pan cook the bird; at the hearth, the fire radiates the heat and should be kept stoked. Battery-powered or electric rotisserie units suitable for use at a fireplace are available where outdoor-cooking supplies are sold. To support the rotisserie, set bricks on the hearth at the edge of the firebox to form two parallel stacks 12 inches [30 cm.] high and far enough apart to accommodate the spit rod. Halve a cored brick—one with a round cavity—and set the halves on the stacks to hold the spit. Build two more stacks of bricks at right angles to one of the first stacks to enclose the rotisserie motor and shield it from heat.

When the drip pan is in place, lay the spitted bird on the brick supports; let the motor hang free. A 3- to 4-pound [1½- to 2-kg.] chicken will require a roasting time of about one and one half hours, a 6- to 8-pound [3- to 4-kg.] capon or turkey will need two and one half to three hours.

1 **Seasoning the chicken.** Rub the vent cavity of the bird—here, a 4-pound [2-kg.] chicken—with olive oil in which sprigs of a fresh herb such as rosemary have steeped for at least three hours. Sprinkle the cavity with salt and black pepper, and fill it loosely with aromatics—in this case, slices of lemon and sprigs of lovage.

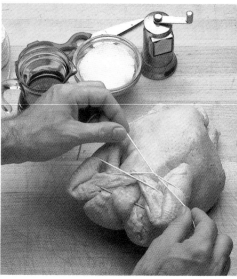

2 **Trussing the chicken.** Pull the flap of neck skin to the back of the chicken and thread a small skewer through the flap to secure it to the back. Tuck the wing tips behind the back. Loop kitchen string around the wings in a figure eight; tie the ends of the string. Tie the tips of the drumsticks together, knot the string and cut off the excess string.

5 **Roasting.** Put a drip pan between the bricks and rake hot coals forward from the fire. Pour ½ inch [1 cm.] of water into the pan and add aromatics—here, black olives, lemon peel and rosemary. Position the chicken over the pan and turn on the rotisserie. Baste the bird with pan juices every 10 minutes for an hour and a quarter. Roast without basting for 10 minutes, turn off the rotisserie and roast for five minutes longer.

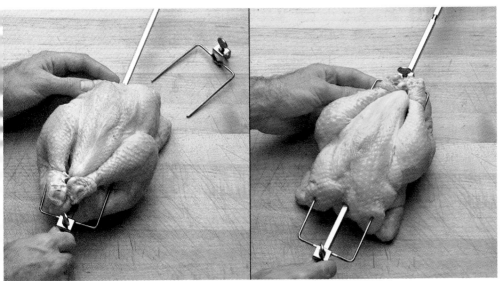

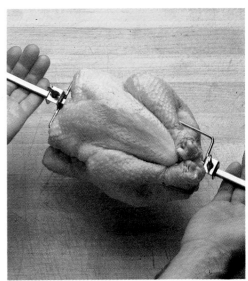

3 **Spitting the chicken.** Slip a holding fork onto the spit with the prongs pointing away from the spit handle. Push the spit into the tail flesh of the chicken, then through the vent cavity and the flap of skin at the neck opening. Push the prongs of the fork through the drumsticks and into the sides of the chicken (above, left). Slip the second fork onto the spit, prongs pointing toward the chicken, and press them into the bony front end of the bird (right). Tighten the forks to secure them to the spit.

4 **Balancing the chicken.** Slip your hands under the spit rod on either side of the bird and lift it. Roll the spit back and forth across your hands. If the chicken and spit do not rotate together in a smooth motion, loosen the forks and reinsert them. Test for balance again. Rub the bird with the oil, and sprinkle it with salt and pepper.

6 **Removing the spit.** Transfer the chicken to a carving board to rest for 10 minutes. Discard the lemon peel and rosemary, but reserve the olives. Skim the excess fat from the pan juices. Turn thick slices of crusty bread—rye bread is used here—about in the pan juices and put them on the carving board. Then pull off the holding forks and use the back of a carving fork to push the bird off the spit.

7 **Cutting off a leg.** Cut off the trussing strings and set the chicken on its back. To remove a leg, steady the bird with a carving fork and cut through the skin between a thigh and the breast. Bend the thigh outward and slice down through the hip joint. To remove a wing, slice diagonally down through the corner of the breast toward the wing. Bend the wing outward and cut through the shoulder joint.

8 **Carving the breast.** Press the fork against one side of the breast to steady the chicken, and slice downward diagonally through the breast meat. Lift off each slice between the fork and knife. Carve the other side of the bird similarly and, if desired, sever the thighs from the drumsticks. Cut the bread into portions, then serve the chicken with the bread and reserved olives.

A Fruit Complement for Duck

Unlike other poultry, ducks and geese are liberally endowed with internal fat. Whether cut into pieces and grilled by the method shown for chicken on pages 54-55 or spit-roasted as demonstrated here, the birds must be handled in such a way that most of this fat is released—leaving the skin crisp and crunchy and the flesh succulent, but not greasy.

The first step in preparing a duck or goose, therefore, is to remove all visible fat and pierce the fatty deposits under the skin with a skewer or needle. Although puncturing the skin all over makes the fat drain fast, it also may sacrifice some of the bird's juices. For tender meat, puncture only the four large concentrations of fat above the thighs and under the wings; the skin in these areas looks opaque and creamy. Always pierce just deep enough to puncture the fat without penetrating the flesh beneath it.

During either grilling or roasting, the fat that the bird releases will make the coals blaze up unless a drip pan is set under the duck or goose. The pan will also catch the liquid used to baste the bird and, in spit-roasting, conserve its juices and fat as part of the liquid. For basting, choose an acidic liquid that will help break down the bird's fat and draw it out. Here the duck is basted with apple cider. Other kinds of fruit juice—grape, cranberry, orange or grapefruit, for example—will work, as will wines.

Like all poultry, a duck or goose has such a large cavity that a conventional stuffing would not cook through in the time required to roast the bird. However, for enrichment, the cavity can be filled with sliced fruit, pieces of onion or celery, or sprigs of herbs—flavorings that also can be added to the basting liquid.

No duck is too large for spit-roasting, but a goose should not exceed 10 pounds [5 kg.] (a larger goose is probably an old bird that needs to be tenderized by the moist heat of braising). On a spit, a 4- to 5-pound [2- to 2½-kg.] duck will roast in about two hours, a 6- to 7-pound [3- to 3½-kg.] goose in two and one half hours and an 8- to 10-pound [4- to 5-kg.] goose in three hours. The bird is done when its thigh juices run clear, or when a meat thermometer indicates an internal temperature of 170° F. [75° C.].

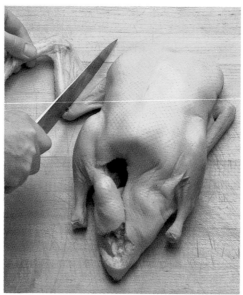

1 **Preparing the bird.** Pull off and discard the large chunks of fat around the neck opening and tail vent of the bird—here, a 4-pound [2-kg.] duck. Using a sharp, heavy knife, cut off the tip and first joint of each wing: Although they have little meat, they can be reserved for making stock.

2 **Trussing the wings.** Pull the flap of neck skin over the opening and secure it to the duck's back with a small skewer. Pull the wings behind the back and tie them together firmly with a piece of kitchen string.

5 **Roasting.** Set the spitted duck over the drip pan. Baste the duck every 10 minutes; after one hour, replace the pan drippings with fresh cider and apple wedges. Baste for 40 minutes more, then discontinue basting to let the skin crisp for 20 minutes. Stop the spit—with the legs toward the coals—for the last five minutes.

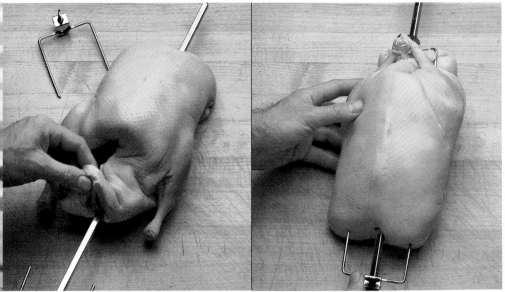

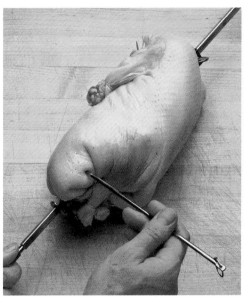

3 **Spitting the duck.** Slide a holding fork onto the spit rod, prongs pointing away from the handle. Thrust the tip of the spit into the duck's tail vent and body cavity so that it emerges through the flap of skin at the neck opening *(above, left)*. Tie the ends of the legs together with string, then push the holding fork deep into the bony parts of the legs and thighs. Slide the other fork onto the spit and push the prongs into the bony area around the wings *(right)*. Check the balance of the spitted duck *(page 59, Step 4)*.

4 **Piercing.** Push a trussing needle or skewer into the fatty deposits above the thighs and beneath the wings. Center a drip pan in the firebox of a grill and rake coals around it *(pages 8-9)* or place the pan between bricks stacked on a hearth *(page 58)*. Pour a ½-inch-deep [1-cm.] layer of cider into the pan and add a few bay leaves.

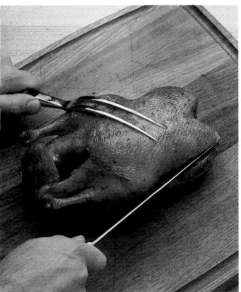

6 **Removing a wing.** If the juices run clear when a thigh is pierced with a skewer, the duck is done. Transfer the duck to a carving board, remove it from the spit, cut the trussing strings, and let the duck rest for 10 minutes. Then move one wing to locate the shoulder joint and cut down through the joint with a heavy knife to remove the wing.

7 **Removing a leg.** Cut through the skin of the duck where the leg joins the body. Push the thigh downward and outward to expose the joint, then cut through it to remove the leg.

8 **Carving the breast.** Holding the carving knife at a slight angle to the breastbone, carve the breast meat into slices ¼ inch [6 mm.] thick. Remove the wing and leg from the other side of the bird, and carve the remaining breast meat similarly. Separate the thighs from the drumsticks before serving.

Quail Arrayed on a Spit

Threaded sideways onto a spit rod, a brace or more of such little birds as quail, squabs or Rock Cornish game hens can be simultaneously roasted to a golden mahogany finish in 30 to 40 minutes, depending on size. The number of birds is limited only by their girth in relation to the length of the spit. In this demonstration, the spit easily holds eight quail.

Because little birds tend to be lean, they must be oiled before they are spitted, and basted frequently with fat or oil as they roast. An easy way to keep them moist is to use a rotisserie that can hold two spits one above the other, as shown here. The top spit, which may be stationary, is strung with lean salt pork that has been cooked just enough to begin to release fat. The bottom spit, which must rotate, holds the birds. As they turn, they brush against the melting pork.

To ensure that the birds rotate smoothly, they should be packed tightly on the spit by alternating the direction in which their legs point. The holding forks must be pushed tightly against the end birds; if the birds are too small to be impaled by the prongs, turn the forks outward.

1 **Trussing the birds.** Rub the cavity of each quail with oil, season it and add fresh herbs—here, parsley and thyme. Tuck the wing tips of each bird behind the back. Loop the middle of a 12-inch [30-cm.] string around the end of first one drumstick and then the other and tie the two together (above, left). Pull the two ends of the string toward the neck opening of the bird and tie them so that the legs will be pulled snugly against the body (right). Cut off the excess string. Oil the surfaces of the birds.

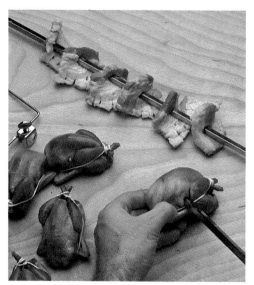

2 **Spitting.** Cut thickly sliced salt pork into six 2-inch [5-cm.] squares. Blanch for five minutes, slash the edges every ¼ inch [6 mm.] and spit the squares. Thread the birds in alternating directions on the second spit, inserting it behind the rib cage of each quail. Press the flat edge of each holding fork against the birds.

3 **Roasting.** Attach the spit of salt pork to the rotisserie motor and place two drip pans beneath it. Roast the pork until it begins to drip—about 10 minutes—then transfer the spit to a higher support and attach the spitted quail to the motor. Basting the birds frequently with the pan juices—applied here with thyme sprigs held in tongs—roast them for 30 to 40 minutes, or until juices run clear when a thigh is pricked with a fork.

Smoking a Turkey for Moist Tenderness

When roasted in the gentle, moist heat of a charcoal-water smoker, poultry and game birds emerge juicy and flavorful without the benefit of any basting whatsoever. Except for replenishing fuel or water, the smoker must be kept covered to hold in the smoke and maintain an average temperature of 200° F. [100° C.]. Even so, the process is lengthy. The 10-pound [5-kg.] turkey used in this demonstration requires eight hours of smoking, and a 20-pound [10-kg.] bird needs 12 hours. A 5-pound [2½-kg.] chicken or duck needs at least six hours, and a 2-pound [1-kg.] pheasant or guinea hen about four hours.

For faster results, you can smoke the bird for two hours or so and then transfer it to the oven to complete the cooking at 325° or 350° F. [160° or 180° C.]. In any case, the smoking will give the meat a pinkish color when it reaches an internal temperature of 170° F. [75° C.] and is fully cooked. The juices, however, will still run clear if tested with a skewer.

1 Oiling the turkey. Start the fire in the smoker (pages 46-47). Rub the cavity of the bird—here, a 10-pound [5-kg.] turkey—with oil, season it, and add flavorings such as the onion halves, strips of orange peel and sprigs of mint used here. Coat the skin with oil—flavored in this demonstration with rosemary.

2 Inserting the turkey. Tuck the tips of the wings behind the bird's back. Leave the legs untrussed so that smoke and steam can circulate freely around them. Wearing heavy mitts, lower the water pan into the smoker. Fill the pan with hot water. Oil the rack, set it in place and put the turkey on it.

3 Smoking the turkey. Roast the turkey undisturbed in the covered smoker for eight hours, or until the juices run clear when a thigh is pricked or a meat thermometer inserted in a thigh registers 170° F. [75° C.]. Lift the turkey, on the rack, out of the smoker. Place the turkey, breast side up, on a carving board; let it rest for 10 minutes.

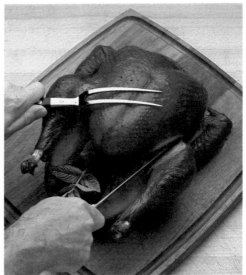

4 Removing a leg. Remove the aromatics from the cavity of the bird and discard them. Holding the turkey steady with a carving fork, cut through the skin between the thigh and the breast. Push down on the thigh to expose the hip joint. Cut through the joint, severing the leg. Then separate the drumstick from the thigh.

5 Slicing the breast. Cut down diagonally through the corner of the breast to remove the wing at the shoulder joint. To carve the breast, steady the turkey with the fork and cut down at an angle to the breastbone to form slices that are about ¼ inch [6 mm.] thick. Then carve the opposite side of the turkey in the same way.

4
Fish and Shellfish
Preserving Natural Delicacy

Nestled in a fish-shaped basket, a striped bass stuffed with lemon slices is bedded between aromatic pine sprigs. For grilling, the basket will be closed and set directly among the coals, where the pine will release its perfume. Legs that extend from both halves of the hinged basket allow the fish to be turned easily midway through the cooking process.

Naturally tender fish and shellfish taste delectable when scented by wood smoke. But because they need cooking only to develop their flavor and firm their flesh—and will toughen if they dry out—fish and shellfish need gentle treatment: The coals must be no closer than 4 inches [10 cm.] nor more than medium hot.

Anatomically, fish divide into two types—roundfish such as bass or trout and flatfish such as fluke or turbot. All can be grilled whole, with the skin left on to help keep the flesh moist *(pages 66-67)*. However, most cooks find it easier to serve fish that has already been divided into fillets or steaks. If these are to remain juicy in the direct heat of the coals they must be at least ¾ inch [2 cm.] thick, but no more than 2 inches [5 cm.] lest they char before they cook through. Most roundfish are plump enough to yield fillets of such dimensions *(pages 68-69)*. True to their name, most flatfish produce thin fillets that require packeting in foil, a limitation that can become an advantage if complementary flavorings are cooked with the fish *(pages 72-73)*.

Fish also differ in their fat content. The fatty types, including salmon, bluefish, tuna and swordfish, resist drying best and thus become prime candidates for kebabs. Nonetheless, all whole or cut-up fish need an advance coating of oil or butter and at least one basting while they grill. Fish can be marinated if the process is kept short—no more than half an hour at room temperature or two hours in the refrigerator—to preserve the freshness and delicate flavor of the flesh.

Shellfish, too, can be grilled whole or cut apart *(pages 76-77)*. Crustaceans such as lobsters or shrimp need lubricating or marinating with oil—and periodic basting; so do shucked bivalves such as oysters or scallops. Nuggets of shellfish meat can be packeted in foil to steam in their own juices or, providing they are firm enough to skewer, grilled on a rack covered with perforated foil *(page 72)*.

Depending on their type and form, shellfish will cook in about five to 15 minutes, and are done as soon as their flesh looks opaque or—in the case of whole bivalves—their shells open. Fish are ready to eat when their flesh flakes easily. As a general rule, they will require 10 minutes of cooking for each inch [2½ cm.] of thickness, although fish kebabs, being small, need less time, and foil-wrapped fish need more.

A Whole Striped Bass Grilled Intact

Crisp on the outside and moist within, a whole fish grilled over coals ranks as one of the simplest, yet most splendid, offerings of outdoor cooking. Fish of any type or size can be grilled whole on a rack. But—because fish break apart easily when cooked—grilling them in a hinged basket will help keep them intact.

A rectangular basket will do for flatfish and small roundfish. Larger roundfish need a fish-shaped basket such as the one shown. Available where fine kitchen supplies are sold, such baskets range in length from 10 to 21 inches [25 to 53 cm.]. This basket is 16 inches [40 cm.] long and the bass weighs 4 pounds [2 kg.].

Before grilling roundfish, remove the scales, fins and viscera, then trim the tail and cut off the head, if necessary, to make the body fit in the basket. For flatfish, slice off the head just behind the gills and press the body gently to squeeze out the viscera. Female fish often yield eggs, or roe—which can be grilled separately (*pages 70-71*) or used to enrich a mayonnaise (*box, opposite; recipe, page 165*).

A preliminary coating of oil and a thorough basting midway through grilling will keep the fish's skin moist. A marinade that incorporates aromatics will enhance the fish's flavor.

The fish can be further perfumed by lining the basket with sprigs of herbs or such nonpoisonous evergreens as the pine shown here. Common juniper, incense cedar, or red spruce are safe substitutes for pine. Because some evergreens, such as yews and holly, are toxic, be sure you identify the sprigs. You may consult a library to determine their safety.

A fish-shaped basket can stand directly amidst the coals if the legs are long enough to keep the fish 4 inches [10 cm.] above them. Otherwise place it—like a rectangular basket—on a rack 4 to 6 inches [10 to 15 cm.] from the fire. Allow 10 minutes of grilling time for each inch [2½ cm.] of thickness, measured at the plumpest part of the fish. The internal temperature of a perfectly done fish is 140° F. [60° C.]; you can test it by inserting a rapid-response thermometer.

1 **Scaling the fish.** Rinse the fish—in this case, a striped bass—and leave it wet. Lay the fish on a flat surface, start from the tail and scrape the back of a knife or fish scaler against the scales with short, firm strokes. Work all the way up the body and then turn the fish over to scale the other side. Use scissors to snip off the fins and trim the tail.

5 **Preparing for grilling.** Open a fish-shaped hinged grill basket and oil it. Line one side of the basket with pine sprigs— here, eastern white pine—that have been dipped in water. Place the fish on the sprigs, cover it with more sprigs, close the basket and clamp the handle. Wearing a flame-resistant mitt, set the basket amidst medium-hot coals.

6 **Grilling the fish.** Grill the fish until half-cooked, then baste it with leftover marinade, turn the basket and baste again. When the pine needles begin to burn, use tongs to pull them from the basket and throw them onto the coals. To test for doneness, insert a knife tip at the backbone; if the flesh flakes easily, remove the basket from the coals.

7 **Transferring to a platter.** Before opening the basket, run a knife along the wires to make sure that the fish is not stuck to them. Open the basket and place a platter upside down over the fish. Wearing mitts, hold the lower half of the basket and the platter together and invert the fish onto the platter.

2 **Gutting the fish.** Slit the belly of the fish from the tail vent to the head. Pull out the viscera and discard them. If you find a pair of roe sacs *(above)*, remove the membrane and thick vein that join them; reserve the roe. Run the tip of the knife along both sides of the backbone inside the belly cavity to release any blood pockets.

3 **Removing the head.** To cook the fish with its head on, lift each gill cover and remove the gills. To remove the head, first sever each gill flap at the base of the head. Then position the fish on its belly and slice through the backbone to cut off the head. Rinse and dry the fish.

4 **Marinating the fish.** Cut diagonal slashes about ¼ inch [6 mm.] deep at 2-inch [5-cm.] intervals across each side of the fish. Place the fish in a shallow dish and rub it with a marinade—a blend of thyme, parsley and olive oil is used here. Push lemon slices into the belly cavity and marinate the fish for up to 30 minutes, turning it occasionally.

8 **Serving.** Garnish the fish with fresh lemon slices and parsley sprigs and present it with roe mayonnaise *(inset)*. To serve, slide a narrow metal spatula along the backbone to free the top fillet. Cut the fillet crosswise into portions and, starting from the tail end, lift off each piece *(above)*. Lift away the backbone before serving the lower fillet.

A Rich Roe Sauce

Whisking. Gently rinse fresh roe—in this case, from striped bass—and poach it for five minutes in lightly salted water. Place the roe in a bowl and use a whisk to mash it together with egg yolks and lemon juice. When the mixture is smooth, gradually whisk in enough olive oil to form a thin mayonnaise. Add salt and pepper.

Bluefish Filleted for Grilling

Most roundfish can be easily divided into two fillets plump enough to cook to golden perfection over coals. Free of bothersome bones and skin, the fillets are a delight to serve and an invitation to colorful garnishes and sauces.

For best results, choose large fish that produce fillets at least ¾ inch [2 cm.] thick—the minimum size for grilling. Varieties with simple skeletons—snapper, sunfish, trout or the bluefish used in this demonstration—will readily yield tidy fillets. Pike, shad and carp have so many tiny bones that only a skilled chef or fisherman can fillet them successfully.

To free the flesh of the fish, you will need a sharp knife with a long, narrow blade that is flexible enough to ride closely over the fish's bones. Once each fillet has been removed from the backbone and ribs, check it for any additional small bones; cut these away with the knife, or pick them out individually with tweezers or your fingers. To skin the fillets, switch to a knife with a broad, stiff blade that will help to prevent you from cutting into the skin.

Because the flesh of fish begins to dry rapidly as soon as it is exposed to air, fillet the fish as close to grilling time as possible. Coat the fillets with oil or clarified butter to keep them moist, or rub on an oil-based marinade.

The fillets can be grilled in a hinged rectangular basket or—if turned carefully with a long, broad spatula as shown here—directly on a rack. In either case, the fillets will tend to stick to the wires unless the basket or rack is oiled well.

Fillets from fatty fish require basting only when they are turned, but lean fish should be basted frequently. As with whole fish, plan to grill the fillets for about 10 minutes for each inch [2½ cm.] of thickness, but watch them carefully lest they overcook.

1 **Cutting along the backbone.** Scale and gut the fish—in this case, bluefish—following the process shown in Steps 1 and 2, pages 66-67. Position the cleaned fish on one side, with its tail toward you. Cut down to the backbone just behind the gill to sever the upper fillet from the head. Then steady the fish with one hand as you slice along the backbone from head to tail with a sharp, flexible knife, cutting deep enough to expose the backbone.

4 **Marinating the fillets.** Place the fillets on a large plate and sprinkle them with salt, pepper and freshly chopped herbs—here, parsley is used. Pour olive oil over the fillets and turn them so that they are well lubricated on both sides. Let the fillets marinate for up to 30 minutes. With a long, broad spatula, place the fillets on an oiled rack set 4 to 6 inches [10 to 15 cm.] above medium-hot coals.

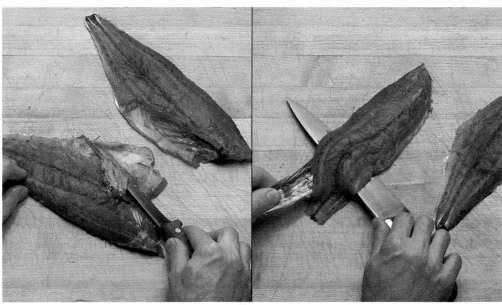

2 **Freeing the fillets.** Pull up the head end of the upper fillet and insert the knife between the fillet and rib. With the blade parallel to the ribs, make short cutting strokes down to the tail to detach the fillet. Pull up the backbone and slice below it to free the lower fillet. Remove the head, bones and tail.

3 **Trimming and skinning the fillets.** If the fillets contain additional bones, hold the knife at a slant to slice them out *(above, left)*. Place each fillet with the skin side down and use a heavy, stiff-bladed knife to cut ½ inch [1 cm.] of flesh away from the skin at the tail end. Holding the exposed skin taut, insert the knife blade beneath the flesh at a shallow angle and make short cutting strokes to free the fillet *(right)*. Trim the fillets neatly.

5 **Grilling and serving.** After four or five minutes, baste the fillets with oil or leftover marinade. Use the spatula to turn the fillets *(above)*, then baste them again. Cook the fillets until the flesh flakes when prodded with a fork. Use the spatula to lift the fillets onto a platter. Serve the fish at once, garnished—if you like—with sliced avocado and topped with a tomato vinaigrette *(recipe, page 162)*.

Strategies for Cooking Fish at the Fireplace

Any whole fish, fillet or steak that can be grilled over coals can be cooked at a fireplace. A whole roundfish in a fish-shaped grill basket *(pages 68-69)* can simply be placed amidst the coals in the firebox. A whole flatfish or fish fillets or steaks fitted into a rectangular basket can be supported by bricks stacked on the hearth *(right, top)*. And—in a variation on a technique American Indians used at bonfires—fillets can be planked, or nailed to a board, and propped upright in front of the fire to cook *(right, bottom)*.

Whatever method is chosen, fillets and steaks must, of course, be at least ¾ inch [2 cm.] thick. For grilling, fillets usually are skinned by the technique shown in Step 3 on page 69. Steaks, on the other hand, are best grilled with their central bones and outer skin left in place to protect the flesh from breaking.

If fillets are to be planked, they should not be skinned: Their skin will hold the flesh intact during cooking. Any sturdy hardwood board—for example, the cutting board shown here—will serve as the plank. Avoid plywood, which ignites easily because of the adhesives it contains. To secure the fish to the plank, you should use common steel, stainless-steel or aluminum nails; the coatings on galvanized nails may be toxic.

Oiling the surfaces of the fish is always a necessity and can be a means of flavoring it. Here, the swordfish steaks are marinated in an herb-laced paste; the shad fillets are brushed with sprigs of thyme that have been saturated with oil.

Follow the standard rule of 10 minutes per inch [2½ cm.] of thickness to grill fish. But allow anywhere from 15 to 25 minutes an inch for planked fillets because these will cook by radiant rather than direct heat. Here, shad roe is grilled in a hinged basket as an accompaniment to the fillets; the roe needs eight to 10 minutes of cooking.

Swordfish Steaks Enclosed in a Basket

1 **Marinating the steaks.** Place fish steaks—here, swordfish—in a dish and coat them with marinade; a paste of thyme, chervil, salt, pepper and olive oil is shown. Let the steaks marinate for up to 30 minutes. Meanwhile, pile bricks in two parallel stacks 7 or 8 inches [18 or 20 cm.] high on the hearth at the edge of the firebox *(pages 32-33)*.

2 **Grilling the steaks.** Rake coals from the fire to form a layer about 2 inches [5 cm.] deep between the stacks of bricks. Place the steaks in the basket section of an oiled hinged grill. Cover the basket and clamp the handle. Rest the grill on the bricks. Cook the steaks until half-done, baste them, turn the grill and baste again.

Shad Fillets Fastened to a Plank

1 **Planking the fish.** Place fish fillets—in this case, shad—skin side down on a piece of sturdy hardwood such as the cutting board shown here. Drive a stainless-steel nail through both ends of each fillet, hammering the nail only partway into the wood so that it will be easy to remove later.

2 **Oiling the fillets.** Tie sprigs of fresh herbs—thyme is used here—into two bunches. Soak the sprigs in olive oil for two or three minutes to saturate them thoroughly, then use them to brush a generous coat of oil onto the fillets. Season the fillets with salt and pepper.

3 **Serving.** When the steaks flake easily, place the grill on its lid next to a platter. Unclamp the handle and lift the basket section off the grill. Slide the steaks onto the platter and garnish them with basil leaves. Top the steaks, if you like, with a spoonful of tomato-basil mayonnaise *(recipe, page 165).*

3 **Grilling.** Stand the plank at a slight angle on the hearth close to the fire, setting the bottom of the plank inside a baking pan and propping the back with bricks. Arrange the thyme on the top nails. Meanwhile, rinse shad roe and remove the membrane and vein that connect its lobes. Oil the roe and set it in an oiled basket grill.

4 **Grilling the roe.** Cook the fillets for about 10 minutes, then turn the plank upside down and baste the fillets again—using the thyme sprigs to brush on the oil. Hold the basket grill containing the roe directly over the coals in the firebox and cook the roe for four or five minutes on each side.

5 **Serving.** When the fillets flake easily, pull out the nails with pliers and use a spatula to transfer the fillets to a serving board or platter. Remove the roe from the basket and place it beside the fillets; garnish with parsley and lemon wedges. Then spread red-pepper compound butter *(pages 14-15)* over the fillets and serve at once.

Protective Packets for Flatfish Fillets

Used as a wrapping or as a support, aluminum foil extends the outdoor cook's repertoire by making it possible to grill fish and shellfish too thin—or tiny—to be cooked directly over coals. Flatfish such as the fluke shown here, for example, yield fillets that are rarely more than ½ inch [1 cm.] thick. When enclosed in packets of foil, such fillets will retain their natural moisture while absorbing the flavors of the aromatics that steam with them to form a ready-made garnish.

The same strategy can be applied to roundfish fillets or steaks, small whole fish, even shelled or shucked shellfish. The only proviso is that the fish or shellfish must be no more than an inch [2½ cm.] thick if it is to cook through evenly. Nonetheless, the cooking time will be longer than usual: Allow seven or eight minutes for each ½ inch of thickness.

Foil also can be used to cover the grill rack so that skewered or loose morsels of shellfish such as small shrimp, shucked hard-shell clams or the bay scallops in the box below do not fall between the wires onto the coals. Poking holes in the foil allows smoke from the fire to reach the shellfish and imbue it with flavor.

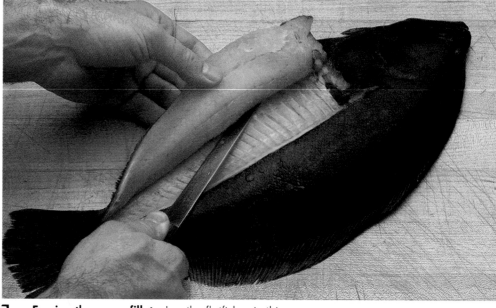

1 **Freeing the upper fillets.** Lay the flatfish—in this case, a fluke—with its eyes facing up and its tail toward you. Using a sharp, flexible knife, cut down the center of the fish along the backbone from head to tail. Insert the knife blade at a shallow angle between the flesh and the ribs at the head end of one upper fillet and lift the fillet free as you cut along the fish with short strokes. Sever the fillet at the tail. Remove the second upper fillet in the same way.

Foil to Cover a Rack

Grilling scallops. Cover a grill rack with heavy-duty foil; puncture the foil all over. Set the rack 4 to 6 inches [10 to 15 cm.] above medium-hot coals. Oil, season and skewer bay scallops. Turning them frequently, grill the scallops for four or five minutes, or until they are firm and opaque.

4 **Preparing packets.** For each fillet, lay two sheets of heavy-duty foil together and generously butter the center of the top sheet. Sprinkle chopped shallots and sliced mushrooms over the buttered area and set the fillet on top. Place lemon slices on the fillet and top them with chopped tomatoes (above, left); place a tarragon sprig on the assembly and season with salt and pepper. Bring the sides of the foil up over the fillet and fold them together two times (right). Make a double fold at both ends of the packet to enclose the fillet securely.

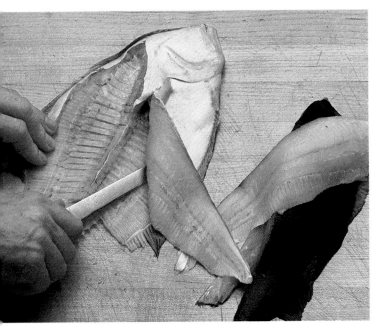

2 **Filleting the underside.** Turn the fish over and remove the two fillets from the underside of the fish. Trim off any remaining fins and ragged edges from the fillets. Reserve the fish head and skeleton, if you like, for preparing stock.

3 **Skinning the fillets.** Place each fillet with its skin side down and cut about ½ inch [1 cm.] of flesh away from the skin at the tail end. Grasp the exposed tail skin in one hand and insert the stiff blade of a heavy knife beneath the flesh at a shallow angle. Hold the tail end taut as you cut away from yourself with short strokes to separate the fillet from its skin.

5 **Grilling the packets.** To avoid breaking the fillets, use a long metal spatula to place the foil packets on a rack 4 to 6 inches [10 to 15 cm.] above medium-hot coals. Cook the fillets— without turning the packets over—for seven or eight minutes.

6 **Serving the fillets.** Using the spatula, remove the packets from the grill. Carefully open one packet at a time by unfolding the ends and top, and gently slide its contents—including the accumulated juices—onto a platter. Serve the fillets immediately.

Chunky Kebabs of Fish and Vegetables

For an interplay of tastes and textures, small pieces of fish and vegetables can be strung onto skewers and grilled together as kebabs. Any fish fillet or steak that is at least ¾ inch [2 cm.] thick can be used. But because bite-sized pieces will dry out quickly when grilled, the best types of fish to choose are naturally fatty ones—trout, catfish, swordfish or the salmon used in this demonstration.

Cucumbers, summer squashes, onions or peppers all would complement the fish. To make sure that every ingredient grills at the same rate, the vegetables should be parboiled for a minute or two. Both vegetable and fish pieces need oil to keep their surfaces moist. Steeping them beforehand in an oil-based marinade lubricates them thoroughly and introduces flavor too.

The kebabs will need only seven or eight minutes of grilling, but must be turned often to cook evenly. Serve them hot from the grill with a compound butter or basil mayonnaise *(pages 14-15)*.

1 **Preparing ingredients.** Remove the skin and any bones from fish fillets or steaks 1 inch [2½ cm.] thick. Cut the fish—in this case, salmon fillets—into bars about 1 inch wide and 1 ½ inches [4 cm.] long. Cut red onions into six or eight wedges. Parboil the wedges for two minutes in lightly salted water, drain them and separate the layers.

2 **Marinating.** Place the fish and onion pieces in a shallow dish. Sprinkle chopped fresh herbs—here, sage—over them and season with salt and pepper. Pour in enough olive oil to coat the fish and onions lightly. Let them marinate at room temperature for up to 30 minutes, turning the pieces frequently to keep them well coated.

3 **Forming the kebabs.** Beginning and ending each kebab with a piece of onion, impale the fish and onion pieces alternately on skewers. Push the pieces close together as you go.

4 **Grilling the kebabs.** Place the kebabs on an oiled rack 4 to 6 inches [10 to 15 cm.] above medium-hot coals. To ensure that the pieces brown evenly on all sides, loosen the kebabs every minute or so with a spatula and turn them with tongs that have long gripping ends. Grill the kebabs for seven minutes, or until the fish is firm and opaque.

5 **Serving.** While the kebabs are grilling, coat a serving platter with basil mayonnaise. To serve the kebabs, grasp the handle of each skewer with a cloth napkin or towel, and hold the kebab over the platter. Then push the fish and onion pieces off the skewer onto the platter with a carving fork.

Shucked Oysters in Bacon Wrappers

Freshly shucked oysters are at their succulent best when wrapped in bacon and grilled over coals in a hinged basket. The bacon contributes a smoky taste, and its crispness counterpoints the tender texture of the shellfish. More important, the melting bacon fat bastes the oysters and keeps them moist as they cook.

Before shucking oysters, check to see if the shells are tightly shut. Discard any with gaping shells—a sign that the oyster is dead. Scrub the oysters, then use an oyster knife to free the flesh from the shells. Available at kitchen-equipment stores and seafood markets, an oyster knife has a strong, short blade and a pointed tip to pierce the shell's thick hinge and force it open.

Once shucked, the shellfish should be quickly wrapped and grilled. Here, a small basil leaf and a square of grilled red pepper are tucked into each package. For other flavor accents, lovage, marjoram, savory or thyme might replace the basil leaf, and small pieces of scallion or onion could be used instead of the pepper.

1 **Opening oysters.** Scrub the oysters under cold running water. Place one oyster at a time on a folded cloth towel, positioning the oyster with its flatter shell uppermost and its hinged end toward you. Grasp the broad end of the oyster with the cloth, then insert the tip of an oyster knife into the hinge and twist the blade to force the shells apart.

2 **Severing the muscles.** Slide the knife along the inside surface of the top shell to cut the muscle that attaches the shell to the flesh. Discard the top shell. Slide the blade of the knife under the oyster to release the flesh from the bottom shell. Use the tip of the knife to clean out any bits of shell. Empty the oyster, with its juices, into a bowl.

3 **Wrapping the oysters.** Grill, seed and peel a red pepper (page 19); cut it into small squares. Pull the small leaves from sprigs of fresh basil. Halve thick bacon slices crosswise. For each assembly, place an oyster at one end of a bacon slice. Lay a basil leaf and pepper square on the oyster. Roll the oyster in the bacon slice.

4 **Securing the bacon.** Insert a wooden pick that has been soaked in water for 10 minutes into the exposed end of the bacon. Press the pick through the roll at a diagonal until its point emerges on the underside. Wrap the remaining oysters in bacon in the same way.

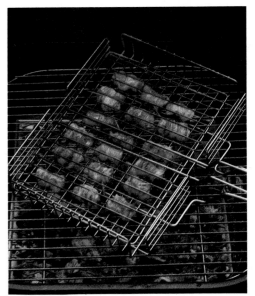

5 **Grilling the oysters.** Place the bacon-wrapped oysters side by side in the basket section of an oiled, hinged grill. Close the grill and clamp it shut. Place the grill on a rack 4 to 6 inches [10 to 15 cm.] above medium-hot coals. Turning the basket frequently, grill the oysters for about six minutes, or until the bacon is crisp and brown on all sides.

Orchestrating a Selection of Grilled Shellfish

For a glorious outdoor feast, a mélange of shellfish can be grilled in their shells and all presented together on a huge platter. The shells are not only decorative, but also protective. They shield the fragile flesh from the drying heat of the coals and help the shellfish retain their juices.

Lobsters, crabs, crayfish, shrimp, Malaysian prawns, oysters, mussels and all kinds of hard-shell clams are suitable for grilling. To ensure freshness, look for live shellfish: Lobsters close their tails when lifted, crabs and crayfish wave their claws, bivalves should be closed tight. Shrimp and prawns are seldom sold live, but be sure those you buy feel firm and smell sweet.

Bivalves are ready for grilling as soon as they are scrubbed and, in the case of mussels, debearded by pulling the rope-like strands from their shells. Lobsters and crabs must be killed as shown in this demonstration. Lobsters then should be halved and eviscerated, crabs cleaned and separated from their top shells.

Smaller crustaceans such as shrimp need to be rinsed, and will be easier to handle if skewered. Impaling them cross-wise on parallel skewers *(Step 3)* will hold them flat so that they cook evenly.

To keep the flesh moist, all of the crustaceans need to be oiled before they are grilled and basted at least once while they cook. Rubbing them with an oil-based marinade will add flavor as well as lubrication; the leftover marinade can be used for basting.

To make sure that everything is ready at the same time, start with the shellfish that need the longest cooking and add others in successive stages. Allow 12 to 15 minutes for lobsters; 10 to 12 minutes for Dungeness crabs; eight to 10 minutes for blue crabs, oysters and clams; six to eight minutes for crayfish; and four to five minutes for shrimp, Malaysian prawns and mussels. Crustaceans are done when their flesh is firm and opaque; bivalves when their shells open.

Traditionally, grilled shellfish are accompanied by melted butter. Here, the butter is enhanced by adding the coral (roe) and tomalley (liver) of the lobsters as well as crab fat, and simmering for five minutes. The mixture is then laced with lemon juice and whisked until smooth.

1 **Preparing lobsters.** Place each lobster right side up. Steady it, then use the tip of a large knife to pierce through the shell and flesh at the center of the cross-shaped mark behind the head to kill the lobster quickly. Turn the lobster over and force the blade of the knife through the center of its body and tail to halve it lengthwise *(above, left)*. Discard the gravel sac from the body and the intestinal vein from the tail. Remove and reserve the blackish roe, if any, and the greenish tomalley *(right)*. Cut off the claws.

4 **Preparing a marinade.** In a large bowl, assemble an oil-based marinade—in this case, a spicy combination of sliced fresh hot chilies, chopped green pepper, sliced garlic, olive oil, salt and pepper. Add the crabs and turn them in the marinade to coat them thoroughly. Then transfer the coated crabs to a shallow dish.

5 **Marinating the crustaceans.** Rub the marinade over the skewered shrimp and add the shrimp to the crabs. Then rub the exposed flesh of the halved lobsters with the marinade. Set the crustaceans aside and let them marinate for up to 30 minutes.

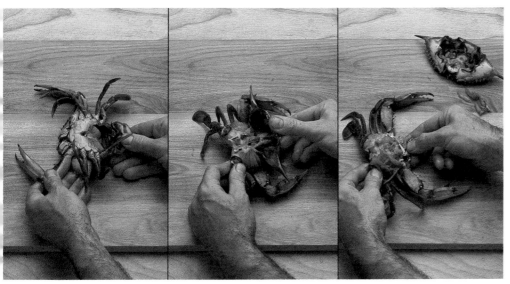

2 **Preparing crabs.** Kill each crab—here, a blue crab—by stabbing it just behind the eyes with a knife point. Turn the crab upside down and pry up, twist off and discard the triangular tail flap, or apron *(above, left)*. Turn the crab over and pry off its top shell *(center)*. Pull off and discard the spongy gills that lie along each side of the crab's exposed top *(right)*, as well as the grayish sandbag in its center. Remove any soft yellowish matter—crab fat—from the body and top shell, and add it to the lobster roe and tomalley. Reserve the top shell, if desired, for a garnish.

3 **Skewering shrimp.** Rinse shrimp under cold running water and pat them dry. Then thread the shrimp onto pairs of skewers, alternating the direction in which the tails point to fit the shrimp close together. Use a stiff brush to scrub the shells of live oysters and clams under running water.

6 **Grilling.** Place the lobsters flesh side up on an oiled rack 4 to 6 inches [10 to 15 cm.] above medium-hot coals. After two minutes, add the crabs and bivalves. After five minutes, add the shrimp, baste the lobsters and crabs, and turn all the shellfish *(left)*. Turn and baste the shrimp occasionally for five minutes, or until all the shellfish are done. Serve with melted butter enriched by the roe, tomalley and crab fat *(inset)*.

5
Special Presentations

Outdoors or at a fireplace, an adventurous approach to ingredients and techniques can be highly rewarding. Cheese, for example, might seem an improbable candidate for the grill because it melts on exposure to heat. Yet hard and soft cheeses alike can be transformed into epicurean delights if their melting is controlled by enclosing slices in a hinged grill basket *(pages 80-81)* or in leafy wrappers *(opposite)*. And a large wedge of cheese can become the basis for the Swiss classic called *raclette* if it is simply set beside the fireplace and scraped onto a plate as it melts.

The delicacy of domesticated rabbit may provide another surprise. Although available from most butchers and supermarkets, rabbit is neglected by many cooks. It may, however, become a family favorite when introduced as a spit-roasted meat. The gentle heat preserves the rabbit's tender texture and the smoke enhances its mild flavor *(pages 82-83)*.

Because a whole rabbit is small, it fits easily on a conventional rotisserie spit and cooks quickly. But large animals—pigs, lambs or goats—also can be spit-roasted whole *(pages 84-87)*. The basic tactics of marinating and trussing the animal ahead of time, then turning and basting it as it cooks remain the same. Only the scale changes: The spit for a pig, lamb or goat is a ½-inch [1-cm.] steel rod, and its supports are two stacks of cinder blocks. Instead of a modest mound of coals, you will need a bonfire of kindling and—over the four to six hours of roasting often necessary—50 to 60 pounds [22½ to 27 kg.] of charcoal lumps.

A lavish fire is also the secret of success for that most American of all outdoor banquets, a clambake at the beach. Originated by the Indians of what came to be known as New England, a clambake is a unique technique for blanketing foods with seaweed and cooking them in a pit lined with hot stones *(pages 88-90)*. Besides clams, such shellfish as lobsters and crabs are traditional ingredients, as are corn and potatoes. To ensure that the foods cook evenly, the stones must be heated uniformly—a process that takes at least two hours. In order to create and sustain a fire of the necessary intensity, about 30 pounds [13½ kg.] of fuel is minimal. Traditionally the fuel is driftwood, but any other dry wood will serve, of course, as will charcoal. Whatever the choice, the embers from the fire must be raked away before seaweed and food can be placed in the pit and the cooking begun.

Spiked with herbs and closely wrapped in grape leaves, rounds of montrachet—a soft goat's-milk cheese—melt slowly to a creamy smoothness on a rack set over glowing embers. The leaves prevent the cheese from dripping onto the coals and imbue it with a unique tanginess.

Warming Cheeses at the Fire

Surprisingly, perhaps, the simplest food to prepare over coals or beside a fireplace is cheese. It only needs gentle heating to give it a soft, melting texture and to bring out its flavor.

As demonstrated here, the best tactics for accomplishing this vary from type to type. Hard cheeses—Parmesan, Romano and well-aged Cheddar, for instance—are sturdy and dry enough to be grilled directly over medium-hot coals if cut into thick slices *(top demonstration)*. A hinged grill basket makes it possible to turn the cheese as quickly and frequently as needed to keep the melting edges from dripping into the coals.

Softer cheeses, however, melt too fast for such handling. When sliced or cut into chunks, these must be wrapped up before they can be set on a rack or in a basket. Foil may, of course, be used for the packages, but grapevine leaves offer an attractive and flavorful alternative and give a tangy flavor to the cheese *(bottom demonstration)*. Appropriate cheeses include firm, semisoft and soft types: Gruyère and Fontina, feta and Bel Paese, Camembert and montrachet—the creamy goat's-milk cheese that is used here.

Large wedges of firm cheeses such as Bagnes, belalp, belsano and gomser also form the base for the Swiss specialty known as *raclette (box, far right),* named for *racler,* the French verb meaning "to scrape." The cheese is placed on a hearth before a fire and, as the exposed edge melts, it is scraped off, transferred to a warm plate and quickly eaten—traditionally with small potatoes boiled in their jackets and tiny sour gherkins.

Softening Aged Parmesan

1 Preparing cheese slices. Use a sharp, heavy knife to trim the dried edges and rind from a block of hard cheese such as the Parmesan used here. Reserve the scraps for grating. Turn the block of cheese on edge and slice it into slabs about ⅓ to ½ inch [8 mm. to 1 cm.] thick. Use your fingers to spread olive oil on both sides of each slice of cheese.

2 Grilling the cheese. Place the cheese slices inside an oiled hinged grill basket. Rest the basket 4 to 6 inches [10 to 15 cm.] above medium-hot coals on a grill rack or, as here, on bricks stacked before a fireplace *(pages 36-37).* Cook the cheese for about three minutes, turning it frequently to prevent it from dripping.

Enfolding Creamy Montrachet in Leaves

1 Preparing the cheese. Pour olive oil onto a plate and roll fresh thyme sprigs in the oil. Cut cheese—in this case, montrachet—into slices ½ to ¾ inch [1 to 2 cm.] thick. Turn the cheese slices in the oil to coat them thoroughly.

2 Wrapping the cheese. Rinse fresh grapevine leaves, as here, or grapevine leaves preserved in brine. Pat the leaves dry with paper towels. Center an oil-coated cheese slice on the dull-colored underside of one leaf and top with an herb sprig. Fold the two leaf sections nearest the stem over the cheese, then the two middle sections.

3 Serving. As soon as the cheese is soft and slightly colored, turn it onto a warmed serving platter and sprinkle it with herbs; here, whole oregano leaves are used, but chopped sage, rosemary or basil would also be suitable. Sprinkle the cheese with freshly ground pepper and dribble olive oil over it. Serve immediately.

A Swiss Specialty

Melting the cheese. Place a large wedge of *raclette* cheese on a cutting board set on bricks in front of a fire. As cheese melts along the edge exposed to the fire, scrape it off onto warmed individual plates and serve it immediately with boiled potatoes.

3 Securing the leaf packages. If you are using a fresh leaf, bring the top leaf point over the cheese and push the stem through it to secure the package. With preserved leaves, use a wooden pick that has been soaked in water for 10 minutes to pin the top leaf point in place. Wrap the remaining cheese slices in the same way.

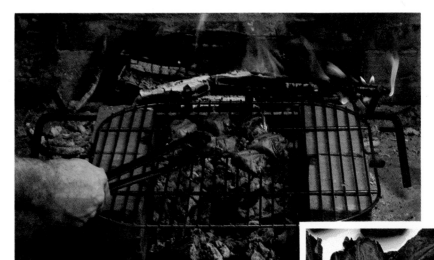

4 Grilling and serving. Place the packages on an oiled rack 4 to 6 inches [10 to 15 cm.] above medium-hot coals. Grill the packages for four minutes on each side, turning them with tongs *(above)*. When the packages feel very soft, arrange them on a platter with chunks of crusty bread. Open each leaf to eat the cheese *(inset)*.

Larding and Basting to Keep Rabbit Succulent

The fine texture and delicate flavor of rabbit's lean, light-colored meat invite comparisons to chicken. However, rabbit is always skinned and therefore requires special handling to prevent the meat from drying out and toughening as it cooks. When cut into pieces and grilled by the technique shown for chicken on pages 54-55, rabbit must be oiled and basted with a lavish hand. When spit-roasted whole—over a grill or, as demonstrated here, at a fireplace—it also should be larded by stitching strips of pork fat, or lardons, into the thighs of its hind legs. For extra flavor, the lardons can be rolled in herbs or spices.

Rabbits usually weigh from 3 to 5 pounds [1½ to 2½ kg.], but are so slender that they require only about one to one and one half hours of roasting. Because of this slenderness, enough heat will penetrate the body cavity to warm a precooked stuffing. Here, the rabbit is filled with mushrooms, bacon and herbs (recipe, page 167). A stuffing of fresh bread crumbs, shallots, celery, and the heart and liver of the rabbit would also be appropriate, as would lightly browned sausage meat, apples and onions.

1 **Stuffing the rabbit.** Chop fresh mushrooms—in this case, 2 pounds [1 kg.] were used—and sauté them in butter for 15 minutes, or until they give up all their liquid. Transfer them to a bowl. Chop sliced bacon into small bits and fry them until crisp—about five minutes; drain the bacon and add it to the mushrooms with chopped savory and thyme. Cut away any chunks of fat from the cavity of a cleaned rabbit. Season the cavity with salt and pepper, and fill it loosely with the mushroom stuffing.

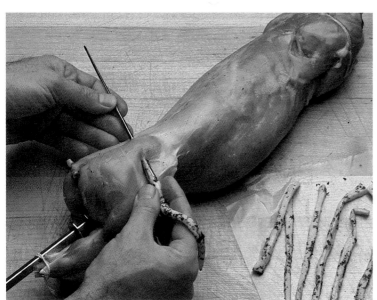

5 **Larding the hind legs.** Cut chilled fatback into 10 lardons ¼ inch [6 mm.] wide and 4 inches [10 cm.] long. Roll the lardons in chopped herbs—here, savory and thyme. Clamp one lardon in a larding needle and push it through one thigh to make a stitch. Trim the lardon, letting about ½ inch [1 cm.] protrude at both ends. Repeat to insert five lardons into each thigh. Wrap string twice around the midsection of the rabbit and tie it.

6 **Roasting the rabbit.** Set a drip pan in the center of a grill (page 9) or between bricks stacked at a fireplace (page 58). Pour in a ½-inch [1-cm.] layer of water. Position the rabbit above the pan. Brush the rabbit every 10 minutes with the pan juices—in this case, applied with lemon peel and rosemary sprigs grasped in tongs. Roast the rabbit for one to one and one half hours, or until the juices from the thigh run clear.

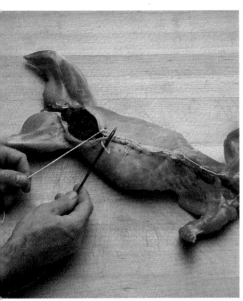

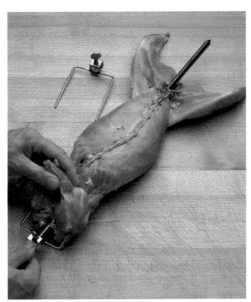

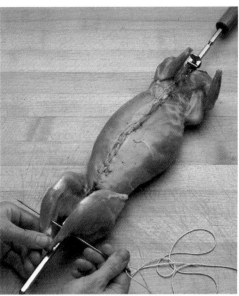

2 **Closing the cavity.** Thread a trussing needle with 18 inches [45 cm.] of kitchen string. Join the edges of the cavity at the neck end with a few stitches, passing the string through the loop of each preceding stitch as you sew. Make stitches at 1-inch [2½-cm.] intervals from the neck to the tail end. Cut off the string and knot it.

3 **Spitting the rabbit.** Slide a holding fork onto the spit rod, prongs pointing away from the handle. Push the spit through the rabbit from the neck to the tail end, keeping the spit as close to the center of the cavity as possible. Lift the forelegs and push the prongs of the fork into the shoulders.

4 **Trussing the legs.** Slide the second holding fork onto the spit and insert the prongs into the thighs. Extend the hind legs, push the threaded needle through them, then tie the legs to the spit. Fold the forelegs against the chest, loop string around the body and tie it tightly. Check the spitted rabbit for balance (page 59, Step 4).

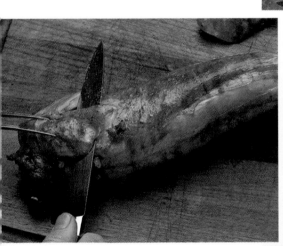

7 **Carving.** Remove the spit, cut off the strings and let the rabbit rest for 10 minutes. Steadying the rabbit with a fork, slice through the joint between the thigh and body to remove each leg (above). To carve each loin, make a cut from backbone to belly just behind the ribs. Slice along the ribs to the neck (right) and from the ribs to the tail. Slit the belly, scoop out the stuffing and serve it with the meat.

Spit-roasting on a Grand Scale

The most spectacular centerpiece for an outdoor feast is a whole animal spit-roasted over coals. Calves and beeves are too large for an amateur cook to handle, but pigs, lambs and goats all are obtainable in suitable sizes.

Even so, producing such a treat is not easy: The animal must be ordered specially from a butcher or ethnic market— usually a week or more ahead of time. Since only the smallest suckling pig will fit onto the spit of a rotisserie, the roasting apparatus generally must be secured from a rental service or improvised with a steel rod and cinder blocks, as demonstrated here and on the following pages.

The dressed weight of lambs and goats ranges from 12 to 50 pounds [5 to 22½ kg.], pigs from 7 to more than 150 pounds [3½ to 67½ kg.]. However, an animal of 100 pounds [45 kg.] or more demands special support apparatus, and the 70-pound [31½-kg.] pig shown here is about the largest size practicable. An animal of such dimensions will not fit into a home refrigerator. Ask the butcher to defrost it if it has been frozen. Then keep it chilled in an ice-filled bathtub.

Several days in advance, buy a ½-inch [1-cm.] stainless- or cold-rolled steel rod about 4 feet [120 cm.] longer than the animal's length when its legs are extended. (Avoid galvanized steel; its coating may be toxic.) Have a blacksmith or welding shop make two right-angle bends at one end of the rod to form a handle, and drill a pair of ⅛-inch [3-mm.] holes through the rod to secure the wires that will hold the animal's feet *(Steps 6 and 7)*. Finally, erect cinder-block supports—broadly based to be stable and high enough to raise the spitted animal about 2½ feet [75 cm.] above the fire.

Start the fire about two hours before you plan to roast the animal. During roasting, keep the fire stoked so the temperature at spit level is constant. Allow three hours for the heat to penetrate any animal. One of up to 15 pounds [6¾ kg.] may be fully cooked at this stage. Roast a larger animal about one hour longer for each additional 15 pounds. When the estimated time has almost elapsed, make a thermometer test *(Step 14)* to ensure well-done pork—and lamb or goat that is cooked to the degree you prefer *(page 42)*.

1 **Starting the fire.** Build two parallel graduated stacks of cinder blocks about 3 feet [90 cm.] high and 4 feet [120 cm.] apart. Top each stack with a halved block. Midway between the stacks, form a tepee of kindling around a wad of crumpled newspaper. Ignite the paper and, when the kindling is burning well, begin to add charcoal gradually—using a total of about 30 pounds [13½ kg.] of charcoal. When all of the charcoal is burning, use a metal-tined rake to spread it into a layer 8 inches [20 cm.] deep.

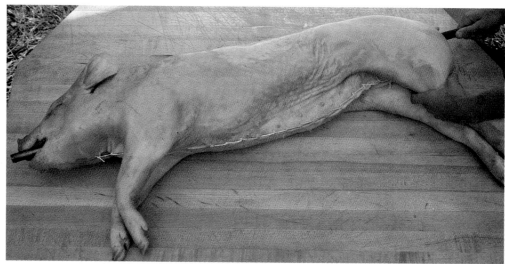

5 **Spitting the pig.** Using another string, sew the neck cavity shut with a few stitches. Lay the pig on its side and push the spit—in this case, a ½-inch [1-cm.] steel rod—through the tail end into the body cavity. Pushing gently, guide the spit so that it emerges through the mouth of the pig. Wrap the pig's ears with foil to prevent them from burning.

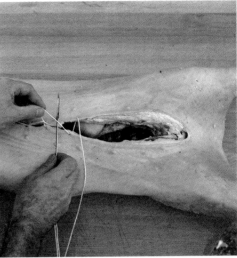

2 **Preparing the marinade.** To flavor the pig, make a marinade—here, a lime, orange and garlic mixture *(recipe, page 162)*. Chop the cloves of several garlic bulbs and place them in a large bowl. Add several bay leaves. Squeeze limes and oranges and strain the juice into the bowl. Stir in olive oil, coarse salt and black pepper.

3 **Marinating the pig.** Rub the marinade into the body cavity and the skin of the pig, making sure it is thoroughly coated. Alternatively, place the pig in a large tub and pour the marinade over it. Let the pig marinate for up to two hours, brushing marinade over its skin occasionally to keep it moist.

4 **Closing the cavity.** Brush the garlic and bay leaves from the skin and place them in the body cavity along with lime and orange rinds and a handful of coarse salt. Tie 3 feet [90 cm.] of string to a trussing needle. Starting at the front end of the pig, close the body cavity by making stitches at 2-inch [5-cm.] intervals—passing the string beneath the preceding stitch each time. Tie and cut the string.

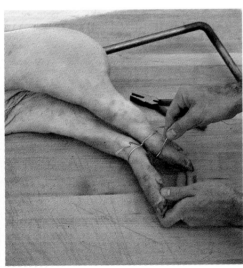

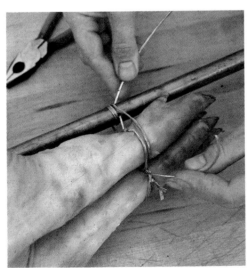

6 **Trussing the feet.** Using a 2-foot [60-cm.] length of 16-gauge cold-rolled or stainless-steel wire, make a loop around one hind foot of the pig. Tighten the loop with pliers, then pass the wire around the other hind foot and draw it close to the first. Twist the two ends of the wire together tightly and cut off any excess. Truss the front feet similarly.

7 **Binding the feet to the spit.** Wrap the middle section of another 2-foot [60-cm.] piece of wire around the spit several times next to the hole drilled nearest the handle. Twist the wire tight with the pliers, then pass it through the hole. Pull the hind feet tight to the spit and loop the wire around them in a figure eight. Twist the ends of the wire together and cut off the excess. Repeat with the front feet.

8 **Tying chicken wire.** To further support the pig, place it on a rectangle of chicken wire long and wide enough to wrap around it loosely. Pull the sides of the chicken wire over the pig. Join the overlapping portions with short pieces of wire, twisting the ends of the pieces together with pliers. ▶

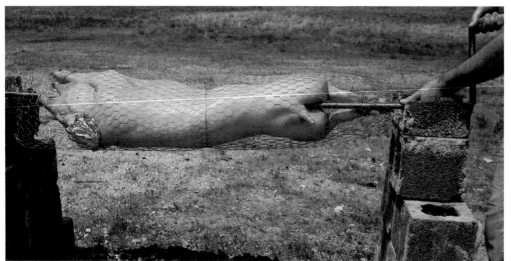

9 **Setting the spit in place.** When the charcoal is covered with white ash—after about two hours—rake the embers into two parallel banks almost as long as the spit and about 18 inches [45 cm.] apart. Restoke the fire if necessary. With the aid of a helper, center the spitted pig between the banks of coals, resting the ends of the spit in the upturned hollows of the split cinder blocks. To hold the pig steady, brace the handle of the spit with a wooden stake that is wedged against an extra cinder block.

10 **Basting the pig.** Strain the leftover marinade and set it aside in a convenient place. When fat begins to drip from the pig—after about 20 minutes of roasting—baste it with the marinade. Then rotate the spit to give the pig a quarter turn. Continue to baste and turn the pig every 20 minutes or so.

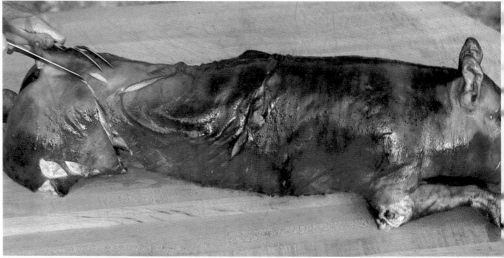

14 **Testing for doneness.** After the pig has roasted for the estimated time—almost seven hours, in this case—insert a meat thermometer into the thickest part of one hind leg. When the thermometer registers 165° to 170° F. [75° C.], take the spitted pig off the fire with the aid of a helper. Wear heavy mitts in order to handle the spit safely.

15 **Removing one hind leg.** Lay the pig on a large work surface and pull out the spit. Let the pig rest for 15 to 20 minutes to facilitate carving. Then, steadying the pig with a carving fork, use a sharp, heavy knife to cut off a hind leg, slicing from the front of the haunch toward the tail.

11 **Removing the wire cage.** After an hour or so of roasting, the flesh of the pig will be firm and you can remove the chicken-wire cage. Wearing flame-resistant mitts, cut the wire ties on the cage with pliers. Then carefully unfold the chicken wire and lift it off the pig.

12 **Rearranging coals.** As the pig roasts, some parts may brown faster than others—here, a dark patch is visible on the belly. If this happens, rearrange the coals so that less heat reaches those parts. In this instance the coals have been raked into banks parallel to the cinder-block supports.

13 **Wrapping in foil.** For extra protection, wrap the browned parts of the pig in heavy-duty aluminum foil—the entire midsection is covered here. Leave the foil in place until the pig is almost done. Periodically add more charcoal to the fire to keep the temperature at spit level constant.

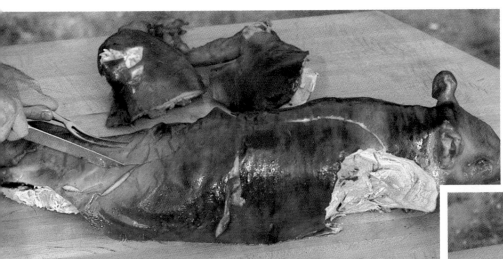

16 **Carving the loin.** To remove the foreleg, cut into the shoulder where it joins the leg. Slice behind the shoulder blade to about 1 inch [2½ cm.] behind the ear, then cut straight down to sever the leg. Make an incision the length of the spine, pressing the knife down to the bone (above). Press the back of the carving fork against the loin and slice down, keeping the knife blade against the ribs, to detach the loin in one piece. Carve each loin crosswise into pieces about 3 inches [8 cm.] wide. Cut through the knee joint to divide the leg in two, then carve the thigh into thin slices, holding the knife parallel to the bone. Carve the other side of the pig in the same fashion.

The Clambake: A Traditional Seaside Feast

A clambake is one of the true extravaganzas of outdoor cooking. Despite its name, it involves no baking: The food is sheathed in seaweed and steamed in a pit lined with hot stones. Preparation and cooking may take upward of six hours, but the quantity of food produced is typically enough for a feast.

The ingredients are usually diverse as well as abundant. Clams are indispensable, but all manner of shellfish, fish, vegetables, poultry and meats can also be included. In this demonstration, the menu consists of soft-shell clams, lobsters, striped bass, potatoes and corn—in amounts to serve 12 generously.

For any clambake, finding a suitable site is the first requirement. Landlocked chefs may dig their pit in earth, but a sandy beach is traditional. Because local rules and ordinances vary widely, be sure to check them and obtain a permit, if necessary, before you begin to dig.

To line the pit, you will need hundreds of smooth, dry and regularly sized large stones—wet rocks or shale may explode when heated. The wood for heating the stones must be dry—and sufficient to maintain a fire over the entire pit for about two hours. The seaweed, on the other hand, must be wet and washed well if sandy. To cover the seaweed and hold in the heat from the stones, you will also need a tarpaulin or other large cloth.

Preparing the food itself is comparatively simple. Clams and other bivalves should be scrubbed; like lobsters and crabs, they are added live and they steam in their shells. For easy handling, fish, meats or poultry may be wrapped in foil. Here, bass fillets are seasoned, buttered and topped with lemon slices before being wrapped. Potatoes cook in their skins; corn should have the silk removed and be rewrapped in its husks (page 22).

The critical stage of a clambake occurs when you add the food. To keep the stones hot, you must work fast to rake out the embers of the fire, cover the stones with seaweed, distribute the foods, cover them with more seaweed and top the assembly with a tarpaulin. Then, you simply wait for about three hours as the hidden ingredients gently steam to doneness.

1 **Digging the pit.** Drive four sticks into a level stretch of sand or earth to mark out a rectangle of about 5 by 8 feet [150 by 240 cm.]. Dig out the sand or earth within the rectangle to a depth of about 18 inches [45 cm.]. If you are digging in earth, mound and pack it to form an embankment around the perimeter of the pit.

2 **Leveling the pit.** Use the back of a metal-tined rake to smooth the bottom o the pit. If you are digging in sand, stand as far back as possible to avoid breaking down the edges of the pit. If you are digging in earth, line the pit with c double layer of heavy-duty aluminum foil to prevent the earth from becoming muddy when you add wet seaweed.

6 **Removing the coals.** Let the wood burn until only glowing coals remain. With the back of the rake, carefully pull the coals out of the pit without disturbing the stones beneath them. To extinguish the embers, cover them with a thick layer of sand or douse them with water.

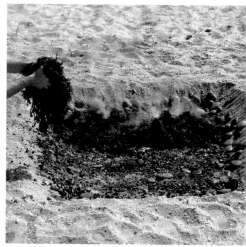

7 **Spreading seaweed.** Working quickly, spread wet and well-washed seaweed evenly over the bottom of the pit to form a layer about 6 inches [15 cm.] deep. In this case, three bushels of seaweed were used.

3 **Lining the pit.** Line the bottom and sides of the pit with smooth, dry stones. If necessary, stones can be purchased from a garden-supply store; in this instance, 400 pounds [180 kg.] of stones were used. Alternatively, line the pit with bricks. Even common bricks will do; they may crumble when heated, but will not explode.

4 **Laying a fire.** Remove the sticks used as corner markers. Place a pile of crumpled newspaper in the center of the stone-lined pit. Starting with small twigs and finishing with larger sticks and branches, build a tepee of kindling on top of the newspaper. Then ignite the newspaper with a match or lighter.

5 **Extending the fire.** When the kindling has begun to burn, gradually add logs to the fire until it fills the entire pit. Keep the fire stoked for at least an hour, then let it burn down for an additional hour to ensure that the stones are heated thoroughly.

8 **Distributing the food.** Lay the prepared foods in a single layer on top of the bed of seaweed. To simplify serving them later, arrange the foods in rows according to type. Here, corn is followed by potatoes, foil-wrapped bass fillets, lobsters and clams.

9 **Covering with seaweed.** Still working as quickly as possible, to conserve the heat from the stones, spread a 6-inch [15-cm.] layer of wet seaweed evenly over the foods. A total of six bushels of seaweed were used in this demonstration. ▶

10 **Covering the pit.** Spread a heavy-duty canvas drop cloth or a tarpaulin, as shown here, over the pit. To effectively trap the heat inside, the cover must be large enough to extend at least 1 foot [30 cm.] beyond each of the sides of the pit. Weight the corners of the cloth with stones to hold the cover in place.

11 **Testing for doneness.** Let the food cook undisturbed for about three hours. Then lift off the cloth cover. Use heavy gloves to remove enough seaweed to check each food in turn for doneness. When ready to eat, the clams will be opened, the small legs of the lobsters will pull away easily, and the fish will flake easily when a packet is opened and the flesh prodded with a fork. The potatoes will offer no resistance to a fork, and the ears of corn will steam when the husks are pulled away.

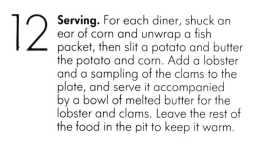

12 **Serving.** For each diner, shuck an ear of corn and unwrap a fish packet, then slit a potato and butter the potato and corn. Add a lobster and a sampling of the clams to the plate, and serve it accompanied by a bowl of melted butter for the lobster and clams. Leave the rest of the food in the pit to keep it warm.

Anthology
of Recipes

Drawing upon the cooking literature of more than 30 countries, the editors and consultants for this volume have selected 230 published recipes for the Anthology that follows. The selections comprise simple dishes such as garlic-broiled shrimp as well as elaborate ones—for example, a spit-roasted extravaganza featuring pork chunks, chicken pieces, quartered squabs, whole quail, sausages and caul-wrapped liver packets.

Many of the recipes were written by world-renowned exponents of the culinary art, but the Anthology also includes selections from rare and out-of-print books and from works that have never been published in English. Whatever the sources, the emphasis in these recipes is always on fresh, natural ingredients that blend harmoniously.

Since many early recipe writers did not specify amounts of ingredients or cooking times, the missing information has been judiciously added. In some cases, clarifying introductory notes have also been supplied; they are printed in italics. Modern recipe terms have been substituted for archaic language and some instructions have been expanded, but to preserve the character of the original recipes and to create a true anthology, the authors' texts have been changed as little as possible. Although some instructions have necessarily been expanded, in any circumstance where the cooking directions still seem abrupt, the reader need only refer to the appropriate demonstrations in the front of the book to find the technique explained.

In keeping with the organization of the first half of the book, the recipes in the Anthology are categorized according to major ingredients. Standard preparations—marinades, sauces and basic meat stock among them—appear at the end of the Anthology. Unfamiliar cooking terms and uncommon ingredients are explained in the combined General Index and Glossary.

Apart from the primary components, all ingredients are listed within each recipe in order of use, with both the customary U.S. measurements and the metric measurements provided in separate columns. All quantities reflect the American practice of measuring such solid ingredients as flour by volume rather than by weight, as is done in Europe.

To make the quantities simpler to measure, many of the figures have been rounded off to correspond to the gradations on U.S. metric spoons and cups. (One cup, for example, equals 237 milliliters; however, wherever practicable in these recipes, the metric equivalent of 1 cup appears as a more readily measured 250 milliliters—¼ liter.) Similarly, the weight, temperature and linear metric equivalents have been rounded off slightly. Thus the American and metric figures do not exactly match, but using one set or the other will produce the same good results.

Vegetables and Fruits

Grilled Artichokes

Alcachofas Asadas

To serve 4

4	large artichokes, stems cut off	4
	salt	
	olive oil	
	vinegar	

Open up the artichokes by spreading the leaves apart gently, without breaking them off. Sprinkle the artichokes with salt and pour oil and vinegar over them; be sure the dressing runs down between the leaves. Place the artichokes, stem side down, on a rack and grill them over coals. The heat should be gentle so that the artichokes cook through without burning. Turn the artichokes onto their sides after 10 minutes or so, and roll them over frequently until they are done—about 30 minutes in all. Before serving the artichokes, remove the charred outer leaves.

VICTORIA SERRA
TÍA VICTORIA'S SPANISH KITCHEN

Skewered Asparagus and Pork

Yachae Sanjuk

To serve 4

12	fresh asparagus tips, about 3 inches [8 cm.] long	12
¼ lb.	boneless lean pork, sliced ½ inch [1 cm.] thick and cut into strips ½ inch wide and 3 inches [8 cm.] long	125 g.
1	garlic clove, crushed to a paste	1
1 tsp.	sesame-seed oil	5 ml.
1 tsp.	sesame seeds	5 ml.
½ tsp.	salt	2 ml.
	black pepper	

Parboil the asparagus tips for about five minutes, or until crunchy but edible. Drain and set them aside. In a large bowl, combine the garlic with the sesame-seed oil, sesame seeds, salt and black pepper to taste. Add the pork strips and asparagus tips, and mix them well until all sides of the pork are coated with the sauce. Thread the pork and asparagus alternately onto four small skewers. Grill the kebabs over medium-hot coals for 10 minutes until the pork is well done.

JUDY HYUN
THE KOREAN COOKBOOK

Small Bean-and-Bacon Rolls

Bohnen-Speck-Röllchen

To serve 4

1 lb.	green beans, trimmed, blanched in salted water for 5 minutes, drained and cooled	½ kg.
8	lean bacon slices	8

To form each roll, lay two bacon slices flat, one overlapping the other slightly. Gather one quarter of the beans into a neat bundle, place it at one end of the slices and roll the beans up in the bacon. Wrap the roll in heavy-duty aluminum foil, folding the edges of the parcel together tightly. Place the parcels directly on the coals at the edge of the grill, or set them on the center of the rack over very hot embers. Turning the parcels repeatedly with tongs, grill them for about 20 minutes to cook the bacon thoroughly.

ANNETTE WOLTER
DAS PRAKTISCHE GRILLBUCH

Grilled Belgian Endive

Radicchio vom Grill

To core a Belgian endive, insert the point of a small knife about 1 inch [2½ cm.] into the plant's base and cut around the core with a circular motion.

This is an excellent accompaniment to mixed grilled fish.

To serve 4

1½ lb.	Belgian endive, cored and the leaves separated	¾ kg.
1 cup	oil	¼ liter

Brush each of the endive leaves with oil, then place them over a hot grill and cook for five minutes only, turning the leaves frequently. They should still be slightly crisp.

GIULIANA BONOMO
LA BUONA CUCINA

Grilled Corn on the Cob

To serve 6

6	ears of corn, husks and silk removed	6
8 to 12 tbsp.	butter, softened and mixed with salt	120 to 180 ml.
½ cup	grated Cheddar cheese	125 ml.

Spread the ears of corn with the butter and sprinkle them with the grated Cheddar cheese. Double-wrap each ear in foil. Grill 6 to 8 inches [15 to 20 cm.] from the coals, turning the ears every three or four minutes, until the corn is roasted and the cheese melted—about 15 to 20 minutes in all.

NANCY FAIR MC INTYRE
IT'S A PICNIC!

Campfire Corn Roast

To serve 4

4	ears of corn, husks pulled back, silk removed, husks closed tightly	4
	butter	

Bury the ears of corn in the hot ashes of the fire. Leave them for 30 minutes, or until the kernels are tender. Remove the husks and butter the kernels. Serve at once.

FERNE SHELTON (EDITOR)
PIONEER COOKBOOK

Eggplant and Pepper Salad

Escalivada Gironina

To serve 4

2	eggplants	2
2	red or green peppers	2
4 tbsp.	oil	60 ml.
	salt	
1	garlic clove, chopped	1
3 tbsp.	finely chopped fresh parsley	45 ml.

Cook the eggplants and peppers over a wood fire for 15 minutes, turning them often, until the skins are charred and the flesh is soft. When they are well cooked, remove the skins and the seeds from the peppers. Cut both the peppers and eggplants into long strips and arrange them on a serving dish. Season them with oil and salt, and sprinkle the garlic and parsley over them.

M. DEL CARME NICOLAU
CUINA CATALANA

Broiled Eggpla

To serve 6

1	large eggplant, cut lengthwis 6 wedges	
1	garlic clove	
2 tsp.	salt	10 ml.
	dried oregano leaves	
¼ cup	olive oil	50 ml.
1 tbsp.	red wine vinegar (optional)	15 ml.

Crush the garlic clove in a mortar with the salt; add a pinch of oregano, the olive oil and, if you like, the red wine vinegar. Paint this mixture onto the cut surfaces of the wedges and broil the eggplant slowly, over embers, until the cut surfaces are brown and tender.

HELEN EVANS BROWN
HELEN BROWN'S WEST COAST COOK BOOK

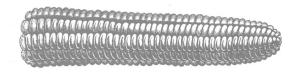

Barbecued Eggplant

Barbecued zucchini is prepared similarly, but the zucchini is not peeled. Both of the vegetables go well with barbecued meat, fowl or fish.

To serve 4

2	medium-sized eggplants, peeled and cut crosswise into ½-inch [1-cm.] slices	2
½ cup	oil	125 ml.
1 tsp.	finely chopped garlic	5 ml.
½ tsp.	paprika	2 ml.
4	peppercorns, crushed	4
¼ tsp.	oregano	1 ml.
	salt	

Brush the eggplant slices with a marinade made of the oil, garlic, paprika, peppercorns, oregano and salt to taste. Marinate the eggplant for seven minutes. Broil the slices over a slow charcoal fire for seven minutes on each side, or until they are well browned.

THE BROWN DERBY COOKBOOK

Marinated Mushrooms

To serve 6 to 8

2 lb.	small fresh mushrooms	1 kg.
	Oil and vinegar marinade	
½ cup	white wine vinegar	125 ml.
⅔ cup	olive oil	150 ml.
1 tbsp.	finely chopped fresh parsley	15 ml.
1	garlic clove, finely chopped	1
1 tbsp.	fresh lemon juice	15 ml.
½ tsp.	sugar	2 ml.
½ tsp.	pepper	2 ml.
½ tsp.	salt	2 ml.

In a large jar, combine all of the marinade ingredients. Shake vigorously. Add the mushrooms and refrigerate for 24 hours. Drain off the marinade, skewer the mushrooms and grill them, turning them frequently, until golden brown—about five minutes.

ED CALLAHAN
CHARCOAL COOKBOOK

Mushroom Kebabs, Tyrolean-Style

Pilzspiesschen Tiroler Art

All the pieces of mushroom, tomato, onion, bacon and sweet pepper should be of similar size.

To serve 4

1½ lb.	large mushrooms, cut into thick slices	¾ kg.
5 tbsp.	butter	75 ml.
4	plum tomatoes, quartered and seeded	4
1 tsp.	ground basil	5 ml.
2	onions, quartered lengthwise and separated into layers	2
4	thick slices lean bacon, cut into 1-inch [2½-cm.] squares	4
1	sweet red pepper, halved, seeded, deribbed and cut into squares	1
	salt and pepper	
2 tbsp.	oil	30 ml.
¼ cup	finely chopped fresh parsley	50 ml.

Heat the butter and stew the mushrooms in it for five minutes, or until all the liquid from the mushrooms has evaporated. Season the tomato pieces with the basil.

Thread the mushrooms, tomato, onion, bacon and red pepper onto four skewers. Sprinkle the kebabs with salt and pepper and brush them with the oil. Grill the kebabs over very low heat for about 10 minutes, turning them frequently. Serve them sprinkled with the chopped parsley.

MECHTHILD PIEPENBROCK
GRILL VERGNÜGEN DRAUSSEN UND DRINNEN

Barbecued Herbed Onions

To serve 4

4	large white onions, slashed into quarters but not cut completely apart	4
4 tbsp.	butter, softened	60 ml.
1 tbsp.	finely chopped fresh parsley	15 ml.
1 tbsp.	finely cut fresh chives	15 ml.
1 tbsp.	finely chopped fresh tarragon leaves	15 ml.

Mix the butter, parsley, chives and tarragon well. Stuff equal portions of the herb mixture into each onion. Wrap the onions in pieces of foil and roast them over hot coals for 20 to 30 minutes.

LOIS M. BURROWS AND LAURA G. MYERS
TOO MANY TOMATOES, SQUASH, BEANS AND OTHER GOOD THINGS

Baked Onion and Potato Salad from Huesca

Ensalada de Cebollas y Patatas

To serve 4

4	onions, unpeeled	4
4	potatoes, scrubbed but unpeeled	4
¾ cup	oil	175 ml.
4 tbsp.	white wine vinegar	60 ml.
	salt	

Place the onions and potatoes in the embers of a fire to bake. When they are tender, after about 45 minutes, remove the skins and eat them while they are still warm, dressed with oil and vinegar, and seasoned with salt.

DELEGACION NACIONAL DE LA SECCION FEMENINA DEL MOVIMIENTO
COCINA REGIONAL ESPAÑOLA

Barbecued Onion Slices

To serve 4

2	large onions, cut into slices ½ inch [1 cm.] thick	2
2 tbsp.	oil	30 ml.
1 tsp.	wine vinegar	5 ml.
½ tsp.	paprika	2 ml.
¼ tsp.	dried oregano leaves	1 ml.
	celery salt	

Combine the oil, vinegar, paprika, oregano and celery salt to taste. Marinate the onion slices for about one hour. Barbecue them over a slow charcoal fire for five minutes on each side.

THE BROWN DERBY COOKBOOK

Roasted Plantain
Platano Asado

To serve 1

1	ripe plantain	1
	butter	

Wash the plantain well and slit the skin from end to end. Place the plantain on a grill rack over charcoal embers and grill for 15 to 20 minutes, turning the plantain often to be sure it cooks on all sides. A skewer inserted in the slit should meet no resistance when the plantain is done. Remove the skin quickly and serve the plantain garnished with butter.

ST. MARY'S CATHEDRAL LADIES GUILD
CARACAS ¡BUEN PROVECHO!

Grilled Potatoes with Caraway
Grillkartoffeln

To serve 1 or 2

2	medium-sized potatoes	2
	salt	
	caraway seeds	

Scrub the potatoes and prick them several times with a knife. Lightly butter or oil two large, double-thick pieces of heavy-duty foil. Place a potato on each piece of foil, sprinkle salt and caraway seeds on it and wrap the foil tightly around it, sealing the packet carefully. Place the potatoes close together on red-hot charcoal and let them cook for 30 to 40 minutes. Serve the potatoes with a little butter or some salt, or sour cream or herb-flavored butter.

FRISCH VOM GRILL

Cheese Potatoes in a Parcel
Käsekartoffeln im Paket

Cheddar, Gruyère, Edam, Gouda, provolone, Jarlsberg, feta and Fontina cheeses are all suitable.

To serve 4

6	medium-sized potatoes, peeled and sliced	6
½ lb.	cheese, cut into ¼-inch [6-mm.] cubes	¼ kg.
	salt and pepper	
	paprika	
½ lb.	slab bacon with the rind removed, cut into ¼-inch [6-mm.] cubes	¼ kg.
2	onions, thinly sliced and separated into rings	2
4 tbsp.	butter, cut into pieces	60 ml.

Brush four large, double-thick pieces of heavy-duty aluminum foil with oil. Lay the potatoes on the foil, distributing the slices evenly, and season the potatoes with a little salt, pepper and paprika. Scatter the cheese and bacon cubes and the onion rings evenly over the potatoes, and sprinkle the butter pieces on top. Fold the foil to form four parcels, closing the edges carefully.

Cook the cheese potatoes over a charcoal grill for 50 minutes, turning the parcels repeatedly.

ANNETTE WOLTER
DAS PRAKTISCHE GRILLBUCH

Zucchini Parcels

To serve 4

4	medium-sized zucchini	4
½ tsp.	fresh oregano leaves	2 ml.
4	tomatoes, peeled, seeded and finely chopped	4
6 tbsp.	butter	90 ml.
	salt and freshly ground black pepper	

Parboil the zucchini for approximately four minutes in salted water to which the oregano has been added. Drain, then slice each zucchini lengthwise into quarters. For each portion, place four quarters on a sheet of heavy-duty aluminum foil. Add about a quarter of the chopped tomato, a few pieces of butter, salt and pepper. Wrap the foil securely around the vegetables, and barbecue over medium-hot coals for approximately 15 minutes, turning the parcels once.

JAMES F. MARKS
BARBECUES

Zucchini and Tomato Kebabs

To serve 2

2	medium-sized zucchini	2
8	cherry tomatoes	8
4 tbsp.	butter, melted	60 ml.
2 tbsp.	freshly grated Parmesan cheese	30 ml.
½ tsp.	dried oregano leaves	2 ml.
	salt and pepper	

Parboil the zucchini in 2 cups [½ liter] of salted water for two minutes. Remove them from the water and cut each into four chunks. Thread the zucchini alternately with the cherry tomatoes onto two small skewers. Baste the vegetables with the melted butter and cook them 8 inches [20 cm.] above hot coals, turning and basting them frequently, until tender and browned on all sides—about 10 minutes. Serve them sprinkled with the cheese, oregano, and salt and pepper.

ED CALLAHAN
CHARCOAL COOKBOOK

Baked Squash

To serve 1

1	acorn squash, halved and seeded	1
2 tbsp.	molasses	30 ml.
2 tbsp.	butter	30 ml.
4 tsp.	brown sugar	20 ml.

Wrap each squash half loosely in heavy-duty aluminum foil. Double-fold the open edges to seal the parcel. Place the squash on a grill rack, cut side down. Grill for about 30 minutes, or until the flesh of the squash is tender. When the squash is done, unwrap it and put half of the molasses, butter and brown sugar into each squash cavity.

STAFF HOME ECONOMISTS, CULINARY ARTS INSTITUTE
THE OUTDOOR GRILL COOKBOOK

Grilled Vegetables

Verdure alla Griglia

To serve 8

4	large potatoes	4
2	eggplants	2
4	sweet green or red peppers	4
4	large underripe tomatoes, halved	4
1 lb.	large mushrooms, stems removed	½ kg.
	olive oil	
	salt	
	fresh lemon juice	

Salt the potatoes lightly. Steam them over boiling water in a tightly covered pan for 30 to 45 minutes, or until they are just tender. Cool them slightly. Peel the potatoes; cut them into thick slices and brush them with oil. If you wish, cut the eggplants into thick slices, salt them and let them drain for 30 minutes. Then rinse the eggplant slices under cold water and pat them dry with paper towels.

Brush the peppers and the eggplants (slices or whole) with oil, and grill them over hot coals for about 20 minutes, turning them often. Oil the tomatoes and place them, cut side up, on the grill five minutes after the peppers. Sprinkle them with salt. Rub the mushrooms with lemon juice, brush them with oil, and grill them for about 10 minutes, turning them halfway through. Salt them after cooking. Grill the potato slices on one side only, until they are toasted.

When the peppers are cooked, peel and halve them and remove the seeds. Sprinkle them with salt. If you grilled the eggplants whole, cut them into quarters and season them with salt, oil and lemon juice before serving them.

ANNA BASLINI ROSSELLI
100 RICETTE PER LA COLAZIONE SULL'ERBA

Pumpkin Kebabs

Kürbis-Kebab

To serve 4

2 lb.	pumpkin, peeled, seeded and cut into 1½-inch [4-cm.] cubes	1 kg.
8	small tomatoes, halved	8
2	medium-sized potatoes, boiled for 10 minutes and cut into 1½-inch [4-cm.] cubes	2
	oil	

Thread the pumpkin cubes onto skewers, alternating them with the tomato halves and the cubes of half-cooked potato. Brush the skewers with oil and cook them on the grill for 15 minutes, or until thoroughly cooked and browned.

THEODOR BÖTTIGER
DAS GRILL-BUCH

———————◆———————

Geraldine's Apple Slices

Apfelscheiben Geraldine

To serve 4

2	large apples, peeled, cored and cut into rings ¾ inch [2 cm.] thick	2
3 tbsp.	fresh lemon juice	45 ml.
4 tbsp.	butter, melted	60 ml.
¼ cup	sugar, mixed with 1 tbsp. [15 ml.] ground cinnamon	50 ml.

Dip each apple slice in the lemon juice and let the excess juice drain off. Place a large piece of heavy-duty aluminum foil on the rack of a grill and brush it lightly with melted butter. Place the apple rings on the foil in a single layer, then brush them with some of the remaining butter. Grill the apples for three to four minutes. Sprinkle a little of the cinnamon sugar over the apple rings. Turn the rings and cook them for another three to four minutes, or until they are tender, brushing them with the remaining butter and sprinkling them with a little more cinnamon sugar.

Before serving, dip the cooked apple rings into any remaining cinnamon sugar.

ANNETTE WOLTER
DAS PRAKTISCHE GRILLBUCH

———————◆———————

Mixed Fruit Skewers

The author suggests that a selection of the following fruit should be used: quartered peaches, halved apricots, unripe bananas cut into 1-inch [2½-cm.] slices, chunks of pineapple, orange segments, apples and pears cut into wedges and sprin-kled with lemon juice to prevent them from darkening, pitted plums or cherries.

A very attractive alternative to the caramel is to brush the skewers frequently with a mixture of 8 tablespoons [120 ml.] of melted butter, 1 tablespoon [15 ml.] of sugar and 1 teaspoon [5 ml.] of cinnamon or powdered ginger or the seeds from a cardamom pod. Or squeeze lemon or orange juice into the melted butter. Serve the skewers with a little of the basting sauce poured over them.

To serve 4

1½ lb.	mixed fresh fruits	¾ kg.
¼ cup	sugar	50 ml.

Thread the fruits alternately onto skewers. Cook them over a medium fire, turning the skewers frequently, for five to 10 minutes. Then sprinkle them with the sugar and let it caramelize over the fire.

CLAUDIA RODEN
PICNIC: THE COMPLETE GUIDE TO OUTDOOR FOOD

———————◆———————

Fruit Kebabs

Brochettes de Fruits

To serve 6

3	barely ripe bananas, peeled and cut into quarters	3
2	oranges, cut into quarters	2
1	lemon, quartered	1
1	small pineapple, peeled, quartered, cored and thickly sliced	1
2 tbsp.	rum	30 ml.
⅔ cup	superfine sugar	150 ml.
1	loaf stale, firm-textured white bread, cut into ¾-inch [2-cm.] slices, crusts removed	1
7 tbsp.	butter, melted	105 ml.

Macerate the fruits for a few minutes in a mixture of the rum and 2 tablespoons [30 ml.] of the sugar. Cut each slice of bread into eight rectangles. Brush the pieces of bread with the butter and roll them in the remaining sugar.

Thread all of the ingredients onto six skewers, alternating the bread and the fruits. Cook over coals for about 10 minutes, or until the surfaces are caramelized, turning the skewers occasionally and sprinkling the bread and fruits with the rest of the sugar without letting the granules fall onto the coals. Serve hot.

MYRETTE TIANO
LES MEILLEURES RECETTES: PIQUES-NIQUES, BARBECUES

Bananas in Their Skins

Bananes en Robe

To serve 8

8	barely ripe bananas	8
3 tbsp.	granulated sugar	45 ml.
½ cup	kirsch	125 ml.

With a sharp knife, cut the skin of the bananas lengthwise and carefully remove half of the skin, making sure not to damage the flesh.

Place the bananas, skin side down, on a grill over coals that are not too hot. Cook them for about 10 minutes, or until the flesh is soft and the skin blackened.

Put the bananas on a heatproof platter and sprinkle them with the sugar. Heat the kirsch, set it alight and pour it over the bananas. When the flame dies, serve the bananas immediately.

MYRETTE TIANO
LES MEILLEURES RECETTES: PIQUES-NIQUES, BARBECUES

Meats

Tangy Barbecued Beef

To serve 6 to 8

4 lb.	boneless beef chuck	2 kg.
⅓ cup	red wine vinegar	75 ml.
¼ cup	tomato ketchup (recipe, page 163)	50 ml.
¼ cup	soy sauce	50 ml.
2 tbsp.	oil	30 ml.
1 tbsp.	Worcestershire sauce	15 ml.
½ tsp.	dry mustard	2 ml.
1	garlic clove, finely chopped	1
1 tsp.	salt	5 ml.
¼ tsp.	pepper	1 ml.

In a small mixing bowl, combine all the ingredients except the beef. Put the meat in a baking dish or a heavy-duty plastic bag. Pour the marinade over the meat and turn the meat until it is completely coated. Cover with plastic wrap or close the bag securely. Refrigerate it overnight.

About six hours before serving, remove the meat from the refrigerator. To prepare the smoker, soak two or three chunks of wood or a handful of wood chips in water for an hour or so. Fill the fire pan with charcoal and start the fire.

When the coals turn gray, drain the wood pieces and add them to the coals. Put the water pan in place and fill it almost full with hot water. Put the grill rack in place.

Lift the meat from the marinade and put it in the center of the rack. Pour the marinade into the water pan. Cover, and smoke the beef for about five hours, or until the meat is firm to the touch. After about four hours, check the water pan and—if necessary—add hot water. To serve, cut the beef into thin slices.

THE EDITORS OF CONSUMER GUIDE
SMOKE COOKERY

Beef Shanks and Summer Squash

To serve 4

4	slices beef shank, each 1 inch [2½ cm.] thick	4
4	medium-sized crookneck or zucchini squash, cut into halves lengthwise	4
2 cups	water	½ liter
½	medium-sized onion, sliced	½
1	carrot, sliced	1
1	bay leaf	1
8 to 10	black peppercorns	8 to 10
1 tsp.	salt	5 ml.
6 tbsp.	butter	90 ml.
1 tbsp.	prepared mustard	15 ml.
½ tsp.	prepared horseradish	2 ml.
½ tsp.	dried basil leaves	2 ml.
½ to ¾ cup	dry bread crumbs	125 to 175 ml.
	salt	

In a wide, shallow pan, combine the slices of beef shank, the water, onion, carrot, bay leaf, peppercorns and salt. Bring to a boil, cover and simmer slowly for about one and one half hours, or until the beef is tender. Cool the slices in the liquid, then bone them.

Melt the butter and blend in the mustard, horseradish and basil. Dip the beef slices in the seasoned butter; coat them with the bread crumbs. Sprinkle the squash halves with salt, then coat them with seasoned butter and crumbs.

Place the beef and the squash, cut side down, on a grill rack about 6 inches [15 cm.] above the coals. Turn them as needed. The meat will be browned and the squash tender in about 10 to 15 minutes. Pour the remaining seasoned butter over the meat and squash, and serve them.

ED CALLAHAN
CHARCOAL COOKBOOK

Smoked Rarified Brisket

To serve 8

4 to 5 lb.	beef brisket, trimmed of excess fat	2 to 2½ kg.
3	garlic cloves, cut into slivers	3
2	thick slices bacon, chopped	2
¼ cup	finely chopped fresh parsley	50 ml.
	paprika	
	crumbled dried thyme leaves	
	salt and freshly ground pepper	

Cut gashes in the meat and poke into each one a sliver of garlic and a little bacon that has been mixed with the parsley. Dust the meat generously on both sides with paprika, thyme, salt and pepper. Set the brisket in a smoker and cook for 35 to 45 minutes a pound, or until a meat thermometer inserted into the center of the brisket registers 150° F. [65° C.]. To serve, slice the meat diagonally across the grain.

MAGGIE WALDRON
FIRE & SMOKE

Roast Beef Done on a Spit

Pieczeń z Rożna

To serve 6 to 8

3 to 4 lb.	boneless beef rump or top-round roast	1½ to 2 kg.
2 tbsp.	olive oil	30 ml.
1½ tbsp.	fresh lemon juice	22½ ml.
3 or 4	onions, sliced	3 or 4
	salt and pepper	
	melted butter	
1 tbsp.	flour	15 ml.

Rub the meat with the olive oil, and sprinkle it with the lemon juice. Place half of the onion slices in a dish, put the beef on top of them and cover it with the remaining onion slices. Let the meat stand for three hours. An hour before cooking, season the meat with salt and pepper.

Fix the meat on a spit and place a drip pan beneath the spit to catch all of the drippings. Roast the meat over very hot coals, brushing it frequently with melted butter. When the meat is well browned, after about 20 minutes, dust it with the flour; let the flour dry, and again brush it with butter. The roast should be ready in 35 to 50 minutes, depending on its size and how well cooked you prefer it.

Slice the meat thin and serve it with potatoes and vegetables. Skim the fat from the juices in the drip pan and present them separately.

MARJA OCHOROWICZ-MONATOWA
POLISH COOKERY

Steak with Sky Ranch Steak Glaze

To serve 6

6	beef top-loin or shell steaks, cut 1 inch [2½ cm.] thick	6
6 oz.	Roquefort or other blue cheese, softened (about ⅓ cup [75 ml.])	175 g.
6 tbsp.	butter, softened	90 ml.
6 tbsp.	grated onion	90 ml.
2 tbsp.	Worcestershire sauce	30 ml.
1 tbsp.	fresh lemon juice	15 ml.
1 tbsp.	salt	15 ml.
2 tsp.	pepper	10 ml.
	Tabasco sauce	

To make the glaze, combine and cream together the cheese, butter, grated onion, Worcestershire sauce, lemon juice, salt, pepper and Tabasco sauce to taste. Grill the steaks over coals until they are done to your taste—about seven minutes for rare. Immediately spread the glaze on one side of the steaks at a time and grill the steaks for five seconds longer on each side, or just enough to make the cheese-butter mixture start to sizzle.

NANCY FAIR MC INTYRE
IT'S A PICNIC!

Barbecued Flank Steak

To serve 4

2 lb.	beef flank steak	1 kg.
1	garlic clove, crushed to a paste	1
2 to 3 tbsp.	soy sauce	30 to 45 ml.
1 tbsp.	tomato paste	15 ml.
1 tbsp.	oil	15 ml.
¼ tsp.	pepper	1 ml.
½ tsp.	fresh oregano leaves	2 ml.

Score the flank steak diagonally on both sides. Blend all of the remaining ingredients together until they are smooth. Pour the sauce over the steak, and marinate it in the refrigerator overnight. Grill the steak over hot coals for four to seven minutes on each side.

JUNIOR LEAGUE OF EL PASO, INC.
SEASONED WITH SUN

Barbecued Steak

Churrasco

In this specialty of Argentina, Uruguay, and parts of southern Brazil, the steaks are cooked on special grids set diagonally over a wood fire that has burned down to vivid coals.

To serve 6

two 3½ to 4 lb.	beef sirloin steaks, cut 3 inches [8 cm.] thick, excess fat removed	two 1½ to 2 kg.
½ lb. plus 2 tbsp.	butter	¼ kg. plus 30 ml.
2 cups	finely chopped scallions or 1½ cups [375 ml.] finely chopped onions	½ liter
½ tsp.	crumbled dried rosemary or oregano leaves, or a combination of both	2 ml.
1 cup	dry white wine	¼ liter
½ cup	wine vinegar or cider vinegar	125 ml.
1 tbsp.	freshly ground black pepper	15 ml.
1½ tsp.	salt	7 ml.

To make the sauce, melt ½ pound [¼ kg.] of the butter over medium heat and in it sauté the scallions or onions, stirring them often, for 10 minutes, or until they are soft but not brown. Add the rosemary and/or oregano, the wine, vinegar, pepper and salt. Stirring constantly, bring the sauce to a boil, then reduce the heat and simmer the sauce for five minutes. Remove the sauce from the heat, correct the seasoning and add the remaining butter.

Broil the steaks over hot coals until done to taste—about 15 minutes on each side for rare steaks. To serve, carve the steaks and pour the sauce over the slices.

ALEX D. HAWKES
THE FLAVORS OF THE CARIBBEAN & LATIN AMERICA

Steak au Poivre

To serve 6

6	beef top-loin or shell steaks	6
3 tbsp.	black peppercorns	45 ml.
¼ cup	Cognac, warmed	50 ml.
	salt	

Crush the peppercorns in a mortar with a pestle until coarsely ground. Dry the steaks with a paper towel. Rub the crushed peppercorns into both sides of the meat with the palm of your hand. Grill the steaks to individual taste and remove them from the rack. Pour the warm Cognac over them, stand back, and ignite it. The flame will burn for just a few minutes. When it goes out, scrape off the excess pepper, season the steaks with salt, and serve them.

NANCY FAIR MC INTYRE
IT'S A PICNIC!

Grilled Steak and Vegetables à l'Orientale

Egg-roll wrappers are obtainable at Chinese food stores.

To serve 4

one 1½ lb.	beef T-bone or sirloin steak, cut 1 inch [2½ cm.] thick, trimmed of excess fat	one ¾ kg.
	soy sauce	
5 tbsp.	olive or peanut oil	75 ml.
4	garlic cloves, thinly sliced	4
2	large onions, cut into ½-inch [1-cm.] slices and separated into rings	2
	salt	
4	sweet red peppers, stemmed, quartered and seeded	4
3	medium-sized zucchini, cut diagonally into 1-inch [2½-cm.] slices	3
6	egg-roll wrappers	6
Spicy sauce		
½ cup	soy sauce	125 ml.
½ tsp.	fresh lemon juice	2 ml.
1	garlic clove, finely chopped	1
	ground ginger	

Combine 1 tablespoon [15 ml.] of the soy sauce, 2 tablespoons [30 ml.] of the olive oil and the garlic in a shallow dish. Add the steak and turn it over several times to coat it with the mixture. Marinate the steak at room temperature for two hours.

Parboil the onion rings in salted water for five minutes. Drain them and place them on a large sheet of aluminum foil. Sprinkle the onions with salt and 1 teaspoon [5 ml.] of soy sauce; fold the foil over them to form a thin packet. Parboil the peppers for five minutes and drain them. Sprinkle both the peppers and the zucchini with soy sauce.

Cut each egg-roll wrapper in half. Rub the remaining 3 tablespoons [45 ml.] of oil over both sides of the wrappers, salt them, and fold them into squares. Prepare the sauce by combining the soy sauce, lemon juice, chopped garlic and ginger to taste.

Place the steak, peppers, zucchini and the onion packet over medium-hot coals and grill them for six minutes on each side, or until the steak is rare and the peppers and zucchini are well browned. Remove them to a warmed platter and grill the egg-roll wrappers briefly until they are lightly browned and bubbled on both sides.

To serve, cut the steak into thin slices and arrange the vegetables and crisp wrappers around them. Strain the sauce and present it on the side.

JUDITH OLNEY
SUMMER FOOD

Peter Hyun's Barbecued Korean Beef
Bul-Kogi

	To serve 4	
2 lb.	beef sirloin, rib or flank steak	1 kg.
3	scallions, finely chopped	3
4	garlic cloves, crushed to a paste	4
5 tbsp.	soy sauce	75 ml.
2 tbsp.	sesame-seed oil	30 ml.
1 tbsp.	sesame seeds	15 ml.
¼ cup	sugar	50 ml.
2 tbsp.	sherry or consommé	30 ml.
⅛ tsp.	black pepper	½ ml.

Slice the steak very thin across the grain, diagonally from top to bottom. Score each piece lightly with a cross. Combine the remaining ingredients in a bowl and mix this marinade well. Add the meat to the marinade, making sure that all the sides are well coated. Grill immediately or later; it is best to marinate the meat for at least two hours. A charcoal grill will give the best results, an open electric grill is very good or, failing this, the oven broiler.

NIKA HAZELTON
THE PICNIC BOOK

Beef Rib Steaks, Gypsy-Style
Entrecôte auf Zigeunerart

	To serve 4	
4	beef rib steaks, cut 1 inch [2½ cm.] thick, excess fat removed	4
2 tbsp.	red wine vinegar	30 ml.
2 tbsp.	Dijon mustard	30 ml.
1	onion, chopped	1
4	garlic cloves, crushed to a paste	4
1	small sweet red pepper, halved, seeded, deribbed and finely chopped	1
½ tsp.	dried thyme leaves	2 ml.
	salt and pepper	
8 tbsp.	lemon compound butter (recipe, page 165)	120 ml.

With a sharp knife, slit the border of fat around each steak at 1½-inch [4-cm.] intervals—cutting right through to the meat. Mix the vinegar, mustard, onion, garlic, red pepper

and thyme. Spread the steaks with this mixture, wrap them in foil and let them marinate for several hours. Then drain the steaks, reserving the marinade. Pat the steaks dry and grill them for three to five minutes on each side, or until they are browned on the outside but still pink in the middle. Remove the steaks from the grill and season them with salt and pepper. Spread on the remaining marinade, place a piece of lemon butter on each one and serve.

ULRIKE HORNBERG
SCHLEMMEREIEN VOM GRILL

Thai Beef Barbecue

	To serve 6	
2 lb.	boneless lean beef, thinly sliced	1 kg.
½ cup	soy sauce	125 ml.
¼ cup	sugar	50 ml.
6	garlic cloves, finely chopped	6
2 tbsp.	sesame seeds, toasted	30 ml.
¼ cup	thinly sliced scallions	50 ml.
¼ cup	finely chopped fresh coriander leaves	50 ml.
1 tbsp.	grated fresh ginger	15 ml.
	Dipping sauce	
⅓ cup	sugar	75 ml.
2 tbsp.	cornstarch	30 ml.
⅓ cup	soy sauce	75 ml.
3 tbsp.	vinegar	45 ml.
¾ tsp.	crushed red pepper	4 ml.

Combine the soy sauce, sugar, garlic, sesame seeds, scallions, coriander and ginger to make a marinade. Add the sliced beef, cover, and let the meat marinate in the refrigerator for up to two hours.

To make the dipping sauce, mix the sugar and cornstarch in a saucepan. Add the soy sauce, vinegar and crushed red pepper. Stirring constantly, cook the mixture until it bubbles and thickens slightly. Cool, cover and set aside at room temperature. Cook the beef slices on a hibachi for two minutes and serve them with the dipping sauce.

ELINOR SEIDEL (EDITOR)
CHEFS, SCHOLARS & MOVABLE FEASTS

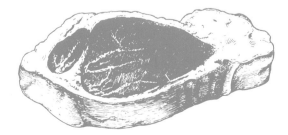

Extraordinary Barbecued Short Ribs

To serve 4 to 6

4 lb.	beef short ribs, excess fat removed	2 kg.
¼ cup	water	50 ml.
⅓ cup	tomato ketchup *(recipe, page 163)*	75 ml.
⅓ cup	oil	75 ml.
¼ cup	brown sugar	50 ml.
¼ cup	vinegar	50 ml.
1 tbsp.	finely chopped onion	15 ml.
1 ½ tsp.	chili powder	7 ml.
1 ½ tsp.	salt	7 ml.

Put the short ribs in a heavy plastic bag or deep bowl. Combine all of the remaining ingredients and pour them over the ribs. Close the bag tightly and turn it to coat the ribs completely; or spoon the marinade over the ribs in the bowl. Chill for at least several hours, preferably overnight.

To cook the ribs, lift them from the marinade and arrange them on the cooking rack of a smoker. Reserve the marinade. Smoke the ribs for four to five hours, until they are tender. Bring the reserved marinade to a boil and serve it as a sauce.

GEORGIA ORCUTT
SMOKE COOKERY

Judy Hyun's Marinated Korean Short Ribs

To serve 4

4	large beef short ribs, excess fat removed	4
2	large scallions, including the green tops, finely chopped	2
2	large garlic cloves, finely chopped	2
½ cup	soy sauce	125 ml.
¼ cup	sesame-seed oil	50 ml.
1 tsp.	sesame seeds	5 ml.
¼ tsp.	white vinegar	1 ml.
2 tbsp.	sugar	30 ml.
¼ tsp.	dry mustard	1 ml.
¼ tsp.	freshly ground black pepper	1 ml.

Score the meat almost to the bone at ½-inch [1-cm.] intervals. Combine the remaining ingredients to make the mari-

nade. Pour the marinade over the ribs, making sure it penetrates to the bone. Turn them over, scored side down, in the sauce. Cover, allow to stand at room temperature for two hours or—if possible—in the refrigerator overnight. Broil the ribs over charcoal for about 15 minutes. They will be well done and crisp on the outside and rarer near the bone.

NIKA HAZELTON
THE PICNIC BOOK

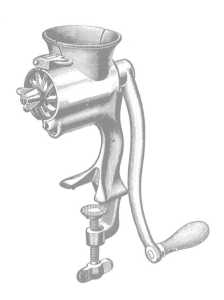

Mixed Skewered Meat, Yugoslav-Style

Ražnjići

To serve 4 or 5

1 lb.	lean boneless beef, cut into 1-inch [2½-cm.] cubes	½ kg.
1 lb.	lean boneless lamb, cut into 1-inch [2½-cm.] cubes	½ kg.
	salt and pepper	
5 tbsp.	rendered bacon fat	75 ml.
2 tbsp.	oil	30 ml.
1 or 2	onions, chopped	1 or 2

Thread the cubed meat, alternating beef and lamb, on skewers. Season the meat with salt and pepper. Heat the bacon fat and oil in a small saucepan and, using a pastry brush, paint the meat with some of the mixture. Charcoal-broil the skewers, turning and brushing them with the fat mixture until the meat is evenly browned—about 10 minutes.

MARIA KOZSLIK DONOVAN
THE BLUE DANUBE COOKBOOK

Five-flavored Kebabs

Spiedini dei Cinque Sapori

To serve 4

14 oz.	beef tenderloin	425 g.
7 oz.	lean slab bacon with the rind removed	200 g.
4	slightly underripe small tomatoes, halved	4
2	small onions, quartered lengthwise	2
8	large stuffed green olives	8
	olive oil	
	salt and pepper	

Salt the cut sides of the tomatoes and let them drain, cut sides down. Cut the beef into eight cubes and the bacon into eight small blocks.

Thread the ingredients onto four skewers in the following order: tomato, bacon, onion, beef, olive, bacon, onion, beef, olive, tomato. Brush the kebabs with oil, and cook for about eight minutes on a hot grill rack, turning them halfway through the cooking time. Season them with salt and pepper and serve at once.

ANNA BASLINI ROSSELLI
100 RICETTE PER LA COLAZIONE SULL'ERBA

Kebabs from Anguilla

To serve 4

2 lb.	boneless beef rump or top round, cut into 12 cubes of about 1½ inches [4 cm.] each	1 kg.
⅓ cup	unsweetened pineapple juice	75 ml.
3 tbsp.	distilled white vinegar	45 ml.
2 tbsp.	molasses	30 ml.
2 tsp.	salt	10 ml.
	freshly ground black pepper	
12	boiling onions, simmered in water for 5 minutes and peeled	12
12	cherry tomatoes	12
2	green peppers, halved, seeded, deribbed and cut into 1½-inch [4-cm.] squares	2
12	1-inch [2½-cm.] cubes fresh pineapple	12

Combine the pineapple juice, vinegar, molasses, salt and several grinds of pepper. Add the cubes of beef and let them

marinate at room temperature for one hour. Drain the meat and reserve the marinade to use as a basting sauce.

Thread the meat, onions, tomatoes, green peppers and pineapple cubes alternately onto four skewers. Brush the skewers with the marinade. Grill the kebabs about 4 inches [10 cm.] above the coals, turning the skewers every three minutes, for about 10 minutes, or until the beef is cooked to the required degree. Baste the kebabs with the marinade each time you turn them. Serve them with plain boiled white rice and pour any remaining marinade over the kebabs.

ELISABETH LAMBERT ORTIZ
THE COMPLETE BOOK OF CARIBBEAN COOKING

Coated Skewered Beef

Tsitsinga

The roasted corn flour called for in this recipe is obtainable, as ablemamu, where West African foods are sold. If not available, cut kernels from fresh corn and roast them in a 350° F. [180° C.] oven, stirring them frequently until the kernels are dry to the touch—about 15 minutes. Grind the kernels in a blender or processor until they are reduced to the size of cornmeal. The volatile oils in chilies may irritate your skin. Wear rubber gloves when handling them.

To serve 4

1 lb.	beef round steak, cut into 1-inch [2½-cm.] cubes	½ kg.
1 cup	vegetable oil	¼ liter
2 tbsp.	vinegar	30 ml.
	salt	
1	tomato, peeled and seeded	1
1	onion	1
1 tbsp.	chopped fresh ginger	15 ml.
3	fresh hot chilies, or substitute ½ to 1 tbsp. [7 to 15 ml.] crushed hot red pepper or ½ to 1 tsp. [2 to 5 ml.] cayenne pepper	3
½ cup	roasted corn flour	125 ml.

Marinate the meat in a mixture of ½ cup [125 ml.] of the oil, the vinegar and salt to taste for at least one hour. Skewer the meat and grill it over charcoal until it is half-done—about five minutes. Remove the meat from the skewers. Grind or blend the tomato, onion, ginger and chilies. (If using crushed red pepper or cayenne, add it after grinding the vegetables and ginger.) Coat the meat well with the vegetable mixture. Skewer the meat again and roll it in the roasted corn flour. Dab the coated meat generously with the remaining oil and return it to the grill until done—about five minutes.

HARVA HACHTEN
KITCHEN SAFARI

Little Squares of Fat Strung between Pieces of Meat

The Qodban of Tangier

To serve 6 to 8

2 lb.	tender boneless beef or lamb, or veal liver, cut into 1-inch [2½-cm.] cubes	1 kg.
¼ lb.	beef or lamb fat, sliced ¼ inch [6 mm.] thick and cut into 1-inch [2½-cm.] squares	125 g.
1	large onion, finely chopped	1
2 tbsp.	finely chopped fresh parsley	30 ml.
2 tsp.	salt	10 ml.
2 tsp.	freshly ground pepper	10 ml.
2 tsp.	cumin seeds, crushed	10 ml.

Mix all of the ingredients together with your hands in order to incorporate the spices. Marinate at room temperature for two hours. String the meat on skewers, putting a square of fat between each pair of meat pieces. Grill over hot coals, turning the skewers to brown the meat evenly, until the meat is done but still pink—about 10 minutes.

MAGGIE WALDRON
FIRE & SMOKE

Ukranian Shashlik

Ukranians are fond of combined meats, and even their shashlik calls for a variety.

To serve 6

½ lb.	beef tenderloin	¼ kg.
½ lb.	veal tenderloin	¼ kg.
½ lb.	pork tenderloin	¼ kg.
½ lb.	lean salt pork or slab bacon, rind removed	¼ kg.
6	lamb kidneys, fat and membrane removed, halved and cored	6
	salt and ground black pepper	
	paprika	
6	scallions, halved lengthwise	6
2	lemons, each cut into 6 wedges	2
2	tomatoes, each cut into 6 wedges	2

Cut all the meats into 1-inch [2½-cm.] cubes and thread them onto six skewers, alternating the different kinds of

meat. Sprinkle the meats with the pepper and the paprika, and grill them over glowing coals for 15 minutes, turning the skewers often. Salt the skewers before serving the meats. Garnish with the scallions, lemon and tomato wedges.

BARBARA NORMAN
THE RUSSIAN COOKBOOK

Marinated Beef on Skewers

Basterma Shashlik

To serve 4

2 lb.	beef tenderloin or boneless sirloin, cut into 1½-inch [4-cm.] cubes	1 kg.
1 cup	finely chopped onion	¼ liter
¼ cup	red wine vinegar	50 ml.
1 tsp.	salt	5 ml.
¼ tsp.	freshly ground black pepper	1 ml.
2	medium-sized firm, ripe tomatoes, halved	2
2	medium-sized green peppers, halved, seeded and deribbed	2
8	scallions, including 2 inches [5 cm.] of the green tops, finely chopped	8
	fresh coriander or parsley, finely chopped	

In a large bowl, combine the onion, vinegar, salt and pepper. Add the meat, and toss to coat it thoroughly with the marinade. Cover and let the meat stand at room temperature for about six hours, turning the pieces of meat in the marinade from time to time.

Remove the meat from the marinade, and thread it onto long skewers, leaving a few inches bare at each end. String the tomatoes and green peppers on separate skewers, since cooking time for them varies. Broil the meat and vegetables over charcoal, 3 to 4 inches [8 to 10 cm.] from the heat. Turn the skewers frequently, until the vegetables and meat are browned evenly on all sides. The vegetables cook more quickly; remove them when they are done and keep them warm. For rare meat, allow about 10 to 15 minutes; for well-done meat, allow 15 to 20 minutes.

Using a fork, push the meat and vegetables off the skewers onto warmed individual plates, and garnish with the scallions and coriander or parsley. Serve at once.

SONIA UVEZIAN
THE CUISINE OF ARMENIA

Skewered Spiced Mixed Grill

Satay

Lemon grass is an aromatic tropical grass; it is obtainable dried where Indonesian foods are sold. The volatile oils in chilies may irritate your skin. Wear rubber gloves when you are handling them.

	To serve 4	
½ lb.	boneless lean beef or lamb, thinly sliced and cut into 1-by-2-inch [2½-by-5-cm.] strips	¼ kg.
1 tbsp.	coriander seeds	15 ml.
1 tsp.	anise seeds	5 ml.
¼ tsp.	poppy seeds	1 ml.
4	dried hot red chilies	4
4	small onions, chopped	4
1	garlic clove	1
1-inch	piece lemon grass	2½-cm.
2	macadamia nuts (optional)	2
2	white peppercorns	2
1-inch	piece fresh ginger	2½-cm.
¼ cup	thick coconut milk	50 ml.
	coconut oil	
1 tsp.	dried tamarind, soaked in ¼ cup [50 ml.] water, the liquid strained and reserved	5 ml.
	sugar	
	salt	
1 tbsp.	peeled peanuts, ground	15 ml.
1	cucumber, peeled, halved, seeded and cut into chunks	1
1	tomato, cut into 8 wedges	1
1	large onion, cut into 8 wedges	1

In a mortar, blender or processor, grind together the coriander, anise and poppy seeds, the chilies, onions, garlic, lemon grass, macadamia nuts—if used—peppercorns and ginger. Rub each strip of meat with this mixture and then soak the meat in the coconut milk to soften it.

Heat 2 tablespoons [30 ml.] of the oil in a saucepan until it is smoking and fry the remaining ground spice mixture until it separates from the oil. Add the tamarind liquid and sugar and salt to taste. Bring to a boil, reduce the heat, and simmer the sauce, uncovered, until it is thick enough to coat the back of a spoon. Stir in the peanuts and the coconut milk, and simmer to thicken the sauce. Pour it into a bowl and let it cool.

Thread the meat onto 10-inch [25-cm.] wooden skewers, leaving 1 inch [2½ cm.] free at one end and 5 inches [13 cm.]

at the other. Brush the meat evenly with oil and grill on a well-greased rack over a glowing charcoal fire. Turn the skewers frequently until the meat is cooked and the coating is well puffed up—about 10 to 15 minutes. Serve the meat on the skewers, accompanied by the cold sauce. Garnish each serving with pieces of cucumber, tomato and onion.

LILIAN LANE
MALAYAN COOKERY RECIPES

Polynesian Steak Kebabs

	To serve 6	
2 lb.	beef round steak, cut into 1-inch [2½-cm.] cubes	1 kg.
¾ cup	pineapple juice	175 ml.
¼ cup	oil	50 ml.
3 tbsp.	soy sauce	45 ml.
2 tsp.	brown sugar	10 ml.
¾ tsp.	ground ginger	4 ml.
1	garlic clove, finely chopped	1
2	medium-sized green peppers, halved, seeded, deribbed and cut into 1-inch [2½-cm.] squares	2
18	mushroom caps	18
18	pearl onions	18
18	cherry tomatoes	18

Combine the pineapple juice, oil, soy sauce, brown sugar, ginger and garlic. Marinate the meat in this mixture overnight in the refrigerator. Drain the meat, reserving the marinade. Thread the meat cubes onto skewers alternately with the squares of green pepper, the mushroom caps, the pearl onions and the cherry tomatoes. Grill over charcoal for 10 to 15 minutes, basting frequently with the reserved marinade.

THE JEKYLL ISLAND GARDEN CLUB
GOLDEN ISLES CUISINE

Spicy Barbecued Meat

Saté Bumbú

Much of the food of the Netherlands Antilles is distinctly spicy-hot. This is due in large part to the Indonesian influence, which is reflected in the almost daily use of a wide variety of volcanic sambal peppers. Here is a good hot Dutch West Indian culinary delight, one of the delightful *satés*, which are exceptionally popular in this part of the globe.

To serve 6

1½ lb.	beef sirloin, cut into 1-inch [2½-cm.] cubes	¾ kg.
4	small white onions	4
2	garlic cloves	2
¼ tsp.	cayenne pepper, or several dashes Tabasco sauce	1 ml.
1 tbsp.	dark brown sugar	15 ml.
1 tsp.	fresh lime juice	5 ml.
1½ tsp.	curry powder	7 ml.
2	whole cloves	2
½ tsp.	grated fresh ginger	2 ml.
3 tbsp.	soy sauce	45 ml.
3 tbsp.	warm water	45 ml.

Peanut saté sauce

¼ cup	peanut butter	50 ml.
2 tbsp.	olive oil	30 ml.
2 tbsp.	grated onion	30 ml.
1 tbsp.	dark brown sugar	15 ml.
1 tsp.	fresh lime juice	5 ml.
⅛ tsp.	salt	½ ml.
1 cup	coconut milk	¼ liter

Grind together the onions and the garlic, using the fine blade of a food mill or a processor. Place the mixture in a bowl along with the cayenne pepper or Tabasco sauce, the brown sugar, lime juice, curry powder, cloves and ginger, then blend in the soy sauce and water. Add the meat cubes, toss, and marinate them in the refrigerator for six hours. To make the peanut sauce, lightly heat the olive oil in a saucepan and cook the onion for five minutes—do not let it brown. Add the brown sugar, lime juice, salt and peanut butter, and blend them well. Add the coconut milk gradually, stirring and cooking the sauce until it is thick and smooth.

Reserving the marinade, arrange the meat on skewers and broil them 3 inches [8 cm.] from the coals for 10 to 15 minutes. Brush the kebabs with the marinade and turn them often. Serve them with the peanut sauce.

ALEX D. HAWKES
THE FLAVORS OF THE CARIBBEAN & LATIN AMERICA

Filled Beef or Lamb Burgers

The authors suggest that instead of using the nut mixture, you could fill each burger with an anchovy and a few capers or with a slice of Roquefort or Cheddar cheese or of liverwurst.

To serve 6

1½ lb.	ground beef or lamb	¾ kg.
6	slices bacon	6
6 tbsp.	chopped nuts	90 ml.
3 tbsp.	finely chopped fresh parsley	45 ml.
2 tbsp.	grated onion	30 ml.

Sauté the bacon slices lightly. Set them aside. Divide the ground beef or lamb into 12 portions and shape them into flat cakes. Combine the nuts, parsley and onion, and spread this mixture on six of the cakes. Top them with those remaining. Bind the edges with the partially sautéed bacon slices and fasten each slice with a wooden pick. Broil the filled burgers for 10 to 15 minutes, turning them once.

IRMA S. ROMBAUER AND MARION ROMBAUER BECKER
JOY OF COOKING

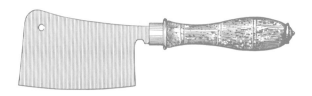

Skewered Beef

Boeuf en Brochette Extraordinaire

To serve 4 to 6

1½ lb.	beef tenderloin, cut into 1½-inch [4-cm.] cubes	¾ kg.
3 tbsp.	olive oil	45 ml.
8 tbsp.	butter, melted	120 ml.
½ tsp.	dried thyme leaves	2 ml.
1 tbsp.	Dijon mustard	15 ml.
⅛ tsp.	dried hot-pepper flakes	½ ml.
	salt and freshly ground black pepper	
6 tbsp.	fresh lemon juice	90 ml.

Divide the beef cubes between two long skewers. You should have about 16 cubes, so eight on each skewer will work well. Because you are not filling space with mushrooms, green peppers or onions in this particular brochette, you will have room on the skewers for all the meat.

Combine the oil, 4 tablespoons [60 ml.] of the melted butter, the thyme, mustard and hot-pepper flakes, and mix well. Brush this combination on all sides of the beef cubes.

Salt to taste, and add a dash of freshly ground pepper. Cook over a charcoal grill for about three minutes per side. Brush more of the seasoned oil-and-butter mixture on the cubes while they are cooking. Combine the remaining melted butter with the lemon juice. Heat this quickly, and pour over the skewered meat just a second before serving.

JOE FAMULARO AND LOUISE IMPERIALE
THE FESTIVE FAMULARO KITCHEN

Molded Beef Kebabs

Kefta

Ras el hanout is a mixture of many spices that is widely used in Moroccan cooking. A version of this exotic spice mixture can be prepared from equal pinches of ground allspice, cinnamon, ginger, nutmeg, cardamom, black pepper and cloves.

Kefta may also be made like hamburger patties. And, of course, they may be made less spicy.

To serve 4 or 8

1 lb.	boneless beef chuck, finely ground twice	½ kg.
½ tsp.	finely chopped fresh coriander leaves	2 ml.
1 tsp.	finely chopped fresh parsley	5 ml.
1 tsp.	salt	5 ml.
¼ tsp.	dried marjoram	1 ml.
½ tsp.	pepper	2 ml.
¼ tsp.	cayenne pepper	1 ml.
1 tsp.	*ras el hanout* or curry powder	5 ml.
1 tsp.	ground cumin	5 ml.
1	onion, finely chopped	1

Combine all of the ingredients and refrigerate them for at least one hour; two would be better.

To cook, pick up enough of the meat mixture to make a ball about the size of an egg. Mold the meat onto an oiled skewer, shaping the meat into a sausage about 4 inches [10 cm.] long and about an inch [2½ cm.] or so in diameter. Two or three sausages should fit onto one skewer. Grill them 4 to 6 inches [10 to 15 cm.] above glowing coals, turning them once, for 10 to 15 minutes, or until the sausages are browned on all sides.

HARVA HACHTEN
KITCHEN SAFARI

Serbian Meat Rolls

Serbischer Cevapcici

To serve 4

1 lb.	lean beef, ground	½ kg.
½ lb.	lean pork, ground	¼ kg.
	salt and pepper	
	chopped onion	

Mix together the ground beef and pork. Add plenty of salt and some pepper, and work the mixture together well with your hands. Mold small sausage-shaped rolls, 2 inches [5 cm.] long and the width of a finger, from the mixture. Place the rolls in a hinged grill basket and cook them quickly, turning them frequently so that they brown evenly, for about six minutes. Serve the rolls with chopped onion.

MARIA HORVATH
BALKAN-KÜCHE

Grilled Hamburger

Yuk Sanjuk Kui

To serve 2

¼ lb.	ground beef	125 g.
¼ lb.	ground pork	125 g.
2	garlic cloves, crushed to a paste	2
1	scallion, finely chopped	1
⅛ lb.	bean curd, diced (about ¼ cup [50 ml.])	60 g.
1 tbsp.	sugar	15 ml.
2 tsp.	sesame-seed oil	10 ml.
1 tsp.	sesame seeds	5 ml.
½ tsp.	salt	2 ml.
	pepper	

In a bowl, combine the ground meats with the rest of the ingredients. Mix well. Shape the mixture into six flat, round patties. Grill the patties over charcoal for 10 to 15 minutes, turning them once.

JUDY HYUN
THE KOREAN COOKBOOK

Veal or Lamb Chops

To serve 3

6	veal or lamb chops, each about 1½ inches [4 cm.] thick	6
½ cup	tomato sauce (recipe, page 163)	125 ml.
⅓ cup	red wine	75 ml.
¼ cup	olive oil	50 ml.
1 tsp.	fresh lime or lemon juice	5 ml.
1 cup	chopped onion	¼ liter
1	garlic clove, crushed to a paste	1
1 tbsp.	chili powder	15 ml.
1 tsp.	salt	5 ml.
½ tsp.	dried thyme leaves	2 ml.
½ tsp.	ground cumin	2 ml.
½ tsp.	dried oregano leaves	2 ml.

Combine all of the ingredients and marinate the chops for at least four hours. Cook the chops over charcoal for eight to 10 minutes on each side, basting them with the marinade.

RONALD JOHNSON
THE AFICIONADO'S SOUTHWESTERN COOKING

Veal Olives on Skewers

Quagliette di Vitello

Serve the skewers on a dish of white rice. Those who find the scent of sage overpowering can replace it with mint or basil, or simply sprinkle the meat with marjoram or thyme before cooking it. This dish can also be made with pork or lamb.

To serve 4

6	thinly sliced veal scallops, each cut into two 3-inch [8-cm.] squares	6
	salt and pepper	
	fresh lemon juice	
12	thin ham slices, each 3 inches [8 cm.] square	12
6	slices lean bacon, halved crosswise	6
1	onion, quartered lengthwise and separated into layers	1
	fresh sage leaves	
2	thick slices stale white bread, cut into ½-inch [1-cm.] squares	2
	melted bacon fat	

Season the veal with salt, pepper and lemon juice. Top each piece of veal with a piece of ham, roll them up together, and wrap a slice of bacon around each little roll. Thread the rolls onto four small skewers, alternately with the onion pieces, sage leaves and bread cubes. Pour a little melted bacon fat over the rolls and grill them for seven to eight minutes, or until they are cooked through, turning them over and basting them two or three times with bacon fat.

ELIZABETH DAVID
ITALIAN FOOD

Cutlets for the Village Festival

Costelles de Fiesta Mayor

A truffle is an edible wild fungus, sometimes available fresh during the winter at specialty markets in large cities, but more commonly found canned.

This is a Catalan regional dish from Rupiá, Gerona.

To serve 6

6	veal cutlets	6
½ cup	vinegar	125 ml.
3	truffles, diced	3
¼ lb.	ham, diced (about ½ cup [125 ml.])	125 g.
1 tbsp.	flour	15 ml.
	fresh lemon juice	
Wine and lemon marinade		
⅔ cup	dry white wine	150 ml.
3 tbsp.	fresh lemon juice	45 ml.
1 tsp.	black peppercorns	5 ml.
	salt	

Combine the marinade ingredients and marinate the cutlets for two hours.

Remove them from the marinade, dry them with a cloth; then strain the marinade and set it aside. Grill the cutlets over hot coals for 12 to 15 minutes, turning them once.

Place the vinegar, truffles, ham and flour in a saucepan and add the remaining marinade. Bring the sauce to a boil and let it thicken for about five minutes. Add a little lemon juice to taste. Arrange the veal cutlets in a serving dish and pour the sauce over them.

DELEGACION NACIONAL DE LA SECCION FEMENINA DEL MOVIMIENTO
COCINA REGIONAL ESPAÑOLA

Veal Sausages in a Cloak

Kalbsbratwürste im Mantel

Veal sausages are obtainable where German foods are sold.

	To serve 4	
4	veal sausages	4
1 tsp.	paprika	5 ml.
4	thin slices bacon	4

Skin the sausages, dust them all over with paprika and wrap them in the bacon slices. Fasten the bacon with wooden picks. Place the parcels on a rack over hot coals and grill them for four to five minutes on each side.

ULRIKE HORNBERG
SCHLEMMEREIEN VOM GRILL

Giant Mixed Grill on Skewers

	To serve 4	
1¼ lb.	boneless lean veal loin	600 g.
1 lb.	boneless beef sirloin	½ kg.
¾ lb.	boneless lean lamb loin	350 g.
6	thick slices bacon	6
2	green peppers, parboiled for 1 minute, halved, seeded and deribbed	2
2	onions, quartered lengthwise and separated into individual layers	2
8	bay leaves, cut into halves	8
	Herb marinade	
1¼ cups	mild-flavored olive oil	300 ml.
2	sprigs thyme or ½ tsp. [2 ml.] dried thyme leaves	2
2	bay leaves, crushed	2
1	sprig rosemary or ¼ tsp. [1 ml.] ground rosemary	1
	freshly cracked pepper	
	dried thyme and oregano leaves	

Cut the veal, beef and lamb across the grain into slices ½ inch [1 cm.] thick. Then cut the meats, bacon and green peppers into 1-inch [2½-cm.] squares. Thread the meats, bacon, peppers, onions and bay leaves onto four long skewers. Start each assembly with a square of green pepper, beef and a piece of onion. Then add squares of veal, green pepper, bacon and half of a bay leaf; followed by squares of lamb and bacon and a piece of onion. Repeat this sequence three or four times to fill each skewer. Push the meats close together.

For the marinade, mix the oil with the herbs and cracked pepper and use a brush to carefully coat the skewered meats and vegetables with marinade. Set the skewers on a rack to drain for 15 to 20 minutes. Sprinkle with a few pinches of dried thyme and oregano and grill the kebabs over medium heat, turning them only once, until the meats brown nicely—about five minutes on each side.

LOUISETTE BERTHOLLE
SECRETS OF THE GREAT FRENCH RESTAURANTS

Spit-roasted Leg of Lamb

Gigot de Mouton Rôti

	To serve 6 to 8	
one 6 lb.	leg of lamb	one 3 kg.
1	garlic clove (optional)	1
8 tbsp.	butter, melted	120 ml.
2 tbsp.	vinegar	30 ml.
2 tsp.	salt	10 ml.

If you wish, insert a garlic clove under the fell at the shank end of the leg. Fix the meat firmly on the spit, running it into the leg beside the bone. When the fire is good and hot, place the spit in front of it with a drip pan underneath. Put the butter, vinegar and salt into the drip pan. Use this mixture, with the drippings from the meat, to baste the leg often.

Roast the leg for one and one quarter to two hours: The cooking time will depend upon the heat of the fire and the degree of doneness desired.

OFFRAY AINÉ
LE CUISINIER MÉRIDIONAL

Spit-roasted Whole Lamb

Arni sti Souvla

To judge when the lamb is cooked through, insert a meat thermometer into the thickest part, without letting it touch the bone. Lamb is medium rare at an internal temperature of 135° F. [60° C.], medium to well done at 145° to 175° F. [63° to 80° C.]. Greek roast lamb is traditionally very well cooked.

If the fire is in a pit, prop sheets of corrugated iron on each side of the fire to deflect the heat onto the lamb.

To serve 40 to 50

one 50 lb.	lamb, cleaned	one 22½ kg.
1	lemon, halved, plus 6 tbsp. [90 ml.] fresh lemon juice	1
	salt and freshly ground black pepper	
	sprigs of fresh thyme, oregano and rosemary	
1⅓ cups	olive oil	325 ml.
3 to 4	garlic cloves, crushed to a paste	3 to 4

Wipe the lamb inside and out with a damp cloth. Rub the cavity well with the lemon halves and with salt and pepper. Put a few sprigs of herbs in the cavity and close it with skewers. Then rub the outer surfaces with the lemon halves, salt and pepper.

Set the lamb on its stomach and push the spit through the center, from between the back legs, along the spine and through the neck. Pull the forelegs forward and tie them securely onto the spit with wire. Press the back legs along the spit and cross them about it, securing them with wire.

Mix together the lemon juice, olive oil, garlic, and salt and pepper. Wrap sprigs of thyme, oregano and rosemary in muslin and tack the package to the end of a long rod. Set the package of herbs in the oil-and-lemon mixture until it is required for basting.

Set a wood fire in a pit or a halved fuel drum and let it burn until the flames die down. Add a layer of charcoal and put the spitted lamb in position. Turn the lamb slowly over the fire. Begin with the spit well away from the fire, if possible, then lower it closer to the fire halfway through the cooking. Baste the lamb occasionally with the soaked package of herbs. Roast the lamb for six to seven hours over the glowing coals, adding more charcoal as needed.

TESS MALLOS
GREEK COOKBOOK

Grilled Breast of Lamb Riblets with Artichokes and Mustard Cream

To serve 6

6 lb.	lamb breast	3 kg.
2 cups	chicken or veal stock *(recipe, page 167)*	½ liter
	salt and pepper	
	Dijon mustard	
	olive oil	
½ cup	fine dry bread crumbs	125 ml.
6	large artichokes	6
1	lemon, halved	1
3	medium-sized ripe tomatoes	3
12	small new potatoes	12
	black Niçoise olives	
	finely chopped fresh parsley	
	fresh thyme leaves	

Mustard cream sauce

3 cups	heavy cream	¾ liter
2 tsp.	Dijon mustard	10 ml.
	salt and pepper	

Trim the breast and poach it, at a bare simmer, in the stock with enough added water to cover it. Test it with a fork and when it is perfectly tender—after about 50 minutes—drain the breast and cut it into riblets. When the riblets are cool, season them and brush them lightly with mstard. Dip them in olive oil and roll them in the bread crumbs. Refrigerate the riblets until the coating is firm—at least two hours.

Break off the stem of each artichoke and pull off the outer leaves until the pale green center is evident. Slice off two thirds of the top with a stainless-steel knife and rub the artichoke with a cut lemon half. Boil the artichokes in salted water acidulated with about 1 tablespoon [15 ml.] of the lemon juice. After about 30 minutes, or when the bases are easily pierced with a knife tip, drain the artichokes. Cool, then trim them by digging out the thistle-like cores and cutting off any tough, dark green exterior. Coat the artichoke bottoms with olive oil.

Cut the tomatoes in two crosswise and gently squeeze out most of the seeds and juice. Season the tomatoes with salt and pepper, and oil them lightly. Scrub the potatoes, then salt and oil them.

To make the sauce, reduce the cream over low heat to about 1½ cups [375 ml.]. Stir in the mustard, and salt and pepper to taste.

Put the potatoes on the grill first, setting them on a rack 4 to 6 inches [10 to 15 cm.] above medium-hot coals. After about 30 minutes, add the lamb riblets, artichoke bottoms and tomatoes. Grill for about 10 minutes, turning the riblets occasionally to brown them evenly. Heap everything in an earthenware dish and garnish with a handful of olives. Sprinkle with parsley, thyme, salt and pepper. Serve the sauce on the side.

JUDITH OLNEY
SUMMER FOOD

Leg of Lamb, Indian-Style

Parcha Seekhi

This dish can also be made with veal.

	To serve 6	
5 lb.	leg of lamb, boned	2½ kg.
3-inch	piece fresh ginger, pounded to a paste	8-cm.
1¼ tsp.	salt	6 ml.
10 tbsp.	clarified butter	150 ml.
1 cup	grated onions	¼ liter
2 tbsp.	ground coriander	30 ml.
5 tbsp.	water	75 ml.
⅔ cup	yogurt, whipped	150 ml.
2 tbsp.	cumin seeds, lightly roasted	30 ml.
½ tsp.	ground cloves	2 ml.
2 tsp.	ground cinnamon	10 ml.
½ tsp.	ground cardamom	2 ml.

Remove as much fat, sinews, gristle and connecting tissue as possible from the boned lamb. Wipe the lamb with a damp cloth, then dry it and prick it all over with a sharp knife. Rub it well with the ginger and salt. Reserve it for the moment.

Heat 2 tablespoons [30 ml.] of the butter, and fry the onions with the coriander until the onions are dark gold— about 15 minutes. Add the water and cook the mixture until it is dry. Place this mixture on the center of the lamb and roll it up, securing it with string. Place the lamb on a revolving spit over a drip pan and cook it in front of a hot fire until it is browned—about 15 minutes, then let the heat die down to medium. As soon as the flesh looks dry, begin to baste it with the remaining butter mixed with the yogurt, cumin, cloves, cinnamon and cardamom.

The lamb should be cooked after about one and one quarter hours. Test it by inserting a sharp kitchen needle; the juices should be clear. Mix the drippings with a little water and reduce this mixture to a paste over medium heat. Serve this as a sauce with the meat.

DHARAMJIT SINGH
INDIAN COOKERY

Leg of Lamb Kebab

Kabab-e Ran-e Bareh

To blanch and peel the nuts called for in this recipe, parboil them for about two minutes. Drain and allow to cool slightly, then squeeze each nut lightly but firmly to pop it from its skin.

	To serve 8	
one 6 lb.	leg of lamb, boned	one 3 kg.
2	large onions, chopped	2
3 tbsp.	butter	45 ml.
10 to 15	chicken livers, trimmed and halved	10 to 15
1 cup	white rice, boiled in salted water for 15 minutes and drained	¼ liter
2 tbsp.	tomato paste, diluted with ½ cup [125 ml.] hot water	30 ml.
2 tsp.	fresh lemon juice	10 ml.
¼ cup	almonds, blanched, peeled and cut into slivers	50 ml.
¼ cup	pistachios, blanched, peeled and cut into slivers	50 ml.
2 tbsp.	candied orange peel, cut into thin strips	30 ml.
2 to 3	garlic cloves, cut into slivers	2 to 3

Sauté the onions in the butter until they are golden. Add the chicken livers and sauté them until they are brown. Pour the diluted tomato paste over the livers. Add the lemon juice, the slivered nuts and the candied orange peel; cover and simmer gently for 15 minutes. Stir in the rice.

Fill the leg of lamb with this stuffing, roll it up, and truss it well with string. Secure the ends well so that the stuffing will not spill out. Prick the outer skin in several fatty places and insert the slivers of garlic under the skin. They may be removed just before serving. Spit-roast the lamb over a charcoal fire for about two hours.

NESTA RAMAZANI
PERSIAN COOKING

Marinated Grilled Lamb
Panggang Kambing

To serve 6 to 8

one 6 lb.	leg or shoulder of lamb, or 16 lamb chops cut 1 inch [2½ cm.] thick	one 3 kg.

Tamarind-water marinade

2 cups	tamarind water, made by soaking 1 cup [¼ liter] dried tamarind in 2 cups [½ liter] water for 20 minutes and straining the liquid	½ liter
1 tbsp.	brown sugar	15 ml.
1 tsp.	cayenne pepper	5 ml.
2 tsp.	salt	10 ml.
1 tsp.	ground coriander	5 ml.

Soy and garlic sauce

3 tbsp.	dark soy sauce	45 ml.
4	garlic cloves, crushed to a paste	4
2 tbsp.	fresh lemon or lime juice	30 ml.
1 tbsp.	olive oil or 1 tbsp. [15 ml.] butter, melted	15 ml.
1 tbsp.	ground roasted peanuts (optional)	15 ml.
½ tsp.	ground ginger	2 ml.

Mix the marinade ingredients together, add the meat, and marinate in the refrigerator for at least five hours or overnight, turning the meat several times. Just before you are ready to start cooking, prepare the sauce by mixing together all of the ingredients.

If using a leg of lamb, place it on a spit and put it over hot charcoal. Cook for about one hour, then score the meat deeply with a knife, brush well with the sauce and continue cooking until the meat is tender—the whole process is likely to take up to two hours.

If using lamb chops, place them over the charcoal and grill for three minutes on each side. Then put sauce on top of the chops, turn them over and grill the sauced side for another three minutes; repeat on the second side.

SRI OWEN
INDONESIAN FOOD AND COOKERY

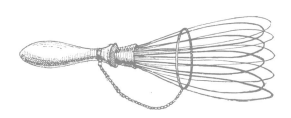

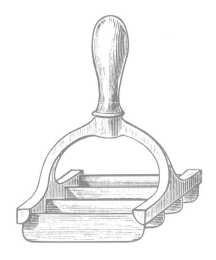

Kid with Garlic
Haedus in Alio

This recipe is from a book first published in 1475. If kid is not obtainable, leg of lamb is a suitable substitute.

To serve 6

3 to 4 lb.	leg of kid	1½ to 2 kg.
¼ cup	olive oil	50 ml.
2	garlic cloves, halved	2
3	large sprigs rosemary or 6 bay leaves, tied together to make a brush	3
3 tbsp.	finely chopped fresh parsley	45 ml.

Saffron-flavored basting sauce

1¼ cups	meat stock (recipe, page 167)	300 ml.
2 tbsp.	fresh lemon juice or vinegar	30 ml.
2	egg yolks, well beaten	2
2	garlic cloves, crushed to a paste	2
¼ tsp.	powdered saffron	1 ml.
	pepper	

Spread the oil over the leg, and rub the leg with the cut sides of the garlic cloves. Put the leg on a spit, set it close to a hot fire and turn the spit steadily.

Make the sauce by mixing together the stock, lemon juice or vinegar, egg yolks, garlic, saffron and a little pepper. As the leg roasts, baste it every 10 minutes with the sauce, dipping the rosemary sprigs or bay leaves into the sauce and using the herb brush to spread the mixture onto the meat.

When the leg is cooked through—after about one and one half hours—pour what is left of the sauce over it and sprinkle it with the parsley. Serve immediately, while the meat is still hot.

PLATINA
DE HONESTA VOLUPTATE

Barbecued Lamb Shanks with Vermouth

	To serve 6	
6	lamb shanks	6
1 cup	dry vermouth	¼ liter
1 cup	oil	¼ liter
1 tbsp.	fresh lemon juice	15 ml.
3	shallots or 1 medium-sized onion, chopped	3
2	garlic cloves, finely chopped	2
1 tsp.	chopped fresh tarragon leaves	5 ml.
1 tsp.	chopped fresh basil leaves	5 ml.
1 tsp.	salt	5 ml.
10	peppercorns, crushed	10

Marinate the lamb shanks in a mixture of the vermouth, oil, lemon juice, shallots, garlic, herbs, salt and pepper. Let the shanks stand at room temperature for at least four hours. During this time, turn the lamb shanks once or twice and spoon the marinade over them. Broil the shanks over hot coals for about 30 minutes, turning them frequently and basting them with the marinade.

PICTURE COOK BOOK

Smoked Stuffed Lamb Shoulder

	To serve 6 to 8	
4 to 5 lb.	lamb shoulder, boned	2 to 2½ kg.
1½ lb.	pork sausage meat	¾ kg.
1	medium-sized onion, chopped	1
1	garlic clove, finely chopped	1
1 tsp.	finely chopped fresh parsley	5 ml.

Combine the sausage, onion, garlic and parsley, and mix them well. Flatten the shoulder and spread the stuffing mixture over the meat. Roll the meat so that the stuffing is completely enclosed, and secure it with string or skewers. Place the stuffed shoulder in a smoker and cook for eight to 10 hours, or until a meat thermometer inserted into the center of the shoulder registers 170° F. [75° C.]. Let the shoulder stand for 20 minutes before slicing it.

ROSE CANTRELL
CREATIVE OUTDOOR COOKING

Lamb Chops with Mustard-and-Garlic Butter
Lamskarbonades met Mosterdboter

	To serve 4	
4	lamb double-rib chops, each about 2½ inches [6 cm.] thick	4
	olive oil	
	garlic cloves, crushed to a paste	
	fresh lemon juice	
	salt and pepper	

Mustard-and-garlic butter

1 tbsp.	Dijon mustard	15 ml.
1	garlic clove, crushed to a paste	1
4 tbsp.	butter	60 ml.
½ tsp.	fresh lemon juice	2 ml.
	salt and pepper	

Brush the lamb chops with olive oil, crushed garlic and lemon juice, and season them with salt and pepper. Set the chops aside for two hours.

Mix all of the ingredients for the mustard-and-garlic butter, and set it aside at room temperature.

Grill the chops 4 inches [10 cm.] above the coals for seven minutes on each side. Serve immediately, with the mustard-and-garlic butter beside them.

HUGH JANS
VRIJ NEDERLAND

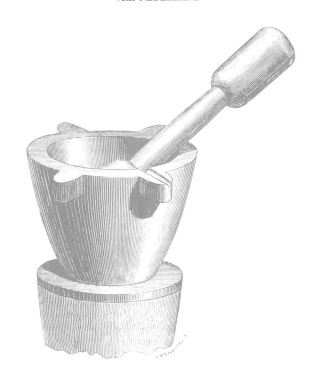

Skewered Lamb
Brochettes d'Agneau de Pré Salé

To serve 8

5½ to 6 lb.	leg of lamb, boned, trimmed and cut into ¾-inch [2-cm.] cubes	2½ to 3 kg.
½ lb.	sliced bacon, cut crosswise into pieces 1 inch [2½ cm.] wide	¼ kg.
4	green peppers, halved, seeded, deribbed and cut into 1-inch [2½-cm.] squares	4
	peanut oil	
	mixed dried herbs (thyme, bay leaf, sage, rosemary and savory)	
16	thin slices prosciutto	16

Thread the lamb cubes onto 16 skewers alternately with the bacon and the green peppers. Brush the skewers with the oil and roll them in the dried aromatic herbs. Cook the skewers over hot coals, turning them once, for a few minutes on each side. Meanwhile, grill the slices of prosciutto. To serve, wrap one slice of prosciutto on the bias around each skewer.

LOUISETTE BERTHOLLE
SECRETS OF THE GREAT FRENCH RESTAURANTS

Chops in Bread Crumbs
Chuletas con Pan Rallado

To serve 4

4	double lamb chops, bones removed and the meat flattened	4
½ cup	oil	125 ml.
1 or 2	garlic cloves, crushed to a paste	1 or 2
3 tbsp.	fresh lemon juice	45 ml.
½ cup	dry white bread crumbs	125 ml.

Make a marinade with the oil, garlic and lemon juice. Then, coat the chops with the marinade and let them stand for about one hour.

When the chops have been well steeped in the marinade, take them out and dust them all over with the bread crumbs. Pat the crumbs in gently. Place the chops on a rack over glowing coals. Cook them for about 15 minutes, turning them several times and basting them with the marinade—using a parsley sprig to brush it on.

LUIS RIPOLL
NUESTRA COCINA

Grilled Lamb on Skewers
Souvlakia

Serve with pilaf, or with fried potatoes and tomato salad.

To serve 6

one 5 lb.	leg of lamb, boned	one 2½ kg.
½ cup	olive oil	125 ml.
4 tbsp.	fresh lemon juice	60 ml.
1 tsp.	salt	5 ml.
	pepper	
	fresh oregano leaves, chopped	

Cut the lamb into 1-inch [2½-cm.] cubes. Mix the oil, lemon juice, salt and pepper, and marinate the lamb in this mixture for about one hour. Thread the cubes onto metal skewers. Turning the skewers once, grill the meat over glowing coals for about 15 minutes. Sprinkle with oregano before serving.

CHRISSA PARADISSIS
THE BEST BOOK OF GREEK COOKERY

Lamb Kebab
Boti Kabab

To serve 8

2 lb.	lamb sirloin, cut into 1½-inch [4-cm.] cubes	1 kg.
5	garlic cloves, coarsely chopped	5
2 tsp.	poppy seeds	10 ml.
1 tsp.	mustard seeds	5 ml.
4 tsp.	ground coriander	20 ml.
2 tsp.	turmeric	10 ml.
1 tsp.	ground ginger	5 ml.
¼ tsp.	cayenne pepper	1 ml.
6 tbsp.	fresh lime juice	90 ml.
½ cup	yogurt	125 ml.
4 tbsp.	butter, melted	60 ml.

In a large mortar, grind the garlic, poppy seeds and mustard seeds together with the coriander, turmeric, ginger and cayenne pepper until they form a thick paste. Blend in 2 tablespoons [30 ml.] of the lime juice, then add the yogurt. Prick the lamb cubes well with a fork, and coat them thoroughly with the yogurt mixture. Marinate the cubes for two hours at room temperature.

Combine the melted butter with the remaining lime juice. Thread the cubes of lamb onto skewers and grill them—turning the skewers frequently and basting the lamb with the lime-flavored butter—for 15 minutes, or until the lamb is well done. If the lamb is grilled only to rare, the spices will have a raw taste.

MOHAN CHABLANI AND BRAHM N. DIXIT
THE BENGAL LANCERS INDIAN COOKBOOK

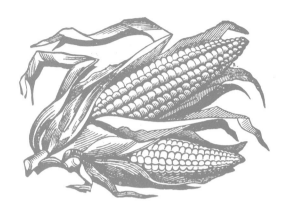

Shish Kebabs

To serve 6

2 lb.	boneless lamb, cut into 1½-inch [4-cm.] cubes	1 kg.
½ cup	fresh lemon juice	125 ml.
¼ cup	olive oil	50 ml.
3	scallions, finely chopped	3
1	garlic clove, finely chopped	1
2 tsp.	curry powder	10 ml.
1 tsp.	ground ginger	5 ml.
1 tsp.	ground coriander	5 ml.
2 tsp.	salt	10 ml.
2	zucchini, cut into rounds 1 inch [2½ cm.] thick	2
2	ears of corn, husks and silk removed, cut into rounds 1 inch [2½ cm.] thick	2
2	green peppers, halved, seeded, deribbed and cut into 1½-inch [4-cm.] squares	2
8	small boiling onions, peeled	8
2 cups	cherry tomatoes	½ liter
2 cups	fresh mushroom caps	½ liter

Combine the lemon juice, olive oil, scallions, garlic, spices and salt. Add the lamb cubes and marinate them, unrefrigerated, for two to three hours. Drain the lamb, reserving the marinade. Thread the lamb cubes onto long skewers, alternately with the zucchini, corn, green peppers and onions. Then alternate the tomatoes and the mushrooms on separate skewers. Barbecue the lamb kebabs over charcoal for 10 minutes. Add the tomato kebabs and grill all the kebabs for five more minutes. Baste all the kebabs with the marinade occasionally.

LOIS M. BURROWS AND LAURA G. MYERS
TOO MANY TOMATOES, SQUASH, BEANS AND OTHER GOOD THINGS

Grilled Lamb Kebabs

To serve 6 to 8

1 to 2 lb.	lean boned lamb, cut into 1-inch [2½-cm.] cubes	½ to 1 kg.
Garlic marinade (optional)		
2	garlic cloves, crushed to a paste	2
2	bay leaves, crushed	2
1 tsp.	dried oregano leaves	5 ml.
1	onion, cut into chunks and squeezed in a garlic press to extract the juice	1
3 tbsp.	fresh lemon juice	45 ml.
3 tbsp.	olive oil	45 ml.
	salt and pepper	
Yogurt and lemon marinade (optional)		
2½ cups	yogurt	625 ml.
3 tbsp.	fresh lemon juice	45 ml.
1 tsp.	ground coriander	5 ml.
1 tsp.	ground cumin	5 ml.
	salt and pepper	

Mix together the ingredients for whichever marinade you choose and pour it over the meat. Let the lamb cubes marinate for a minimum of one hour.

Drain the meat and thread the cubes onto metal skewers. Cook over a glowing charcoal or wood fire for about seven to 10 minutes, depending on how rare you like your meat. Turn the kebabs as they grill so that they cook evenly, and baste them with the marinade to keep them moist. Serve them on a bed of rice, or with *pita* bread, which can be warmed as you cook the kebabs.

HENRIETTA GREEN
THE MARINADE COOKBOOK

Meat-Cheese Sandwiches on Skewers

Kabab Puksand Paneeri

To prepare Indian cheese, bring 2 quarts [2 liters] of milk to a boil in a heavy pan. When foam begins to rise, remove the milk from the heat and add ½ cup [125 ml.] of yogurt and 2 table-spoons [30 ml.] of lemon juice. After the curds separate from the whey, drain them into a bowl through a cheesecloth-lined sieve. Wrap the cloth around the curds and squeeze out the excess liquid. Place the wrapped cheese on a tray, pat the cheese into a rectangle about ½ inch [1 cm.] thick and set a board on top. Weight it with canned foods. Let the cheese drain at room temperature until compact—six to eight hours.

To serve 4

1 lb.	boneless lean lamb, sliced ¼ inch [6 mm.] thick and cut into 2-inch [5-cm.] squares	½ kg.
1 lb.	Indian cheese, cut into 1¾-inch [4½-cm.] squares	½ kg.
1	onion, finely chopped	1
⅓ cup	fresh lime juice	75 ml.
1 tbsp.	cumin seeds	15 ml.
¼ cup	grated fresh ginger	50 ml.
⅔ cup	almonds, blanched, peeled and ground	150 ml.
⅔ cup	yogurt	150 ml.
½ cup	heavy cream	125 ml.
6 tbsp.	clarified butter, melted	90 ml.
1 tbsp.	pomegranate seeds, finely ground	15 ml.
½ tsp.	powdered saffron	2 ml.

Steep the onion in half of the lime juice. Grind the cumin with a few drops of the remaining lime juice, and steep the cumin and ginger in the rest of the juice. Combine the almonds, yogurt and cream with half of the butter.

Coat the cheese with the onion mixture and set aside. Prick the lamb cubes with a sharp fork and rub in the cumin-ginger mixture. Spread the lamb with a little of the liquid from the almond mixture, the ground pomegranate seeds and a light sprinkling of saffron. Drain the cheese and spread the remaining onion mixture over the lamb.

Place a piece of cheese on each cube of lamb and tie them together with thread. Run a long, oiled skewer through four or five of these "open sandwiches" at a time. Grill the sandwiches until the meat becomes dry, then baste them with the remaining almond mixture. Cook them until the meat is russet brown on all sides—about 15 minutes. Brush the sandwiches with the remaining saffron mixed with the remaining butter, and crisp the meat for another few seconds. Remove the sandwiches from the skewers, cut off the threads and serve at once.

DHARAMJIT SINGH
INDIAN COOKERY

Skewers of Lamb, Pineapple, Peppers and Other Things

To serve 4

2 lb.	boneless lamb shoulder, cut into 1½-inch [4-cm.] cubes	1 kg.
16	small onions, parboiled for 5 minutes	16
1	fresh pineapple, peeled, quartered, cored and cut into 1½-inch [4-cm.] cubes	1
3	Italian frying peppers, cored, seeded and cut into 2-inch [5-cm.] squares	3
10	small cherry tomatoes	10
½ cup	soy sauce	125 ml.
2 tbsp.	olive oil	30 ml.
2	garlic cloves, each cut crosswise into 4 pieces	2
1 tsp.	chopped fresh basil leaves or ½ tsp. [2 ml.] dried basil	5 ml.
1 tbsp.	grated fresh ginger or ½ tsp. [2 ml.] ground ginger	15 ml.
	freshly ground pepper	

Mix all of the ingredients in a large ceramic or glass bowl. Marinate in the refrigerator overnight. This is an important step; the time for marination should be from 12 to 24 hours. Remove the bowl from the refrigerator to allow the lamb and the other ingredients to come to room temperature before grilling; this will take about two hours.

On eight 10-inch [25-cm.] skewers, alternate the lamb cubes, onions, pineapple, green peppers and tomatoes. Place the skewers over the charcoal about 4 inches [10 cm.] from the heat, and brush them frequently with the reserved marinade. Turn the skewers often, and cook for 15 minutes, or until the lamb is done to your taste.

JOE FAMULARO AND LOUISE IMPERIALE
THE FESTIVE FAMULARO KITCHEN

Lamb Pinchitos

To serve 4 to 6

2½ lb.	boneless lamb, cut into 1-inch [2½-cm.] cubes	1¼ kg.
¼ lb.	suet, sliced ¼ inch [6 mm.] thick and cut into 1-inch [2½-cm.] squares	125 g.
1 cup	finely chopped onions	¼ liter
½ cup	finely chopped fresh parsley	125 ml.
1 tbsp.	salt	15 ml.
1 tsp.	black pepper	5 ml.

Pinchito hot sauce

1	garlic bulb, the cloves peeled	1
⅓ cup	finely chopped fresh parsley	75 ml.
1 tsp.	ground cumin	5 ml.
1 tsp.	cayenne pepper	5 ml.
1 tsp.	paprika	5 ml.
½ cup	fresh lemon juice or white vinegar	125 ml.
¼ cup	oil	50 ml.
2 cups	water	½ liter
1	lemon or lime, peel included, finely chopped	1
	salt	
1 cup	ripe or green olives, pitted (optional)	¼ liter

For the sauce, pound in a mortar the garlic, parsley, cumin, cayenne and paprika. Blend together the lemon juice, oil, water, chopped lemon or lime and salt to taste. Add the mixture from the mortar and mix well. Toss in the olives if desired. Set the sauce aside.

Pound the onion, parsley, salt and pepper in a mortar to make a paste. Blend the paste with the meat and the suet, and let them marinate for 15 minutes. Then spit the meat and the suet alternately on skewers. Roast the kebabs over hot coals of wood or charcoal for three minutes on each side.

Serve the lamb on plates or still on the skewers, accompanied by the bowl of hot sauce.

IRENE F. DAY
THE MOROCCAN COOKBOOK

Russian Shish Kebab
Shashlyk

To serve 4

2 lb.	boneless lamb	1 kg.
4	lamb kidneys, outer fat and membrane removed, quartered and cored	4
2 cups	vinegar	½ liter
2 cups	water	½ liter
2½ tsp.	pickling spices	12 ml.
	salt	
2	garlic cloves, cut into slivers	2
½ cup	brandy (optional)	125 ml.
2	onions, chopped	2
4	sprigs fresh parsley, finely chopped	4
1 lb.	cherry tomatoes	½ kg.

Boil the vinegar, water and pickling spices together and allow them to cool. Meanwhile, salt the lamb all over and then lard it with the slivers of garlic. Place it in an earthenware bowl, pour on the brandy if you are using it, and sprinkle the chopped onion and parsley over the lamb. Pour the cooled vinegar mixture over the lamb. Cover the bowl and marinate the lamb in a cool place for several hours, turning it frequently.

Drain the lamb, reserving the marinade. Cut the lamb into 1-inch [2½-cm.] cubes, and thread the cubes onto skewers alternately with the quarters of kidney and the cherry tomatoes. Grill the skewered meats over hot charcoal for about 10 minutes, basting them frequently with the marinade and turning the skewers once.

SOFKA SKIPWITH
EAT RUSSIAN

Lamb Satay

Saté Kambing

	To serve 4	
1½ lb.	boneless lean lamb, cut into 1-inch [2½-cm.] cubes	¾ kg.
	salt and pepper	
⅔ cup	soy sauce	150 ml.
1½ tbsp.	fresh lemon juice	22½ ml.
2	garlic cloves, crushed to a paste	2
2	onions, sliced	2

Season the lamb with salt and pepper. Marinate it for about one hour in a mixture of ½ cup [125 ml.] of the soy sauce, the lemon juice and the garlic. Thread the meat onto four skewers and grill it over hot charcoal for 10 minutes, turning the skewers several times. Push the meat off the skewers onto four serving plates, sprinkle it with the remaining soy sauce and garnish it with the sliced onion.

OMA KEASBERRY
OMA'S INDISCHE KEUKENGEHEIMEN

Cypriot Meat Rolls

Sheftalia

Caul is the fatty membranous lining of a pig's stomach. It is obtainable fresh or frozen from specialty butchers, and should be soaked in cold water for a minute or so to soften and separate the pieces.

	To serve 4	
½ lb.	ground lean lamb	¼ kg.
½ lb.	ground lean pork	¼ kg.
1	large onion, finely chopped	1
1 tsp.	finely chopped fresh oregano leaves	5 ml.
	finely chopped fresh parsley	
	salt and pepper	
4 oz.	caul, rinsed and cut into 12 pieces	125 g.

Mix the meats, onion, herbs, salt and pepper together in a bowl. Shape the mixture into 12 small rolls and wrap each roll separately in a piece of caul. Place the rolls on a grill rack over hot coals and grill them for five minutes, turning them frequently so that they brown evenly.

ANDREAS POUROUNAS
APHRODITE'S COOKBOOK

Grilled Arab Meatballs

Koubba Machwiyya

Bulgur is steamed, dried and cracked wheat berries. It is obtainable at health-food stores and wherever Middle Eastern foods are sold.

Instead of forming the meat into balls, you can form it into flat cakes. In that case, you will need to put a slightly larger quantity of fat inside.

	To serve 4	
¾ lb.	lean lamb, ground, plus ¼ lb. [125 g.] finely chopped lamb fat	350 g.
¾ cup	bulgur, soaked in cold water for 10 minutes, drained and squeezed dry	175 ml.
1	small onion, finely chopped	1
3 tbsp.	powdered dried mint	45 ml.
3	slices bacon, finely chopped	3
2 tsp.	freshly ground black pepper	10 ml.
	salt	

Place the lamb meat, bulgur and onion in a mixing bowl and knead them together, rubbing them vigorously against the sides of the bowl. Then add the lamb fat and mix it in well. Sprinkle on the dried mint and knead the mixture again.

Divide the lamb-and-bulgur mixture into 16 or 20 pieces and shape each one into a ball, leaving an opening in the top. Sprinkle the pepper over the bacon, knead and divide the mixture into 16 or 20 pieces. Cupping each ball in the hollow of your half-closed left hand, place a piece of peppered bacon inside, then close the opening. Dip your fingers in a little water, dampen your palms and roll the ball between your palms to make it into a perfect sphere.

Place the balls on a rack over a charcoal fire and grill them for 15 minutes, turning them often so that they brown evenly all over.

RENÉ R. KHAWAM
LA CUISINE ARABE

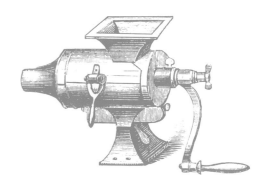

Ground Lamb Kebabs

Seekh Kebab

Garam masala is a mixture of ground spices obtainable from stores specializing in Indian food.

The volatile oils in chilies may irritate your skin. Wear rubber gloves when handling them.

Use lamb that is free from tendons but with a good amount of fat to keep the kebabs moist and juicy. The secret is to work the ground lamb to a paste so that it sticks well together around the skewer; it tends to fall off the skewer if you do not work quickly. It is easier and just as good to shape the meat into round cakes.

To serve 6 to 8

2 lb.	boneless lamb shoulder, cut into pieces	1 kg.
3 tbsp.	yogurt	45 ml.
1	large onion, grated	1
1-inch	piece fresh ginger, crushed in a garlic press	2½-cm.
3	garlic cloves, crushed to a paste	3
1 or 2	fresh hot green chilies, stemmed, seeded and chopped	1 or 2
1 tbsp.	fresh lemon juice	15 ml.
1 tbsp. each	chopped fresh coriander, mint and parsley leaves	15 ml. each
1 tbsp.	ground coriander	15 ml.
2 tsp.	ground cinnamon	10 ml.
1 tsp.	ground cumin	5 ml.
1 tsp.	*garam masala*	5 ml.
½ tsp.	cayenne pepper	2 ml.
	salt and black pepper	
¼ tsp. each	ground mace, cloves and nutmeg	1 ml. each
⅛ tsp.	ground cardamom	½ ml.

Grind the lamb twice through the fine disk of a food grinder or grind it to a paste in a food processor. Add all of the rest of the ingredients, cover, and marinate the lamb in a cool place for two or three hours.

Divide the lamb mixture into six or eight portions. Press each portion into a sausage shape about 1 inch [2½ cm.] in diameter around a skewer that has a wide flat blade so that the meat does not slide. Place the sausages on a grill over medium heat. Cook them gently, turning them over once, until they are browned but still tender and juicy inside—about five minutes on each side.

Serve the sausages with lemon wedges and slices of raw onion softened by sprinkling them with salt for half an hour.

CLAUDIA RODEN
PICNIC: THE COMPLETE GUIDE TO OUTDOOR FOOD

Roast Pork Loin

Àrista di Maiale Arrosto

To serve 6 to 8

4 lb.	pork loin roast	2 kg.
1 tbsp.	finely chopped fresh rosemary leaves or 1 tsp. [5 ml.] dried rosemary	15 ml.
2	garlic cloves, finely chopped	2
1 tsp.	salt	5 ml.
	freshly ground black pepper	

Combine the rosemary and garlic with the salt and plenty of pepper. With the tip of a small, sharp knife, cut deep gashes into the meat, going as close to the bone as possible. Insert some of the rosemary-and-garlic mixture into these gashes, pressing it in firmly. Then sprinkle the outside of the meat with additional salt and pepper. Skewer the meat on a spit and cook, turning, for about two hours, or until the juices run clear when the meat is pierced. Serve the pork hot or cold.

WILMA PEZZINI
THE TUSCAN COOKBOOK

Pork Tenderloin Cooked on a Spit

Polędwicz a Rożna

To serve 6

3 lb.	pork tenderloin	1½ kg.
¼ lb.	salt pork with the rind removed, cut into thin strips (optional)	125 g.
2 tbsp.	olive oil	30 ml.
	salt and pepper	
4 tbsp.	butter, melted	60 ml.
1 tbsp.	flour	15 ml.

If you wish, lard the tenderloin with thin strips of salt pork. Rub the meat with the oil; season it with salt and pepper. Fix the meat to the spit and place a drip pan beneath it. Brushing it frequently with the melted butter, roast the meat for 40 to 50 minutes.

When the meat is well browned, after about 20 minutes, dust it with the flour, allow the flour to dry, then continue to brush the meat with butter.

Slice the meat diagonally and serve it with the drippings from the pan.

MARJA OCHOROWICZ-MONATOWA
POLISH COOKERY

Barbecued Pig

Lechón Asado

Sour, or Seville, oranges are obtainable at some specialty fruit markets and where Caribbean foods are sold. Sweet orange juice mixed with 1 tablespoon [15 ml.] of lemon juice can be substituted for sour orange juice. Annatto oil is made from annatto seeds—a pungent Caribbean spice that imparts an orange color to food. To make the oil called for in this recipe, heat 2 cups [½ liter] of vegetable oil in a small saucepan. Add 1 cup [¼ liter] of annatto seeds and cook them over low heat for five minutes, stirring occasionally. Cool the liquid and strain it before use.

The volatile oils in chilies may irritate your skin. Wear rubber gloves when handling them.

To serve 12 to 15

one 25 lb.	suckling pig, cleaned	one 11¼ kg.
24	garlic cloves, coarsely chopped	24
3 tbsp.	dried oregano leaves	45 ml.
1 tbsp.	black peppercorns	15 ml.
¾ cup	salt	175 ml.
½ cup	sour orange juice	125 ml.
2 cups	annatto oil	½ liter

Sour garlic sauce

16	large garlic cloves	16
16	black peppercorns	16
12	fresh hot chilies, stemmed and seeded	12
2 cups	olive oil	½ liter
1 cup	vinegar	¼ liter
1 cup	fresh lime juice	¼ liter
2 tbsp.	salt	30 ml.

In a large mortar, crush the garlic, oregano, peppercorns and salt, and add the mixture to the sour orange juice.

Make deep gashes in the pig on the neck, just under the lower jaw, on the loin, legs, shoulders and over the ribs. Rub the seasoned orange juice into the gashes as well as all over the skin and cavity of the pig. Cover the pig with cheesecloth and refrigerate it overnight.

Barbecue the pig in the traditional way, by passing a pole through its body. Tie the front legs tightly around the pole. Do the same with the hind legs, stretching them as far as possible. Resting the ends of the pole on Y posts, place the pig over an open charcoal fire that has been built over a bed of stones. Rotate the pole constantly and slowly in order to cook the pig evenly, and baste it frequently with the *annatto* oil. Roast the pig for about seven hours, or until the meat is well done; when a skewer is inserted into a thigh, the juices that run out should be clear.

Meanwhile, prepare the garlic sauce by first crushing the garlic, peppercorns and chilies in a mortar. Add all of the other ingredients; mix thoroughly and set the sauce aside. Carve the roasted pig and serve it with the garlic sauce.

CARMEN ABOY VALLDEJULI
PUERTO RICAN COOKERY

Mixed Grill, Woodcutter's-Style

Il Piatto del Boscaiolo

To serve 6

6	small pork cutlets, pounded flat	6
12	fresh large mushrooms, stems removed from the caps and trimmed	12
6	Italian sausages, halved crosswise	6
	salt and pepper	
¼ cup	olive oil, mixed with ½ tsp. [2 ml.] dried rosemary	50 ml.

Roll each cutlet around two mushroom stems, then put the rolls on skewers with the mushroom caps and the sausages, alternating the ingredients. Brush the meats and mushroom caps with the rosemary-flavored oil.

Place the skewers on a hot grill rack. Grill the skewers slowly about 6 inches [15 cm.] from the heat for about 30 minutes. Turn the skewers frequently so that the meats cook evenly. Season them with a little salt and pepper, and serve them very hot, sprinkled with a little of the flavored oil.

ARNOLDO MONDADORI (EDITOR)
FEAST OF ITALY

Fresh Ham Marinated in Wine

To serve 12

5 to 6 lb.	boned and rolled fresh ham roast	2½ to 3 kg.
¾ cup	dry white wine	175 ml.
2 tbsp.	soy sauce	30 ml.
2 tbsp.	oil	30 ml.
2 tbsp.	chopped onion	30 ml.
1 tsp.	ground ginger	5 ml.

In a large, shallow dish, make a marinade of the wine, soy sauce, oil, onion and ginger. Mix thoroughly. Add the ham, and turn it to coat all surfaces with the marinade. Let the ham stand at room temperature for one hour. Remove it from the marinade, and roast it on a spit over medium-hot coals for six hours, basting frequently with the marinade.

LOUISE SHERMAN SCHOON AND CORINNE HARDESTY
THE COMPLETE PORK COOK BOOK

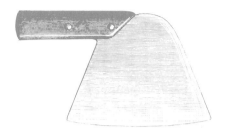

Spit-roasted Fresh Ham

Petits Jambons Frais à la Broche

To lard the ham, clasp the end of each larding strip in the hinged clip of a larding needle and push the needle under the surface of the meat, making a couple of stitches. Release the clip, and trim off the ends of the strip to within about an inch [2½ cm.] of the stitches.

To serve 4

4 lb.	fresh ham shank, rind removed	2 kg.
3½ oz.	pork fatback, cut into thin larding strips	100 g.
4 tbsp.	butter	60 ml.
½ cup	dry white wine	125 ml.
White wine marinade		
2 cups	dry white wine	½ liter
3	shallots, chopped	3
½ cup	olive oil	125 ml.

Lard the shank with the fatback. Combine the marinade ingredients and put the shank into the marinade. Cover and refrigerate for 24 hours, turning the ham from time to time.

Drain the shank; strain and reserve the marinade. Put the shank on a spit, and roast it in front of the fire. Put the butter in the drip pan under the spit, and use it to baste the meat frequently. When the shank begins to turn golden and the drippings are hot, add the white wine and the strained marinade to the drippings. Baste the shank frequently until the meat is done, adding more white wine if necessary. Roast for about 20 minutes per pound [½ kg.]. Deglaze the drippings with water, and serve this sauce with the shank.

ALEXANDRE DUMAINE
MA CUISINE

Chili-flavored Pork Chops

To serve 4

8	pork chops, cut 1 inch [2½ cm.] thick, excess fat removed	8
3 tbsp.	chili powder	45 ml.
3 tbsp.	tomato juice	45 ml.
4	garlic cloves, crushed to a paste	4
1 tsp.	salt	5 ml.
⅛ tsp.	dried oregano leaves	½ ml.
Cold green chili sauce		
¼ cup	finely chopped fresh green chilies	50 ml.
2	pickled jalapeño chilies, stemmed, seeded and finely chopped	2
3	tomatoes, peeled, seeded and finely chopped	3
½ cup	chopped scallions	125 ml.
1	garlic clove, crushed to a paste	1
2 tbsp.	finely chopped fresh parsley	30 ml.
1 tsp.	dried coriander, soaked in 1 tbsp. [15 ml.] hot water and drained	5 ml.
½ tsp.	salt	2 ml.
	black pepper	
	sugar	

Combine the chili powder, tomato juice, garlic, salt and oregano to make a paste, and spread the paste over both sides of the chops. Cover the chops and marinate them overnight in the refrigerator.

Combine all of the sauce ingredients, using a pinch each of the black pepper and sugar. Refrigerate the sauce for at least one hour to chill it thoroughly. Grill the chops over hot coals until tender and browned—about 15 minutes. Serve the chops with the cold chili sauce.

RONALD JOHNSON
THE AFICIONADO'S SOUTHWESTERN COOKING

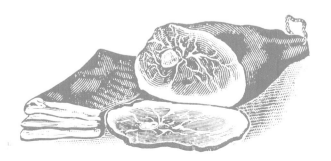

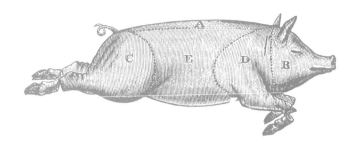

Barbecued Pork Chops

Tightly covered and refrigerated, the sauce can safely be kept for up to two weeks.

	To serve 6	
6	pork chops, cut 1 inch [2½ cm.] thick, excess fat removed	6
1 cup	soy sauce	¼ liter
1	garlic clove, crushed to a paste	1
	freshly ground black pepper	
	Chili sauce	
1½ tbsp.	chili powder	22½ ml.
¾ cup	finely chopped onions	175 ml.
¾ cup	finely chopped green pepper	175 ml.
2	garlic cloves, finely chopped	2
6 tbsp.	butter	90 ml.
4 cups	drained canned tomatoes, crushed into small pieces	1 liter
¾ cup	red wine	175 ml.
	salt and freshly ground black pepper	
2 tbsp.	cornstarch	30 ml.
1 tsp.	sugar	5 ml.
¾ cup	cold meat stock *(recipe, page 167)*	175 ml.

Marinate the chops at room temperature for an hour in the combined soy sauce, garlic paste and black pepper to taste. Turn the chops once or twice and baste with the marinade.

To make the sauce, sauté the onions, green pepper and chopped garlic in the butter for five minutes. Stir in the tomatoes, red wine, chili powder, salt and pepper. Bring the sauce to a boil, then reduce the heat to low.

In a separate bowl, combine the cornstarch and sugar, and whisk in the stock; stir them into the chili mixture. Stirring constantly, cook the sauce until it is thick. Cover and simmer the sauce for 10 minutes.

Grill the chops for 15 minutes on each side, basting them frequently with the sauce.

PICTURE COOK BOOK

Grilled Marinated Chops

	To serve 4	
4	pork rib or loin chops, cut 1 inch [2½ cm.] thick, excess fat removed	4
½ cup	olive oil	125 ml.
½ cup	white wine vinegar	125 ml.
1	garlic clove, finely chopped	1
1	bay leaf, crushed	1
2	peppercorns	2
¼ tsp.	dry mustard	1 ml.
½ tsp.	salt	2 ml.
⅛ tsp.	pepper	½ ml.

Place the chops in a shallow, nonreactive pan. Combine all of the other ingredients, and pour the mixture over the chops. Cover and marinate in the refrigerator overnight or all day, turning the chops occasionally. When ready to use, drain the chops. Grill them over charcoal, turning them once, until they are browned and tender—about 15 minutes.

LOUISE SHERMAN SCHOON AND CORINNE HARDESTY
THE COMPLETE PORK COOK BOOK

Outdoor Pork Chops with Roasted Apples

	To serve 8	
8	pork loin or shoulder chops, each 1 inch [2½ cm.] thick, fat trimmed	8
8	large apples	8
½ cup	vegetable or olive oil	125 ml.
1 tsp.	crushed dried thyme leaves	5 ml.
1 tsp.	crushed dried rosemary leaves	5 ml.
1 tbsp.	paprika	15 ml.
1 tsp.	ground ginger	5 ml.
2 tsp.	salt	10 ml.
1 tsp.	pepper	5 ml.

Combine the oil, herbs, spices, salt and pepper to make a marinade. Brush the pork chops generously with the marinade and let them stand for one hour. Drain the chops, reserving the marinade. Grill them 5 inches [13 cm.] above hot coals—brushing the chops frequently with the marinade—for 15 minutes on each side. While the pork chops are cooking, impale the apples on the tips of long skewers. Set the apples over the coals, and roast them, turning them frequently, until golden brown outside but juicy and slightly soft inside—about 15 to 20 minutes.

CAROL FANCONI
THE OAKS II COLLECTION

Pork in Vermouth

Varkentje in Vermouth

To serve 4

3 to 4 lb.	spareribs, excess fat and membrane removed, or 4 pork shoulder chops cut 1 inch [2½ cm.] thick	1½ to 2 kg.
½ cup	sweet red vermouth	125 ml.
½ cup	dry white vermouth	125 ml.
½ tsp.	fresh lemon juice	2 ml.
2 cups	olive oil	½ liter
3	onions, finely chopped	3
4	garlic cloves, crushed to a paste	4
½ tsp.	dried oregano leaves	2 ml.
1	sweet red pepper, halved, seeded, deribbed and finely chopped	1
2 tsp.	salt	10 ml.
	pepper	

Place the spareribs or chops in an earthenware bowl. Combine all of the remaining ingredients and pour this marinade over the pork. Let it stand for four hours, turning the meat from time to time.

Grill the spareribs or chops about 6 inches [15 cm.] from medium-hot coals until they are nicely browned on both sides, basting them occasionally with the marinade. The spareribs will take about 45 minutes, the chops about 20.

HUGH JANS
VRIJ NEDERLAND

Chinese Barbecued Ribs

To serve 6

6 lb.	lean spareribs, excess fat and membrane removed	3 kg.
¾ cup	*hoisin* sauce	175 ml.
3 tbsp.	yellow bean sauce	45 ml.
1½ tbsp.	black Chinese soy sauce, or Japanese soy sauce	22½ ml.
1½ tbsp.	brown sugar	22½ ml.
1 tbsp.	finely chopped fresh ginger	15 ml.

Place the spareribs in a pot, cover with water and bring to a boil; boil for 30 minutes. Drain and dry the ribs. Combine the remaining ingredients and spread two thirds of this paste on both sides of the ribs. Allow the ribs to marinate in this paste for at least two hours at room temperature or, if desired, overnight in the refrigerator. Grill the ribs 8 to 10 inches [20 to 25 cm.] from hot coals for about 20 minutes, turning them frequently and brushing them with the remaining *hoisin*

paste. The ribs are ready when the juice runs clear if a cut is made between two ribs. Cut the ribs into serving pieces and serve with hot mustard, if desired.

MARIAN BURROS
PURE & SIMPLE

Barbecued Spareribs Canton

To serve 4

3 lb.	lean spareribs, excess fat and membrane removed, cut in half crosswise and the bony ends cracked	1½ kg.
¼ cup	*hoisin* sauce	50 ml.
¼ cup	sugar	50 ml.
1 tbsp.	rice wine or dry sherry	15 ml.
1 tbsp.	oyster sauce	15 ml.
½ tsp.	five-spice powder	2 ml.

Combine the *hoisin* sauce, sugar, rice wine or sherry, oyster sauce and five-spice powder. Rub the spareribs with this mixture and marinate them for at least four hours at room temperature. Set the spareribs over a drip pan on a rack placed 6 to 8 inches [15 to 20 cm.] above medium-hot coals and—turning them occasionally—grill them until they are browned, about 30 to 40 minutes.

MARGARET GIN AND ALFRED E. CASTLE
REGIONAL COOKING OF CHINA

Spareribs Kun Koki

To serve 4

4 lb.	spareribs, excess fat and membrane removed	2 kg.
½ cup	tomato ketchup *(recipe, page 163)*	125 ml.
¼ cup	fresh lime juice	50 ml.
¼ cup	soy sauce	50 ml.
¼ cup	honey	50 ml.

Simmer the spareribs in salted water in a covered kettle for one hour, or just until tender, then drain them. Mix the ketchup, lime juice and soy sauce. Brush part of this sauce mixture over one side of the ribs. Place the ribs—sauce side down—on a grill rack set about 6 inches [15 cm.] above hot coals; brush the other side with the sauce. Grill the spareribs for 10 minutes, turning them over once. Blend the honey into the remaining sauce and brush over the ribs. Grill, turning the ribs and brushing them once or twice with the remaining honey mixture for 10 more minutes, or until the meat is richly glazed.

Remove the ribs to a carving board and cut them into serving-size pieces of one or two ribs each.

THE FAMILY CIRCLE COOKBOOK

Barbecued Country-Style Spareribs

To serve 4

3 to 4 lb.	spareribs, excess fat and membrane removed	1 1/2 to 2 kg.
1 1/2 cups	vinegar	375 ml.
2 tbsp.	cornstarch, dissolved in 1/4 cup [50 ml.] water	30 ml.
1/2 cup	honey	125 ml.
1/2 cup	soy sauce	125 ml.
1/2 cup	tomato ketchup (recipe, page 163)	125 ml.
2	small garlic cloves, finely chopped	2
1/2 tsp.	barbecue spice	2 ml.

Place the ribs in a large, deep roasting pan. Add 1/2 cup [125 ml.] of the vinegar and enough water to cover them. Bring to a boil, cover the pan and simmer the ribs for 45 minutes, or until they are tender; drain.

In a small, nonreactive saucepan, combine the cornstarch solution with the remaining 1 cup [1/4 liter] of vinegar, the honey, soy sauce, ketchup, garlic and barbecue spice. Stirring it constantly, cook this sauce over medium heat until it is thick—about three minutes.

Place the ribs on a grill; brush them with sauce. Turning and basting the spareribs frequently, grill them until they are crisp and brown—about 20 minutes.

THE JEKYLL ISLAND GARDEN CLUB
GOLDEN ISLES CUISINE

Spicy Barbecued Spareribs

To serve 2 to 4

2 lb.	spareribs, excess fat and membrane removed	1 kg.
1/4 cup	soy sauce	50 ml.
1 1/2 tbsp.	vinegar	22 1/2 ml.
1 tbsp.	tomato ketchup (recipe, page 163)	15 ml.
1 tbsp.	chili relish (recipe, page 164)	15 ml.
1 tbsp.	dry sherry	15 ml.
1/2 tbsp.	sugar	7 ml.
1	garlic clove, crushed to a paste	1
1 tbsp.	honey	15 ml.

For the marinade, combine the soy sauce, vinegar, ketchup, chili relish, sherry, sugar and garlic. Lay the spareribs flat in a roasting pan and pour the marinade over them. Turning the ribs frequently, marinate them for at least four hours. Drain the ribs, reserving the marinade. Broil the ribs over charcoal for 20 minutes, turning them often. Mix the honey

into the reserved marinade, and brush it on both sides of the ribs. Grill the ribs for another 20 minutes. Before serving, cut the individual ribs apart.

LADIES' HOME JOURNAL ADVENTURES IN COOKING

Wine-glazed Ham

To serve 4

1	center-cut ham slice, about 1 inch [2 1/2 cm.] thick, excess fat removed	1
1/2 cup	dry white wine	125 ml.
1/4 cup	fresh orange juice	50 ml.
1/4 cup	maple syrup	50 ml.
1 tbsp.	cornstarch, dissolved in 2 tsp. [10 ml.] white wine vinegar	15 ml.
1/2 tsp.	dry mustard	2 ml.
1/4 tsp.	ground ginger	1 ml.

In a nonreactive saucepan, combine all of the ingredients except the ham. Stirring constantly, bring this sauce to a boil, then reduce the heat and simmer it for a few minutes. Grill the ham over charcoal, brushing it frequently with the sauce, for about 10 minutes on each side. Spoon the remaining sauce over the ham when serving it.

LOUISE SHERMAN SCHOON AND CORINNE HARDESTY
THE COMPLETE PORK COOK BOOK

Barbecued Ham Steaks

To serve 6

2 or 3	center-cut ham steaks, cut 1 inch [2 1/2 cm.] thick	2 or 3
4 cups	dry sherry	1 liter
8 tbsp.	butter, melted and cooled	120 ml.
1/2 cup	dry mustard	125 ml.
1/2 cup	brown sugar	125 ml.
2	garlic cloves, finely chopped	2
1 tbsp.	paprika	15 ml.

In a shallow dish, combine the sherry, butter, mustard, brown sugar, garlic and paprika. Stir to mix well. Add the ham steaks and turn them to coat them evenly on both sides. Marinate the ham steaks at room temperature for two hours. Grill the steaks for 10 minutes on each side, basting them frequently with the marinade.

PICTURE COOK BOOK

Pork and Prune Skewers

To serve 2

¾ lb.	boneless pork shoulder, cut into 12 cubes	350 g.
10	soft prunes, pitted	10
2 tbsp.	corn oil	30 ml.
1 tsp.	fresh lemon juice	5 ml.
½ tsp.	finely grated lemon peel	2 ml.

Mix the pork cubes and prunes. Mix the corn oil, lemon juice and lemon peel. Roll the pork and prunes in the corn-oil mixture, and let them stand for 10 minutes or so. Without drying them, skewer the pork and the prunes. Set the skewers close to the coals to sear the pork on all sides. Raise the skewers to about 5 inches [13 cm.] above the coals and, turning them frequently, let the pork cook through to the center—about seven minutes.

MADELEINE KAMMAN
DINNER AGAINST THE CLOCK

Tuscan Mixed Grill

Serve this with a rice pilaf tossed with raisins that have first been plumped up in hot water.

To serve 6

6	small slices pork loin	6
6	small pieces boned chicken	6
6	slices pork liver	6
6	small lamb rib chops	6
12	lean bacon slices, halved	12
24	fresh sage leaves	24
2	sprigs rosemary, ground in a mortar	2
	freshly ground pepper	
6 to 8 tbsp.	olive oil	90 to 120 ml.
3 or 4	juniper berries, crushed, or ½ tsp. [2 ml.] fennel seeds, bruised	3 or 4
	salt	

Thread a piece of pork, chicken, liver and lamb onto each of six skewers, placing a bacon strip and sage leaf between the pieces of meat. Sprinkle with rosemary and pepper.

Place the skewers side by side in a shallow baking dish and pour the olive oil over them. Add the juniper berries (or fennel seeds) and marinate for three to four hours. Grill the meats over charcoal, turning the skewers frequently, for about 15 minutes, or until the meats are cooked but still juicy. Sprinkle the meats with salt.

JANA ALLEN AND MARGARET GIN
INNARDS AND OTHER VARIETY MEATS

Indonesian Skewered Pork

To serve 4 to 6

1½ lb.	boneless lean pork, cut into 1-inch [2½-cm.] cubes	¾ kg.
¼ cup	pine nuts	50 ml.
½	small onion	½
1	garlic clove	1
¼ cup	soy sauce	50 ml.
3 tbsp.	fresh lemon juice	45 ml.
2 tbsp.	ground coriander	30 ml.
1 tbsp.	brown sugar	15 ml.
¾ tsp.	salt	4 ml.
¼ tsp.	freshly ground black pepper	1 ml.
	cayenne pepper	
2	cucumbers, peeled, quartered, seeded and cut into 1-inch [2½-cm.] chunks	2
4	tomatoes, each cut into 8 wedges	4
4 tbsp.	butter, melted	60 ml.

In a blender, combine the pine nuts, onion, garlic, soy sauce, lemon juice, coriander, brown sugar, salt, black pepper and a dash of cayenne. Blend until this marinade is smooth. Pour the marinade over the pork, cover it and marinate it for three hours at room temperature—or better still, overnight in the refrigerator.

Thread the meat and vegetables alternately onto skewers. Cook them slowly over charcoal for 20 to 30 minutes, turning them often and basting the meat and vegetables with the melted butter as needed.

THE JUNIOR LEAGUE OF BOSTON, INC.
PRESENTING BOSTON . . . A COOKBOOK

Pork Tenderloin Grilled on Skewers

Lombello Arrosto

	To serve 4	
¾ lb.	pork tenderloin, cut into ¾-inch [2-cm.] slices	350 g.
3	slices white bread	3
4	slices prosciutto	4

Cut the bread and the ham into pieces of the same circumference as the pork slices. Thread the pork slices onto skewers, alternating them with the bread and ham. Grill the kebabs over medium heat for 12 to 15 minutes, or until the pork is well browned but still juicy inside.

CLAUDIA RODEN
PICNIC: THE COMPLETE GUIDE TO OUTDOOR FOOD

Skewered Pork and Apple

Brochettes de Vierville

	To serve 6	
3 lb.	boneless pork shoulder, cut into ¾-inch [2-cm.] cubes	1½ kg.
4	cooking apples, each cored and cut into 8 chunks	4
1	onion, sliced	1
½ tsp.	dried thyme leaves	2 ml.
1	bay leaf, crushed	1
2 tbsp.	Calvados	30 ml.
2 tbsp.	oil	30 ml.
½ cup	heavy cream, warmed and lightly salted	125 ml.
	salt and cracked black pepper	

Combine the pork cubes, apple chunks, onion, thyme, bay leaf, Calvados and oil, and marinate for 30 minutes.

Skewer the meat and apples, and charcoal-broil them. Sear the meat very well on all sides by placing it very, very close to the coals. Then raise the rack to 5 inches [13 cm.] above the coals and cook the meat for another 10 minutes, turning it at regular intervals.

Place the skewers on a long platter, and season the meat and apples highly with salt and crushed black pepper. Dribble the warmed heavy cream over them.

MADELEINE KAMMAN
DINNER AGAINST THE CLOCK

Belgrade Meat Dumplings with Onions

Belgrader Pljeskavic

	To serve 4	
¾ lb.	boneless lean pork	350 g.
¾ lb.	boneless lean veal	350 g.
	salt and pepper	
4	onions, finely chopped	4
1	red pepper, halved, seeded, deribbed and finely chopped	1

Put the pork and veal through a meat grinder, add salt and pepper, 1 tablespoon [15 ml.] of the chopped onion and all of the red pepper. Mix well with your hands, then leave the mixture for one to two hours.

Form the mixture into small flat patties, like hamburgers. Grill them quickly on a hot rack for about five minutes on each side, or until they are evenly browned. To serve, heap the remaining chopped onions in the middle of a flat dish and arrange the meat patties around the edge.

MARIA HORVATH
BALKAN-KÜCHE

Grilled Hot and Sweet Italian Sausages

	To serve 2	
4 to 6	Italian sausages, hot and sweet	4 to 6
	white wine or dry vermouth	
8 to 12	mushroom caps	8 to 12
8 to 12	small white onions, parboiled for 10 minutes	8 to 12
	olive oil	

Poach the sausages for 10 minutes in wine or vermouth. Drain them well. Thread the sausages onto two skewers, alternating them with the mushrooms and onions. Brush the skewers with the olive oil and cook them over a charcoal fire for 10 to 12 minutes, turning them two or three times.

THE JUNIOR LEAGUE OF THE CITY OF NEW YORK
NEW YORK ENTERTAINS

Country-Style Sausages

Botifarras o Salsitxes a la Pagesenca

Butifarras, a specialty of Catalonia, are pork sausages flavored with white wine, garlic and spices; the black ones also include pig's blood. Each sausage is about 5 inches [12 cm.] long. Butifarras are obtainable where Spanish foods are sold. If not available, other spicy pork sausages can be substituted.

	To serve 4	
4	fresh *butifarras*, white or black, pricked with a fork	4
4	large potatoes, scrubbed but not peeled	4
8	large mushrooms, stems trimmed	8
	salt	
¼ cup	oil	50 ml.
2	garlic cloves, chopped	2
¼ cup	finely chopped fresh parsley	50 ml.
½ cup	garlic mayonnaise (recipe, page 165)	125 ml.

Bury the potatoes in the ashes of the fire and bake them for about one and one half hours.

Place the *butifarras* close together on a rack over hot coals or embers and cook them gently so that they remain whole. Turn them several times; they will take about 10 minutes to cook. Sprinkle the mushrooms with salt, oil, garlic and parsley, and grill them for about seven minutes.

When the potatoes are cooked, cut them in half lengthwise and place them in a dish. Sprinkle them with salt. Put the *butifarras* in another dish, with a thin line of garlic mayonnaise along each one, and the mushrooms by their side.

IGNASI DOMÈNECH
ÀPATS

Grilled Italian Sweet Sausages with Green Peppers

	To serve 6	
2 lb.	sweet Italian link sausages, cut crosswise into halves	1 kg.
4	onions, peeled and quartered	4
4	green peppers, quartered, deribbed and seeded	4
½ cup	olive oil	125 ml.
	salt and pepper	

Coat the onions and peppers with the olive oil. Add salt and pepper to taste. Marinate the vegetables for at least one hour. Thread the sausage halves onto skewers alternately with the onions and peppers. Grill the sausages slowly over coals for 30 to 40 minutes, turning them frequently.

LADIES' HOME JOURNAL ADVENTURES IN COOKING

Sausages and Cheese in a Bag with Potatoes

Cervelas e Formaggio al Cartoccio con Patate

	To serve 4	
4	cervelas or other garlic-flavored pork sausages, each weighing about ¼ lb. [125 g.]	4
½ lb.	Gruyère cheese, rind removed	¼ kg.
4	medium-sized potatoes, scrubbed but not peeled	4

Slice the cheese about ¼ inch [6 mm.] thick, and cut it into 24 squares. Make six deep, crosswise cuts in each sausage, without slicing through them completely. Place a square of cheese in each cut. Oil four sheets of heavy-duty foil and wrap a sausage in each sheet, closing up the ends tightly. Wrap the potatoes individually in oiled foil.

Place the wrapped potatoes in the embers of the fire. After 20 minutes, place the wrapped sausages in the embers. Cook them for 20 minutes and serve them hot, accompanied by the potatoes.

ANNA BASLINI ROSSELLI
100 RICETTE PER LA COLAZIONE SULL'ERBA

Young Rabbit Spit-roasted with Mustard

	To serve 4	
2 to 4 lb.	rabbit, cleaned	1 to 2 kg.
1 tbsp.	chopped fresh thyme leaves	15 ml.
1	bay leaf	1
6 tbsp.	butter	90 ml.
	salt and pepper	
4 tbsp.	Dijon mustard	60 ml.

Place the rabbit on the spit. Put the thyme, bay leaf, butter, salt and pepper into a drip pan underneath the rabbit. Baste the rabbit with this mixture while it is roasting. When the rabbit is three quarters cooked, after about 30 minutes, coat it with the mustard and continue cooking it for about 10 minutes more, or until it is browned and cooked through.

SYLVAIN CLUSELLS
COOKING ON TURNING SPIT AND GRILL

Broiled Young Rabbit

To serve 6 to 8

2	plump young rabbits	2
	oil	
2 tbsp.	fresh lemon juice	30 ml.
½ tsp.	finely chopped garlic	2 ml.
	sage	
1 tsp.	salt	5 ml.
1 tsp.	pepper	5 ml.

Have the butcher hang the rabbits for several days. Split them and pound them flat so that they will be easy to broil. To make a sauce, combine 3 tablespoons [45 ml.] of oil, the lemon juice, garlic, a pinch of sage, and the salt and pepper.

Brush the rabbit halves with oil and place them on a grill. Sear the rabbits over hot coals until both sides are brown. Raise the rack, and broil them slowly for about 25 minutes. Baste the rabbits frequently with the sauce and turn them often. Before serving, test them to be sure there is no redness to the meat.

JOHN AND MARIE ROBERSON
THE COMPLETE BARBECUE BOOK

Kidney Kebabs with Prunes

Kalbsnierenspiess mit Pflaumen

To serve 4

2	veal kidneys, outer fat and membrane removed, halved and inner core of fat removed	2
2 tbsp.	vinegar	30 ml.
16	prunes, soaked in warm water for 20 minutes and pitted	16
16	thin slices bacon	16
	salt	
1 cup	heavy cream	¼ liter
3 tbsp.	Dijon mustard	45 ml.

Place the kidneys in a bowl of water, add the vinegar and leave them for five minutes. Rinse and dry the kidneys and cut them into 24 equal-sized pieces.

Wrap each prune in a slice of bacon. Thread the kidney pieces and the prunes onto eight small skewers, beginning and ending with a kidney.

Grill the kebabs on a hot rack for 15 minutes or until well done. Salt the kidneys at the end of cooking. Serve the kebabs on heated plates. Whisk the cream and mustard together and serve it separately as a sauce.

GIULIANA BONOMO
LA BUONA CUCINA

Kidney Kebab

To serve 4

6	lamb kidneys, outer fat and membrane removed, halved and cored	6
6	thick slices bacon, cut into 1-inch [2½-cm.] pieces	6
24	fresh mushroom caps	24
3	onions, quartered lengthwise and separated into individual layers	3
6	green peppers, halved, seeded, deribbed and cut into 1-inch [2½-cm.] strips	6
½ cup	vinaigrette (recipe, page 162)	125 ml.

Place the meat and vegetables alternately on four long skewers. Baste the skewers well with the vinaigrette. Cook them over coals, turning them often, until the bacon is crisp—about 10 minutes.

BARBARA AND GEORGE REIGER
THE ZANE GREY COOKBOOK

Grilled Tongue Tarragon

To serve 6 to 8

one 3 lb.	fresh beef tongue, soaked in cold water for several hours, parboiled for 10 to 15 minutes, poached for 1½ hours in salted water and peeled, ½ cup [125 ml.] of poaching liquid reserved	one 1½ kg.
2	garlic cloves, crushed to a paste	2
1½ tbsp.	dried tarragon	22½ ml.
1 tbsp.	prepared mustard	15 ml.
2 tbsp.	tarragon vinegar	30 ml.
½ tbsp.	salt	7 ml.
3 tbsp.	butter, melted	45 ml.

Make a paste by mixing together the garlic, dried tarragon, mustard, 1 tablespoon [15 ml.] of the tarragon vinegar and the salt. Rub half of this paste on the tongue. To make a basting sauce, mix the remaining paste with the reserved tongue poaching liquid, the butter and the rest of the tarragon vinegar. Arrange the tongue on a spit from tip to base, fasten and balance it, then roast it over moderate heat for about 45 minutes—basting it periodically with the sauce. The tongue should be brown and crusty on the outside, tender and juicy within.

JAMES A. BEARD AND HELEN EVANS BROWN
THE COMPLETE BOOK OF OUTDOOR COOKERY

Lamb Tongues in Paper Cases

Langues de Mouton en Papillotes

To serve 6

twelve 5 oz.	lamb tongues, poached in salted water for 1 hour or until tender, and peeled	twelve 150 g.
8	scallions, finely chopped	8
2	garlic cloves, finely chopped	2
½ lb.	fresh mushrooms, finely chopped	¼ kg.
2	lemons, thinly sliced	2
¼ cup	olive oil	50 ml.
	salt and coarsely ground pepper	
4 cups	veal stock *(recipe, page 167)*, boiled to reduce it to 2 cups [½ liter]	1 liter

Split the tongues lengthwise almost to the base and open them out. Combine the chopped vegetables, lemon slices, olive oil and seasonings, and marinate the tongues in this mixture for several hours at room temperature or overnight in the refrigerator.

Coat each tongue with the marinated vegetables, and wrap it in oiled parchment paper. Seal the packages tightly so that the juices cannot escape. Lay the packages on the rack of a charcoal grill and cook them over low heat for about 10 minutes on each side. Serve the tongues in the paper cases, accompanied by a well-reduced veal stock.

NOUVEAU MANUEL DE LA CUISINIÈRE BOURGEOISE ET ÉCONOMIQUE

Barbecued Liver and Bacon

To serve 4 to 6

1½ lb.	lamb liver, membrane removed, cut diagonally into slices ½ inch [1 cm.] thick	¾ kg.
4 to 6	thick slices bacon	4 to 6
⅓ cup	olive oil	75 ml.
3 tbsp.	fresh lemon juice	45 ml.
1 tbsp.	finely chopped fresh parsley	15 ml.
	salt and freshly ground pepper	

Combine the olive oil, lemon juice, parsley, salt and pepper. Place the liver in a shallow dish, pour the marinade over it, cover and let it stand for one hour. Drain the liver, and barbecue it over medium-hot coals for 10 to 12 minutes. Grill the bacon until it is crisp and brown. Heat the remaining marinade and serve it with the liver and bacon.

ELIZABETH SEWELL
BARBECUE COOKBOOK

Grilled Veal Liver, Florentine-Style

Fegato alla Griglia

To serve 4

4	large slices veal liver, cut ¼ inch [6 mm.] thick, membrane removed	4
	salt and freshly ground black pepper	
2 tbsp.	olive oil	30 ml.
	lemon wedges	

Preheat the grill rack over the coals and sprinkle it with 2 or 3 teaspoons [10 or 15 ml.] of salt. When the rack is very hot, grill the liver slices for about 45 seconds on each side, or until browned on the outside but pink in the middle. Sprinkle the liver with a little freshly ground black pepper and with olive oil. Garnish with lemon wedges and serve immediately.

GIULIANO BUGIALLI
THE FINE ART OF ITALIAN COOKING

Broiled Lamb or Veal Heart

To serve 2

1 lb.	lamb or veal heart, fat, tubes and fibrous tissue removed, the flesh halved lengthwise	½ kg.
¼ cup	soy sauce	50 ml.
2 tbsp.	wine vinegar	30 ml.
2	garlic cloves, finely chopped	2
1 tsp.	dried rosemary or tarragon leaves	5 ml.
1 tsp.	salt	5 ml.
1 tsp.	coarsely ground black pepper	5 ml.
	vegetable oil	

In a dish, combine the soy sauce, vinegar, garlic, rosemary or tarragon, salt and pepper. Add the heart, turn the halves to coat them well, then marinate the heart for one hour. Drain the halves and brush them with oil. Grill until they are brown on the outside but still rare on the inside—about five minutes on each side.

JAMES A. BEARD AND HELEN EVANS BROWN
THE COMPLETE BOOK OF OUTDOOR COOKERY

Mixed Meat and Poultry Roasted on a Spit

Arrosto Girato alla Fiorentina

Homemade white bread can be substituted for Tuscan bread.

A huge spit over a roaring fire of wood or charcoal is one of the trademarks of the Italian country villas. The spit has given its name, *girarrosto*, to a kind of restaurant in which these specialties are served.

In Italy, a special pan called a *ghiotta* is placed under the spit. Potatoes are put in the *ghiotta* to cook so that they can collect the delicious drippings from the meat. These *patate alla ghiotta* accompany the dish.

The bread commonly used for this dish is a Tuscan bread shaped in the form of a very long loaf, 1½ inches [4 cm.] thick and baked for only 35 minutes. Because of its short baking time, the bread does not form a crust and retains a whitish color, even if the dough is made with whole-wheat flour.

To serve 12

one 3½ lb.	chicken, cut into 12 pieces	one 1½ kg.
1¾ lb.	boneless pork loin, cut into 12 pieces	875 g.
3	squabs, quartered	3
12	quail, cleaned	12
12	spicy pork sausages, pricked with a fork	12
1 lb.	Tuscan bread, sliced ½ inch [1 cm.] thick and cut into pieces 1 inch [2½ cm.] long	½ kg.
12 to 14	bay leaves, halved	12 to 14
18 to 24	fresh sage leaves, halved	18 to 24
	salt and freshly ground black pepper	
1 cup	olive oil	¼ liter

Florentine-style pork liver (optional)

1½ lb.	pork liver, membrane removed, cut into 12 pieces	¾ kg.
½ lb.	caul, soaked in cold water for several minutes, drained and cut into 12 pieces	¼ kg.
¾ cup	fresh white bread crumbs	175 ml.
3 tbsp.	fennel seeds	45 ml.
	salt and freshly ground black pepper	
6	medium-sized bay leaves, halved	6

To prepare the pork liver, if used, combine the bread crumbs, fennel seeds, salt and pepper in a large bowl and mix well. Add the liver and coat it well with the bread-crumb mixture. Place each piece of liver on top of a piece of caul. Add half a bay leaf to each piece, and wrap the liver and bay leaf completely in the caul. Secure the parcels with wooden picks.

Now thread the meats onto the spit in the following order: chicken piece, half a bay leaf, pork-loin piece, half a sage leaf, bread, squab quarter, half a bay leaf, bread, sausage, half a sage leaf, bread, quail, half a bay leaf, bread, pork liver, half a sage leaf, bread.

Season the meats freely with salt and pepper, and place the spit over a charcoal fire (the charcoal should be gray and there should be no flames). Cook the *arrosto* very slowly for about one hour, sprinkling the meats every so often with salt and brushing them with olive oil. When it is ready, remove the *arrosto* from the spit and serve immediately.

GIULIANO BUGIALLI
THE FINE ART OF ITALIAN COOKING

Barbecued Pig's Tail

To serve 10 to 12

5 lb.	pig's tails, cleaned	2½ kg.
1½ tbsp.	salt	22½ ml.
2 cups	dry bread crumbs	½ liter

Chili barbecue sauce

1 tbsp.	chili powder	15 ml.
1 cup	chopped onions	¼ liter
3	garlic cloves, finely chopped	3
8 tbsp.	butter	120 ml.
½ cup	tomato ketchup *(recipe, page 163)*	125 ml.
¼ cup	brown sugar	50 ml.
2 tbsp.	fresh basil leaves or 1 tsp. [5 ml.] dried basil	30 ml.
1½ tsp.	freshly ground black pepper	7 ml.
1 tsp.	salt	5 ml.
¼ tsp.	Tabasco sauce	1 ml.
1 tbsp.	fresh lemon juice	15 ml.

Arrange the tails in a fairly deep pan where they can lie flat. Add the salt, cover them with water and bring them to a boil very slowly. When they have boiled for three to five minutes remove any scum that may have formed. Reduce the heat so that the tails simmer with the barest ripple. Cook them for about one and one half hours. Let them cool in the water for one hour, then remove and chill them.

For the chili barbecue sauce, sauté the onions and garlic in the butter until they are just tender. Add the remaining ingredients, bring to a boil and simmer for five minutes.

To barbecue the tails, brush them well with the barbecue sauce and place them in a hinged grill. Grill them slowly, turning them often and being careful not to break their skin.

When the tails are brown, remove them, brush them with the sauce again and roll them lightly in the bread crumbs. Grill, basting them once or twice, until the crumbs are nicely brown. Serve the tails at once with additional sauce.

JAMES BEARD
JAMES BEARD'S AMERICAN COOKERY

Skewered Lamb Variety Meats

Brochettes d'Abats d'Agneau

Sharpened rosemary branches, with a tuft of leaves left at the unsharpened end, may replace metal skewers, affording much the prettiest and most appetizing presentation.

To serve 4

4	lamb kidneys, outer fat and membrane removed, each cut crosswise into 3 pieces	4
3	lamb hearts, fat, tubes and fibrous tissue removed, halved and each half cut into 3 pieces	3
5	slices bacon, cut into squares (optional)	5
6 oz.	sweetbreads, soaked, parboiled for 5 minutes, membrane removed, pressed under weights for 2 hours, and sliced (optional)	175 g.
6 oz.	lamb liver, membrane removed, cubed (optional)	175 g.
6 oz.	boneless lamb shoulder, cubed (optional)	175 g.
6 oz.	small fresh mushrooms, preferably unopened, the stems cut off and finely chopped	175 g.
2	medium-sized onions, 1 finely chopped and 1 quartered lengthwise and separated into individual layers	2
2	small zucchini, thinly sliced (optional)	2
1	large sweet pepper, cut into 1½-inch [4-cm.] squares	1
2 tbsp.	finely chopped fresh parsley	30 ml.
1 tsp.	crumbled mixed dried herbs	5 ml.
1	large garlic clove, crushed to a paste	1
⅔ cup	olive oil	150 ml.
	salt and pepper	

In a large mixing bowl, combine all of the ingredients, except for half of the oil and the salt and pepper. Mix everything thoroughly but gently so that all of the meat and vegetable pieces are uniformly coated with oil, herbs and chopped vegetables. Marinate the mixture for about two hours, if you like, turning the ingredients around two or three times.

Drain the meats and vegetable pieces; reserve the marinade and mix it with the remaining oil. Thread the meats and vegetables alternately onto four skewers, salt and pepper all sides, and grill over hot coals for 12 to 15 minutes. Turn the skewers every three or four minutes, brushing the surfaces lightly with the marinade after each turn.

RICHARD OLNEY
SIMPLE FRENCH FOOD

Poultry

Chicken on a Spit

To serve 4

one 4 lb.	chicken	one 2 kg.
2 tsp.	salt	10 ml.
2	medium-sized apples, peeled, quartered and cored	2
1 cup	celery leaves	¼ liter
Lemon sauce		
½ cup	fresh lemon juice	125 ml.
12 tbsp.	butter	180 ml.
2 tsp.	paprika	10 ml.
1 tsp.	sugar	5 ml.
1 tsp.	salt	5 ml.
½ tsp.	freshly ground black pepper	2 ml.
¼ tsp.	dry mustard	1 ml.
	cayenne pepper	
½ cup	hot water	125 ml.
	Tabasco sauce	

To make the lemon sauce, melt the butter and stir in the paprika, sugar, salt, pepper, mustard and a pinch of cayenne pepper. Then blend thoroughly into the butter mixture the lemon juice, hot water and a few drops of Tabasco sauce. Set the sauce aside.

Rub the cavity of the bird with the salt. Place the apple quarters and celery leaves in the cavity. Sew up the opening of the cavity, or skewer the edges and lace the opening closed with cord. Fasten the neck skin to the back with a skewer. Tie the wings to the body. Insert a spit through the chicken. Then tie the drumsticks to the spit by looping cord over the tip ends and around the spit. Check to be sure that the chicken is well balanced.

Set the spit in place above the coals; put a drip pan underneath it. Start the motor of the spit. Roast the chicken for about one and one half hours, or until the skin of the bird is well browned and begins to split. Baste the chicken often with the sauce to keep the skin moist and to add flavor.

Heat the remaining lemon sauce and serve it with the roasted chicken.

STAFF HOME ECONOMISTS, CULINARY ARTS INSTITUTE
THE OUTDOOR GRILL COOKBOOK

Galveston-Style Tex-Mex Chicken

To serve 4

3 ½ to 4 lb.	chicken, backbone removed, halved	1 ½ to 2 kg.
1	lemon, halved	1
6	garlic cloves, finely chopped	6
1 tbsp.	cayenne pepper	15 ml.
2 tbsp.	paprika	30 ml.
	salt	

Rub each chicken half well on both sides with half of a lemon. Rub each half with the garlic, then rub in the cayenne pepper and paprika. Place the chicken halves, skin side up, in a shallow baking dish. Let the halves stand, uncovered, in a cool place—not the refrigerator—for 24 hours.

Place the chicken halves, skin side down, on a rack high above the coals of a covered grill. Cover and grill, turning the halves several times, until the chicken is tender—about one and one half hours.

BERT GREENE
HONEST AMERICAN FARE

Grilled Chicken

Pollos a la Parrilla

To serve 6

three 2 lb.	chickens, halved and flattened	three 1 kg.
	salt	
	oil	
3 tbsp.	butter, softened	45 ml.
3 tbsp.	Dijon mustard	45 ml.
	dry white bread crumbs	

Season the chicken halves with salt, and brush them well with oil. Place them on a very hot grill and cook them for approximately 10 minutes on each side, or until they are cooked through. Mix together the butter and mustard to form a paste. Spread the paste all over the cooked chickens and sprinkle them with the bread crumbs. Return the chickens to the rack to cook for another two minutes on each side, or until browned.

MAGDALENA ALPERI
LA COCINA

Manu Chicken

To serve 4

one 3 to 4 lb.	chicken, halved and flattened	one 1 ½ to 2 kg.
6 tbsp.	soy sauce	90 ml.
6 tbsp.	honey	90 ml.
½ cup	finely chopped onion	125 ml.
2	garlic cloves, crushed to a paste	2
1 tbsp.	grated fresh ginger	15 ml.
1 tsp.	salt	5 ml.

Combine the soy sauce, honey, onion, garlic, ginger and salt in a large bowl. Add the chicken and marinate it for two hours. Place the chicken in a hinged grill and cook it over coals. Turn and baste the chicken often, until it is well browned—approximately 25 minutes.

BARBARA AND GEORGE REIGER
THE ZANE GREY COOKBOOK

Grilled Chicken with Asparagus

Coquelets Grillés aux Pointes d'Asperges

To serve 6

six 2 lb.	chickens, halved and flattened	six 1 kg.
½ cup	clarified butter	125 ml.
	salt and pepper	
1 ½ lb.	jumbo asparagus, peeled and boiled in salted water for 5 minutes, drained and patted dry	¾ kg.
	fresh lemon juice	

Build a fire with charcoal, add hickory-wood chips, and as soon as the smoke has burned off, start broiling the chicken—six halves at a time. Brush the halves well with the clarified butter, set them cavity side down and sear them for five minutes, 2 inches [5 cm.] away from the heat. Raise the rack to 4 inches [10 cm.] away from the heat and continue grilling for five more minutes. Season the chicken halves with salt and pepper; turn them over and follow the same grilling procedure. Push the chicken halves toward the center of the rack and put half of the large asparagus spears—well brushed with butter—at the edge of the rack for one or two minutes, or until they are heated through.

Transfer the grilled chicken and asparagus to plates. Salt and pepper each portion, and sprinkle liberally with fresh lemon juice. Grill the other six chicken halves, and heat the remaining asparagus, while you eat the first batch.

MADELEINE KAMMAN
DINNER AGAINST THE CLOCK

Chicken and Beef Kebabs

To serve 6 to 8

2	whole chicken breasts, skinned and boned	2
1½ lb.	beef tenderloin	¾ kg.
¾ cup	dry red wine	175 ml.
2 tbsp.	fresh lemon juice	30 ml.
⅓ cup	olive oil	75 ml.
1	garlic clove, finely chopped	1
1	small onion, thinly sliced	1
2 tbsp.	soy sauce	30 ml.
2 tbsp.	sugar	30 ml.
	freshly ground black pepper	

Cut the beef into 1½-inch [4-cm.] cubes and the chicken into 1-inch [2½-cm.] cubes. (The larger beef cubes should be slightly rare, while the smaller chicken cubes should be thoroughly cooked.) Combine the remaining ingredients in a jar and shake well. Pour this marinade over the cubed meats in a large glass bowl and refrigerate overnight.

Drain the cubes thoroughly and reserve the marinade. Thread the cubed beef and chicken alternately on skewers. Barbecue over hot coals, approximately 3 inches [8 cm.] from the heat, for three to four minutes—turning the skewers often and basting the meats with the reserved marinade.

DIANE D. MAC MILLAN
THE PORTABLE FEAST

Hoosier Chicken

To serve 6 to 8

three 2 lb.	chickens, cut into quarters	three 1 kg.
1 cup	olive oil	¼ liter
½ cup	dry white wine	125 ml.
1 tbsp.	dried oregano leaves	15 ml.
1 tbsp.	dried rosemary leaves	15 ml.
2	garlic cloves	2
	salt	
	fresh marjoram leaves	

Marinate the chickens for one or two hours in a sauce made of the olive oil, wine, oregano, rosemary and garlic. Barbecue the chickens over a slow fire for about an hour, turning the pieces frequently. Sprinkle salt over the chickens during the last half hour of cooking time. Just before the chickens are finished, burn a big handful of marjoram in the fire. The spicy smoke adds a pungent flavor to the meat.

THOUGHTS FOR BUFFETS

Curried Broiled Chicken

To serve 4

two 2 lb.	chickens, cut into serving pieces	two 1 kg.
1 cup	grated onion	¼ liter
½ cup	strained fresh lemon juice	125 ml.
2¼ tsp.	salt	11 ml.
8 tbsp.	butter, melted	120 ml.
2 tsp.	curry powder	10 ml.

Make a marinade with the onion, lemon juice and 1½ teaspoons [7 ml.] of the salt. Add the chicken pieces, cover, and marinate them for two hours at room temperature or for four to five hours in the refrigerator. Mix together the butter, curry powder and the remaining salt. Grill the chicken over coals, 6 inches [15 cm.] from the heat for 20 to 25 minutes—basting the pieces with both the onion and the curry marinades and turning the chicken pieces several times.

SONIA UVEZIAN
THE CUISINE OF ARMENIA

Barbecued Chicken with Polynesian Sauce

To serve 4

two 2 lb.	chickens, cut into quarters	two 1 kg.
6	kumquats, seeded and finely chopped	6
¼ cup	honey	50 ml.
¼ cup	fresh orange juice	50 ml.
¼ cup	soy sauce	50 ml.
2 tbsp.	grated orange peel	30 ml.
2 tbsp.	fresh lemon juice	30 ml.
½ tsp.	ground ginger	2 ml.
¼ tsp.	freshly ground pepper	1 ml.
	melted butter	

Blend the kumquats, honey, orange juice, soy sauce, orange peel, lemon juice, ginger and pepper. Pour this mixture over the chicken pieces and marinate them for four to five hours in the refrigerator, turning the pieces once every hour. Drain the chicken, reserving the marinade.

Place your grill rack 6 to 8 inches [15 to 20 cm.] above hot glowing coals. Grill the chicken, turning the pieces from time to time and brushing occasionally with melted butter, until the juices flow clear when a thigh is pricked—about 45 minutes to one hour. Baste the pieces with the marinade during the last 15 minutes of cooking.

ANN CHANDONNET
THE COMPLETE FRUIT COOKBOOK

Tandoori Chicken

The tandoori coloring and ghee called for in this recipe may be obtained at Indian food stores.

	To serve 6	
three 2 lb.	chickens	three 1 kg.
2½ tsp.	natural meat tenderizer	12 ml.
⅓ cup	fresh lemon juice	75 ml.
2	large garlic cloves	2
1 tbsp.	finely chopped fresh ginger	15 ml.
1 tsp.	ground cumin	5 ml.
½ tsp.	ground cardamom	2 ml.
½ tsp.	cayenne pepper	2 ml.
1 tsp.	*tandoori* coloring or 1 tbsp. [15 ml.] paprika	5 ml.
⅓ cup	yogurt	75 ml.
	ghee or light vegetable oil	

Place the chickens on a cutting board. Cut off the wings and quarter the chickens neatly. Then pull away the skin. (Reserve the wings and skin for the stockpot.) Prick the chicken all over with a fork or a thin skewer. Make diagonal slashes about ½ inch [1 cm.] deep and spaced 1 inch [2½ cm.] apart on the meaty sides of the chicken.

Place the chicken quarters in a large bowl. Add the meat tenderizer and lemon juice, and rub them into the chicken. Cover and marinate the chicken for half an hour.

Put all of the other ingredients except the *ghee* or oil into the container of an electric blender, and blend them until they are reduced to a smooth sauce. (Alternatively, the garlic and ginger may be crushed to a paste and blended with the remaining ingredients.) Pour this marinade over the chicken quarters and mix, turning and tossing, to coat the chicken well. (A note of caution: Since certain brands of *tandoori* coloring tend to stain the fingers, it is advisable either to use a fork to turn the chicken in the marinade or use a pastry brush to spread it over the quarters.) Cover and marinate the chicken for four hours at room temperature or refrigerate the quarters overnight, turning them several times. Take the chicken from the refrigerator at least one hour before cooking it to bring it to room temperature.

Set the fire well in advance and let it burn until a white ash forms over the surface of the coals. Place the rack at least 5 inches [13 cm.] away from the heat, and rub it generously with oil. Place the chicken quarters, slashed side up, on the rack and brush them with *ghee* or oil. Let the chicken cook without turning for 10 minutes. Turn, baste the other side with *ghee* or oil, and cook for 10 minutes. Continue to cook, turning and basting the chicken until it is done—about 30 minutes in all. Serve the chicken immediately, lightly brushed with *ghee* or oil.

JULIE SAHNI
CLASSIC INDIAN COOKING

Chicken in East-West Sauce

The volatile oils in chilies may irritate your skin. Wear rubber gloves when handling them.

This is a Lebanese sauce invented at the Yildizlar restaurant in Beirut. Serve the chicken with a green salad.

	To serve 6	
one 3 to 4 lb.	chicken, cut into 8 serving pieces	one 1½ to 2 kg.
2	medium-sized sweet red peppers, halved, seeded and deribbed	2
2	fresh hot red chilies, stemmed and seeded	2
6 to 8 tbsp.	olive oil	90 to 120 ml.
3 tbsp.	fresh lemon juice	45 ml.
	salt	

Cook the peppers and chilies in boiling salted water until they are tender—about 10 minutes—and then purée them in a blender. Mix the olive oil and lemon juice into this hot purée and add extra salt if necessary. Set it aside to cool.

Rub the sauce over the chicken pieces and let them marinate overnight in the refrigerator. Then grill the chicken with the sauce still on it, over hot charcoal, for about 40 minutes, turning the pieces once.

JANE GRIGSON
JANE GRIGSON'S VEGETABLE BOOK

Chicken Scheherazade

	To serve 4	
one 4 lb.	chicken, cut into 8 serving pieces	one 2 kg.
1 cup	yogurt	¼ liter
¼ cup	finely chopped scallions	50 ml.
1 tsp.	curry powder	5 ml.
1 tsp.	salt	5 ml.

In a small mixing bowl combine the yogurt with the scallions, curry powder and salt. Place the chicken pieces in a shallow pan or baking dish, or in a heavy-duty plastic bag.

Pour the yogurt mixture over the chicken, turning the pieces to coat all the sides. Cover the chicken loosely and let it stand while preparing the smoker.

Soak two or three chunks of wood or a handful of wood chips in water for an hour or so. Fill the fire pan with charcoal and start the fire. When the coals turn gray, drain the wood pieces and add them to the coals. Set the water pan in place and fill it with hot water; then put the grill rack in place. Arrange the chicken pieces on the rack; cover the smoker and cook the chicken for about three to four hours.

THE EDITORS OF CONSUMER GUIDE
SMOKE COOKERY

Chicken Breasts in Red Sauce

Dak Kui

Red bean paste is a thick sweet paste made from soybeans. It is available in cans where Oriental foods are sold and will keep for months refrigerated in a covered jar.

To serve 2 to 4

2	chicken breasts, skinned, boned and halved	2
2	scallions, finely chopped	2
3	garlic cloves, crushed to a paste	3
4 tsp.	red bean paste	20 ml.
1 tbsp.	sesame-seed oil	15 ml.
1 tbsp.	sesame seeds	15 ml.
1 tbsp.	sugar	15 ml.
1 tbsp.	soy sauce	15 ml.
	black pepper	

To flatten the chicken breasts, pound them with the flat side of a knife. Score them diagonally across the grain. Combine the remaining ingredients in a bowl; add the chicken breasts and mix until the breasts are coated with marinade. Grill the breasts over medium-hot coals for three minutes on each side. To serve, cut the breasts into 2-inch [5-cm.] pieces.

JUDY HYUN
THE KOREAN COOKBOOK

Chicken Breasts and Livers on a Skewer

To serve 6

2 lb.	chicken breasts, skinned, boned and cut into 1½-inch [4-cm.] squares	1 kg.
1 lb.	chicken livers, trimmed and halved	½ kg.
6 tbsp.	olive oil	90 ml.
1	garlic clove, crushed to a paste	1
1 tbsp.	chopped fresh thyme, tarragon or rosemary leaves	15 ml.
	cherry tomatoes	

Mix together the olive oil, garlic and herb leaves. Put the meats into a bowl, pour in the flavored oil and mix thoroughly. Alternate pieces of chicken and pieces of liver on skewers, adding cherry tomatoes as often as you like. Put a piece of perforated foil on a grill rack over a very hot charcoal fire, as close to the coals as possible. Put the skewers on the foil and cook the meat rapidly, turning the skewers several times and basting them with the flavored oil left in the bowl. If the fire is hot enough, 10 to 15 minutes should be enough time to cook the meat. Serve at once.

MOLLY FINN
SUMMER FEASTS

Egyptian Chicken Kebabs

To serve 6 to 8

4	large chicken breasts, skinned, boned and each cut into 16 squares	4
1 tbsp.	plain yogurt	15 ml.
¼ tsp.	salt	1 ml.
¼ tsp.	ground turmeric	1 ml.
½ tsp.	curry powder	2 ml.
⅛ tsp.	ground cardamom	½ ml.
1 tsp.	fresh lemon juice	5 ml.
1 tsp.	vinegar	5 ml.
1	onion, quartered lengthwise and separated into individual layers	1
8	small tomatoes, halved	8

Combine the breast squares with all of the ingredients except the onion and tomatoes, and allow them to marinate for at least 30 minutes. Thread on skewers two squares of chicken, one piece of onion, two squares of chicken and half a tomato. Repeat until all of the ingredients are used. Broil over coals, 6 inches [15 cm.] from the heat source, for about five to 10 minutes—or until the chicken squares are evenly browned on all sides.

JANE NOVAK
TREASURY OF CHICKEN COOKERY

Broiled Chicken
Khorovadz Varyag

To serve 4

two 2 lb.	chickens, cut into serving pieces	two 1 kg.
6 tbsp.	olive oil	90 ml.
6 tbsp.	strained fresh lemon juice	90 ml.
2	large garlic cloves, crushed to a paste	2
2 tsp.	dried oregano or thyme leaves	10 ml.
	salt and freshly ground black pepper	

Wipe the chicken pieces with damp paper towels. In a large bowl mix together the remaining ingredients until they are well blended. Add the chicken, turning the pieces to coat them thoroughly with the mixture. Cover, and marinate the chicken at room temperature for two hours or in the refrigerator for four to five hours, turning the pieces occasionally. Remove the chicken from the marinade and broil over coals, about 6 inches [15 cm.] from the heat. Turn the chicken often and brush the pieces with the marinade until they are well browned, crisp and cooked through—20 to 25 minutes.

SONIA UVEZIAN
THE CUISINE OF ARMENIA

Chicken Puu Puu

To serve 10 to 12 as a first course

2	chicken breasts, skinned, boned and cut into 1-inch [2½-cm.] squares	2
½ lb.	fresh button mushrooms, trimmed	¼ kg.
½ cup	oil	125 ml.
¼ cup	soy sauce	50 ml.
2 tbsp.	vinegar	30 ml.
1 tbsp.	honey	15 ml.
½ tsp.	hoisin sauce	2 ml.
1	garlic clove, finely chopped	1
2 tbsp.	cornstarch, dissolved in ¼ cup [50 ml.] water	30 ml.

Combine the oil, soy sauce, vinegar, honey, hoisin sauce and garlic. Add the chicken squares and the mushrooms, cover and marinate them for two to three hours at room temperature or overnight in the refrigerator. Drain the chicken and mushrooms, reserving the marinade, and thread them alternately onto 10 to 12 small bamboo skewers. Broil about 4

inches [10 cm.] from the coals for three to four minutes on each side, or until the chicken is opaque.

Meanwhile, combine the reserved marinade and the cornstarch in a small pan. Stirring constantly, bring the mixture to a boil and cook briefly until this sauce is thick.

Serve the chicken accompanied by the sauce.

ROANA AND GENE SCHINDLER
HAWAII KAI COOKBOOK

Spiced Grilled Chicken
Wakadori No Nanbanyaki

The volatile oils in chilies may irritate your skin. Wear rubber gloves when handling them.

To serve 4

2 lb.	chicken thighs, each slit lengthwise and the bone cut out, the skin left in place	1 kg.
3 tbsp.	soy sauce	45 ml.
1 tbsp.	mirin	15 ml.
1 tbsp.	sake	15 ml.
2	scallions, including 2 inches [5 cm.] of the green tops, finely chopped	2
2	dried hot red chilies, stemmed and seeded	2
1	egg yolk	1
12	small fresh hot green chilies, stemmed and seeded	12
	vegetable oil	
	salt	

Prick the skin of the boned chicken thighs all over with a fork and put them into a bowl. Add the soy sauce, *mirin* and *sake*, and marinate the chicken for 10 minutes, turning it two or three times. Thread the thighs on a skewer, reserving the marinade. Grind the scallions and dried chilies in a mortar until they form a paste. Add the reserved marinade and mix, then beat in the egg yolk. Set this sauce aside.

Using a hibachi or other grill, cook the chicken thighs until about half done—four minutes on each side. Take the skewers off the heat and use a pastry brush to paint the thighs with the scallion sauce. Return them to the grill and cook for one minute on each side. Repeat two or three times until the sauce is used up and the chicken is done.

Paint the fresh chilies with oil. Grill them, turning them once, for about one minute. Sprinkle them lightly with salt. Slice the chicken thighs diagonally and arrange the slices on plates; garnish with the chilies.

ELISABETH LAMBERT ORTIZ
THE COMPLETE BOOK OF JAPANESE COOKING

Chicken Liver Kebabs

Spiedini di Fegatini di Pollo

	To serve 6	
2½ lb.	chicken livers, trimmed and halved or quartered	1¼ kg.
4 tbsp.	butter, melted	60 ml.
1¼ lb.	fresh mushrooms, thickly sliced	600 g.
½ cup	dry bread crumbs	125 ml.

Heat half of the butter in a skillet, add the livers and cook them until they are firm and lightly browned, but not cooked through—about two minutes. Toss the mushrooms with the remaining butter. Thread the livers and mushrooms alternately onto skewers, roll them in the bread crumbs and grill them 6 inches [15 cm.] from the coals for three to four minutes, turning the skewers several times.

VINCENZO BUONASSISI
CUCINA ALL'ARIA APERTA

Skewered Chicken Livers

Brochettes de Foies de Volaille Grillées

	To serve 6	
1½ lb.	chicken livers, trimmed and cut into halves	¾ kg.
6	thick slices ham, cut into 1½-inch [4-cm.] squares	6
1 tsp.	salt	5 ml.
	freshly ground white pepper	
½ cup	oil	125 ml.
12	medium-sized fresh mushrooms, trimmed	12
	fresh lemon juice	
	Mustard butter sauce	
1 tbsp.	Dijon mustard	15 ml.
1 lb.	butter, melted	½ kg.
2 tbsp.	flour	30 ml.

Season the chicken livers with the salt and a generous grinding of white pepper, and sauté them in ⅓ cup [75 ml.] oil until they are firm—one or two minutes. Drain them in a sieve lined with cheesecloth, and let them cool. In a saucepan over low heat, melt the butter. Add the flour and mustard, and stir until this sauce is thick. Set the sauce aside.

Thread the livers and ham onto six skewers alternately—beginning and ending each assembly with a mushroom cap. Brush the skewered ingredients lightly with the remaining oil and grill over charcoal, turning the skewers

from time to time, for two to three minutes. Place the skewers on a long serving platter, and pour the mustard butter sauce over them.

HENRI LE HUÉDÉ
DINING ON THE FRANCE

Angolan Duck with Grilled Papaya

The volatile oils in the chili may irritate your skin. Wear rubber gloves when handling it.

	To serve 4	
5 lb.	duck, halved or quartered	2½ kg.
2	firm papayas, peeled, halved and seeded	2
½ cup	fresh orange juice	125 ml.
2 tbsp.	fresh lime juice	30 ml.
¼ cup	oil	50 ml.
½ cup	finely chopped green pepper	125 ml.
1	fresh hot chili, stemmed, seeded and chopped	1
12	whole cloves	12
¾ tsp.	salt	4 ml.
4 tbsp.	butter, melted	60 ml.
⅛ tsp.	freshly grated nutmeg	½ ml.

Place the duck pieces in a shallow glass dish. Mix together the orange and lime juices, oil, green pepper, chili, cloves and ¼ teaspoon [1 ml.] of the salt, and pour the mixture over the duck. Marinate the duck for two hours at room temperature, turning the pieces occasionally.

Prepare a charcoal fire. When the coals are hot, arrange them in a ring around a drip pan. Grill the duck, centered over the drip pan, until nicely brown—about 15 to 20 minutes on each side. Meanwhile, put the papayas in a bowl with the melted butter, nutmeg and the remaining salt. Turn the papayas in this mixture to coat them evenly. Just before the duck is cooked, place the papaya halves over the coals and grill them on both sides until just heated through.

MAGGIE WALDRON
FIRE & SMOKE

Marinated Duck
Marinierte Ente

To serve 4 to 6

one 4 lb.	duck, washed inside and out and patted dry	one 2 kg.
½ cup	finely chopped fresh parsley	125 ml.
3 tbsp.	red wine	45 ml.
2 tbsp.	sugar	30 ml.
1 tsp.	paprika	5 ml.
	ground ginger, cinnamon and nutmeg	
	freshly ground black pepper	
	soy sauce	
5 tbsp.	oil	75 ml.
2 tbsp.	salt	30 ml.
¼ cup	hot water	50 ml.
1 lb.	grapes, skinned and seeded	½ kg.

Mix together the parsley, wine, sugar, paprika, a pinch each of ginger, cinnamon, nutmeg and pepper, and a dash of soy sauce. Blend this mixture to a paste with 3 tablespoons [45 ml.] of the oil. Spread the paste over the inside and outside surfaces of the duck, then wrap the duck in foil and marinate it in the refrigerator for at least 24 hours.

Pat the duck dry inside and out, brush it with the rest of the oil and grill it on a spit—with a drip pan underneath it—for about 70 minutes, brushing it now and then with the drippings. Fifteen minutes before the end of the cooking time, dissolve the salt in the hot water and baste the duck with this several times so that the skin becomes crisp. Carve the duck and serve it at once, garnished with the grapes.

MECHTHILD PIEPENBROCK
GRILL VERGNÜGEN DRAUSSEN UND DRINNEN

Duck on a Spit

The technique of spit-roasting duck is demonstrated on pages 60-61.

To serve 6 to 8

two 5 lb.	ducks	two 2½ kg.
4	oranges, quartered	4
½ cup	oil	125 ml.
½ lb.	butter	¼ kg.
1 cup	fresh orange juice	¼ liter
2 tbsp.	grated orange peel	30 ml.
2 tbsp.	chopped watercress leaves	30 ml.

Stuff the ducks with the quartered oranges. Brush the ducks with the oil, and spit-roast them for one and one half hours,

or until done. Meanwhile, combine the butter, orange juice, orange peel and watercress and simmer for 15 minutes, stirring occasionally. Serve the roasted ducks with the hot orange-butter sauce.

PICTURE COOK BOOK

Barbecued Lemon Duck

To serve 4

4 to 5 lb.	duck, quartered	2 to 2½ kg.
4	scallions, finely chopped	4
1 tsp.	grated fresh ginger	5 ml.
2 tsp.	ground turmeric	10 ml.
2 tbsp.	dark soy sauce	30 ml.
1 tsp.	sugar	5 ml.
½ tsp.	grated lemon peel	2 ml.
	salt and black pepper	

Marinate the quartered duck for four hours with the scallions, ginger, turmeric, soy sauce, sugar, lemon peel, salt and pepper. Place the duck on a grill rack over hot coals that are arranged in a ring around a drip pan. Grill the duck for about 20 minutes on each side, until the skin is crisp.

MAY WONG TRENT
ORIENTAL BARBECUES

Squab Grilled over Charcoal
Pigeonneau Grillé sur Charbon de Bois

Instead of using skewers, you can place the squabs directly on the grill rack. Turn them several times during cooking.

To serve 6

6	squabs, cleaned and trussed	6
5 tbsp.	butter	75 ml.
2 tbsp.	paprika	30 ml.
1 tsp.	cumin	5 ml.
1	garlic clove, crushed to a paste	1
	salt	
1¼ cups	water	300 ml.

Place the squabs in a saucepan. Add the butter, half of the paprika, half of the cumin and all of the garlic. Salt the squabs lightly. Add the water, cover the pan and put it over low heat. Let the squabs simmer for about 30 minutes, or until they are cooked through. Remove them from the pan, and boil their cooking liquid until it is reduced to about 1 cup [¼ liter]. Let this sauce cool, then stir in the remaining paprika and cumin. Brush the squabs with this mixture. Thread the squabs on separate skewers and grill them, turning them constantly, over charcoal for 10 minutes. Serve the squabs very hot.

AHMED LAASRI
240 RECETTES DE CUISINE MAROCAINE

Roast Guinea Hen

Perlhuhn vom Grill

Serve this dish with grilled tomatoes or grilled bananas. The guinea hen can also be halved and cooked on the grill.

	To serve 2	
1	young guinea hen	1
	salt	
	paprika	
4	sprigs fresh parsley	4
4 tbsp.	butter, melted, or oil	60 ml.

Lightly salt the inside of the guinea hen and rub paprika over the outside. Place the parsley sprigs in the cavity. Truss the bird.

Fasten the guinea hen onto the spit. Baste it with melted butter or oil and cook it for 40 to 50 minutes, continuing to baste it often during the cooking time. It should be evenly browned and cooked through.

ILSE FROIDL
DAS GEFLÜGEL-KOCHBUCH

Burmese-Style Guinea Hens

Perlhuhn auf Burmesische Art

Serve this dish with rice, mango chutney and melted butter.

	To serve 6	
3	guinea hens	3
¼ tsp. each	ground coriander, turmeric, cumin, cinnamon and pepper	1 ml. each
½ cup	olive oil	125 ml.
3 tbsp.	fresh lemon juice	45 ml.
8 tbsp.	clarified butter	120 ml.
6	small bananas, peeled and halved	6
	flour	
6	sprigs watercress	6

Using scissors, split the guinea hens by cutting to one side of the backbone from the tail to the neck. Lay the birds, breast side up, on a flat surface. Place the palm of your hand over the breast and press down firmly to break the breastbone. With a small sharp knife, make a slit in the loose skin between the legs. Gently bend the legs inward and insert them through the slit in the skin.

Mix the spices together well and rub them thoroughly into the guinea hens. Let the birds marinate for at least two hours in the combined oil and lemon juice.

Roast the guinea hens slowly on the grill for 10 minutes on each side, brushing them from time to time with clarified butter. Dip the bananas in flour and grill them for four minutes, brushing them with butter several times. Serve the guinea hens garnished with the bananas and watercress.

WALTER BICKEL AND RENÉ KRAMER
WILD EN GEVOLGELTE IN DE INTERNATIONALE KEUKEN

Smoked Turkey Teriyaki

To serve 10 to 12

one 10 lb.	turkey, cut into serving pieces	one 5 kg.
¾ cup	soy sauce	175 ml.
½ cup	dry sherry	125 ml.
¼ cup	oil	50 ml.
1 tbsp.	ground ginger	15 ml.
1 tbsp.	dry mustard	15 ml.
1 tbsp.	finely chopped garlic	15 ml.

Place the turkey pieces in a large shallow dish or a heavy-duty plastic bag. Combine all of the remaining ingredients in a small bowl until they are blended. Pour the marinade over the turkey pieces and turn them so the marinade coats them completely. Cover with plastic wrap or close the bag securely. Refrigerate the turkey overnight, turning the pieces in the marinade occasionally.

To prepare the smoker, soak two or three chunks of wood or a handful of wood chips in water. Fill the fire pan with charcoal and light the fire. When the coals turn gray, drain the wood pieces and add them to the coals. Put the water pan in place and fill it almost full with hot water. Put the cooking rack in place. Lift the turkey pieces from the marinade and place them on the rack, leaving some space between the pieces. Pour the marinade over the turkey into the water pan. Cover, and smoke the turkey pieces for six to seven hours. Check the water pan after four hours and add some hot water, if necessary.

THE EDITORS OF CONSUMER GUIDE
SMOKE COOKERY

Barbecued Turkey

To serve 8

8 lb.	turkey, cut into 8 serving pieces	4 kg.
¼ cup	vinegar	50 ml.
¼ cup	peanut oil	50 ml.
1 tbsp.	strained fresh lemon juice	15 ml.
½ cup	finely chopped onion	125 ml.
½ cup	finely chopped green pepper	125 ml.
1 tsp.	celery salt	5 ml.
¼ tsp.	dried oregano leaves	1 ml.
½ tsp.	dried basil leaves	2 ml.
½ tsp.	white pepper	2 ml.
¼ tsp.	ground cinnamon	1 ml.
¼ tsp.	ground cumin	1 ml.
1	garlic clove, crushed to a paste	1
	Tabasco sauce	

In a stainless-steel saucepan, combine all of the ingredients except the Tabasco sauce and the turkey. Cook gently until the onion is translucent—about 10 minutes. Remove the sauce from the heat to cool. Add the Tabasco to taste. Place the turkey pieces in a large bowl or a large, flat baking dish. Pour the sauce over the turkey. Cover and refrigerate for six hours or overnight, turning the turkey pieces frequently. Before cooking, remove the turkey and drain it; reserve the marinade. Cook the turkey pieces on a grill, with the rack about 4 inches [10 cm.] from the coals, for 20 to 25 minutes on each side. Baste the pieces several times with the marinade during cooking and again when the turkey is done.

MORTON GILL CLARK
THE WIDE, WIDE WORLD OF TEXAS COOKING

Delicious Charcoaled Dove

To serve 2

2	dove breasts, halved	2
2 tbsp.	soy sauce	30 ml.
2 tbsp.	olive oil	30 ml.
4	slices bacon	4

Combine the soy sauce and the olive oil, and marinate the dove breasts for one hour. Wrap a slice of bacon around each breast half, then grill them on a rack over a low fire until the bacon is crisp—10 to 15 minutes on each side.

THE JUNIOR LEAGUE OF PINE BLUFF, INC.
SOUTHERN ACCENT

Spit-roasted Partridges

Kuropatwy i Przepiórki Pieczone

The same recipe may be used for quail, which require about 15 minutes of roasting time.

To serve 2

2	partridges, cleaned	2
	salt	
4 or 6	sage leaves (optional)	4 or 6
5 oz.	pork fatback, thinly sliced	150 g.
2 tbsp.	butter, melted	30 ml.
2	slices white bread with the crusts removed, fried in 4 tbsp. [60 ml.] butter	2
2 tbsp.	chicken stock (recipe, page 167)	30 ml.

Salt the birds inside and out. Two or three sage leaves may be placed inside each bird. Wrap each bird in thin slices of fatback and tie with cotton thread. Roast the partridges on a spit suspended above a drip pan for about 25 minutes, basting them from time to time with a tablespoonful [15 ml.] of melted butter. Remove the thread from the birds, leaving on the covering of attractively browned fat, and place each bird on a slice of fried bread. Stir the stock into the juices in the drip pan and pour this sauce over the birds.

MARIA LEMNIS AND HENRYK VITRY
W STARO POLSKIEJ KUCHNI

Small Birds, Spit-roasted

Paulákia stin Soúvla

The technique of threading small birds on a spit is demonstrated on page 62.

Small birds, grilled on spits over coals, are served at many Greek village cafés with cheese or fried eggs on the side, a delicacy since ancient times.

To serve 4

12	quail or other small game birds, cleaned and trussed	12
	salt and pepper	
4 tbsp.	olive oil	60 ml.
½ tsp.	dried thyme	2 ml.
1½ tbsp.	fresh lemon juice	22½ ml.

Rub the birds with salt and pepper, and thread them on a metal spit. Combine the olive oil, thyme and lemon juice in a bowl and beat lightly with a fork until blended. Brush the birds with this mixture. Grill them over a charcoal fire for seven to 10 minutes, turning them often to cook all sides, and basting them frequently with the oil-and-lemon mixture.

THEONIE MARK
GREEK ISLANDS COOKING

Quail Grilled over Charcoal

Putpudutsi Pecheni

To serve 2

4	quail, cleaned	4
	salt and freshly ground black pepper	

Place each quail on its back on a chopping board and slice it lengthwise along the breastbone, leaving the two sides joined at the back. Spread the bird open and pound it gently with a wooden mallet to flatten it, at the same time working in some salt and freshly ground black pepper. Arrange the prepared birds on a greased, hot rack over glowing charcoal and grill them, turning once, until they are cooked through and nicely browned—about 10 minutes. Serve them at once.

SEMEYNO SUKROVISHTE

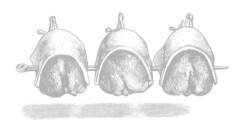

Marinated Grilled Quail or Doves

To serve 4

12	quail or doves, cleaned and split lengthwise	12
1½ cups	dry white wine	375 ml.
1 tbsp.	wine vinegar	15 ml.
1 cup	chopped celery	¼ liter
2	garlic cloves, crushed to a paste	2
1	bay leaf	1
2	sprigs fresh thyme or 1 tsp. [5 ml.] dried thyme leaves	2
	salt and pepper	
8 tbsp.	butter, melted	120 ml.

Mix together the wine, vinegar, celery, garlic, bay leaf, thyme, salt and pepper for the marinade. Add the birds, cover, and marinate them in the refrigerator for eight hours. Remove the birds from the marinade and pat them dry; discard the marinade.

Place the birds, cut side down, on an oiled barbecue grill rack and cook them for about 20 minutes, or until browned, turning them from time to time and basting them with the melted butter.

DOMINIQUE D'ERMO
DOMINIQUE'S FAMOUS FISH, GAME & MEAT RECIPES

Fish and Shellfish

Hawaiian-Sesame Albacore

Bonito or swordfish may be substituted for the albacore.

To serve 4

4	albacore steaks, each about ½ lb. [¼ kg.]	4
8	slices bacon	8
8 tbsp.	butter	120 ml.
6 tbsp.	fresh lemon juice	90 ml.
¼ cup	dry sherry	50 ml.
¼ cup	sesame seeds	50 ml.
	lemon wedges	
Teriyaki marinade		
⅓ cup	soy sauce	75 ml.
¼ cup	dry white wine	50 ml.
4 tbsp.	butter, melted and cooled	60 ml.
2 tbsp.	sugar	30 ml.
¾ tbsp.	grated fresh ginger or ⅓ tsp. [1½ ml.] ground ginger	11 ml.
1	garlic clove, crushed to a paste	1

Combine the marinade ingredients and mix well. Wash the albacore steaks and dry them with paper towels. Place the steaks in a shallow dish, pour in ½ cup [125 ml.] of the marinade, cover and refrigerate for one hour.

Wrap each piece of fish with two bacon slices, and fasten the bacon with wooden picks. This not only keeps the fish neatly together but also adds extra flavor and juiciness. As soon as the fish begins to cook, the meat firms, and can be easily handled.

In a small pan, melt the butter and remove it from the heat. Stir in the remaining marinade, the lemon juice and sherry. Arrange the fish on the grill rack over medium-hot coals. Brush them well with the butter mixture.

When the steaks are done on one side, sprinkle them with sesame seeds, turn them over, and cook them until the other side is brown. Baste the fish again with the butter mixture and sprinkle them with the remaining sesame seeds. Before serving, turn the steaks over once more to toast all the seeds. The total barbecuing time should be about 15 minutes. Garnish with lemon wedges.

KAREN GREEN AND BETTY BLACK
HOW TO COOK HIS GOOSE (AND OTHER WILD GAMES)

Grilled Fresh Anchovies

If anchovies are not available, smelts, herring or sardines may be substituted.

	To serve 4	
16	fresh anchovies	16
3 tbsp.	fresh lemon juice	45 ml.
3 tbsp.	olive oil	45 ml.
2	garlic cloves, finely chopped	2
½ tsp.	paprika	2 ml.
	salt and freshly ground black pepper	
	parsley sprigs and lemon wedges	

Add half of the lemon juice to the oil, garlic, paprika, salt and pepper. Marinate the anchovies for 15 minutes in this mixture. Then place the anchovies on a very hot grill and cook them for four minutes on each side, while basting the fish with the remaining marinade. Before serving, pour the remaining lemon juice over the anchovies, and garnish them with parsley and lemon wedges.

GRANT BLACKMAN
AUSTRALIAN FISH COOKING

Charcoal-broiled Fish

Psári tis Sháras

	To serve 4 to 6	
two 1½ to 2 lb.	whole sea bream, red snapper, grouper or bass, cleaned	two ¾ to 1 kg.
	salt and pepper	
1 tbsp.	chopped fresh oregano leaves or ¼ tsp. [1 ml.] dried oregano leaves	15 ml.
Lemon-oil sauce		
3 tbsp.	fresh lemon juice	45 ml.
½ cup	olive oil	125 ml.
1	garlic clove, halved	1
¼ tsp.	white pepper	1 ml.

Season the cavities of the fish with salt and pepper, rubbing the seasonings in with your fingers. Combine all of the sauce

ingredients in a bowl, and beat them vigorously with a fork or whisk them until they are well mixed. Let the sauce stand at room temperature for one hour before using it.

Using a brush, baste the outside of the fish and the grids of a hinged grill with some of the lemon-oil sauce. When the charcoal is hot, put the fish in the hinged grill and set the grill over the fire. Turning them over and over, baste the fish frequently with the sauce until they are cooked—approximately 20 minutes, depending upon the thickness of the fish. Put the fish on a platter, sprinkle them with the remaining lemon-oil sauce, and garnish them with the oregano.

THEONIE MARK
GREEK ISLANDS COOKING

Egyptian Fish Kebab

Samak Kebab

If sea bass is not available, any fish with firm flesh—drum, grouper, trout, for example—may be substituted.

	To serve 4	
1½ lb.	sea bass fillets, skinned and cut into ½-inch [1-cm.] cubes	¾ kg.
½ cup	fresh lemon juice	125 ml.
3	onions, grated, the juice strained and the pulp discarded	3
4	bay leaves	4
2 tsp.	ground cumin	10 ml.
	salt and pepper	
8	small tomatoes, quartered	8
	olive oil	
	chopped fresh parsley	
	lemon wedges	

In a small dish, combine the lemon juice, onion juice, bay leaves, cumin, salt and pepper. Marinate the cubes of fish for half an hour.

Impale the fish cubes alternately with the tomato wedges on four thin stainless-steel skewers. Brush the fish and tomatoes with a little olive oil and grill them over charcoal for five to six minutes. Serve the skewers on a bed of chopped parsley and garnish with lemon wedges.

ALAN DAVIDSON
MEDITERRANEAN SEAFOOD

Broiled Sea Bass

If sea bass is not available, striped bass, white perch or grouper may be substituted. The technique of filleting a roundfish is demonstrated on pages 66-67.

To serve 6		
two 3 lb.	sea bass, filleted	two 1½ kg.
¼ cup	chopped fresh fennel leaves, plus 4 fennel stalks	50 ml.
½ cup	dry white wine	125 ml.
1 tsp.	fresh lemon juice	5 ml.
	salt and pepper	
8 tbsp.	unsalted butter	120 ml.

Crush the fennel stalks with the back of a knife and insert these stalks between the fillets of each fish. Let them stand in the refrigerator for at least four hours. In a saucepan combine the wine, chopped fennel, lemon juice and salt and pepper to taste. Reduce the sauce over medium heat to 3 tablespoons [45 ml.]; then fluff in the butter.

Let the fish reach room temperature. Broil them for six to eight minutes on each side. Serve the sauce over the fish.

MADELEINE KAMMAN
THE MAKING OF A COOK

Barbecue-steamed Black Bass

If black bass is not available, white perch, grouper or striped bass fillets may be substituted.

To serve 4		
4	black bass fillets, each about 6 to 8 oz. [175 to 240 g.]	4
4	lemon or lime slices	4
¼ cup	finely chopped scallion tops	50 ml.
6 tbsp.	butter	90 ml.
2 tbsp.	fresh lemon or lime juice	30 ml.
1 tbsp.	chopped fresh parsley	15 ml.
1 tbsp.	finely chopped garlic	15 ml.
½ tsp.	salt	2 ml.
¼ tsp.	dry mustard	1 ml.

Place the black bass fillets on individual sheets of heavy-duty foil. Center a lemon or lime slice on each fillet, and sprinkle with the chopped scallion. Melt the butter in a saucepan, and mix in the remaining ingredients. Drizzle some of the butter mixture over each fillet. Fold the foil over the fillets, and seal the packets securely. Place the packets on the rack of a charcoal grill 8 to 10 inches [20 to 25 cm.] from the coals. Cook the bass fillets for 20 minutes.

A. J. MC CLANE
THE ENCYCLOPEDIA OF FISH COOKERY

Grilled Stuffed Striped Bass

If striped bass is not available, bluefish, drum or lake trout may be substituted.

To serve 6 to 8		
8 to 10 lb.	whole striped bass	4 to 5 kg.
1	large onion, quartered	1
2	firm, ripe tomatoes, quartered	2
1	lemon, quartered	1
	salt and pepper	
	paprika	

Wipe the fish thoroughly inside and out. With the tip of a sharp knife, make shallow cuts inside the cavity between the ribs. Dust the onion, tomato and lemon chunks with salt and pepper, put them into the cavity, and close the fish by sewing it with cotton thread or lacing it with small skewers and kitchen string. Rub the outside of the fish with paprika; this will retard the cooking of the layer of flesh just beneath the skin. Grill the fish over medium-bright coals for 20 to 25 minutes on each side. When the skin begins to bubble away from the flesh, the fish is done. Or test for doneness by inserting a knife tip along the dorsal fin; if there is no flow of liquid when the knife is twisted gently, cooking is complete. Lift off the skin, run a knife along the backbone and lift off the top fillet; the ribs and backbone can then be lifted off the bottom fillet and this piece lifted from the skin. Discard the stuffing.

MEL MARSHALL
COOKING OVER COALS

Grilled Cod Fillets

Filety z Dorsza z Rusztu

Haddock or pollock fillets may be substituted for the cod.

To serve 4		
1¼ lb.	cod fillets, skinned	600 g.
	salt and pepper	
3 tbsp.	olive oil	45 ml.
1 tbsp.	white wine vinegar or fresh lemon juice	15 ml.

Dust the fish fillets with salt and pepper. Mix together 1 tablespoon [15 ml.] of the oil and the vinegar or lemon juice and sprinkle this over the fish. Let the fillets marinate for 30 minutes to one hour, turning them over a few times. Drain them and grill them on a hot oiled rack for five minutes on each side, brushing them from time to time with the remaining olive oil.

HELENA HAWLICZKOWA
KUCHNIA POLSKA

Grilled Whole Fish

Machchi Seekhi

A whole cod or six small whiting could be used for this recipe.

	To serve 6	
one 3 lb.	whole fish or 6 small fish, cleaned, heads and tails removed	one 1½ kg.
¼ cup	coriander seeds	50 ml.
½ tsp.	paprika	2 ml.
6	whole cardamoms, pods removed and seeds separated	6
1 tbsp.	anise or dill seeds	15 ml.
½ tsp.	salt	2 ml.
¼ tsp.	freshly ground black pepper	1 ml.
2	onions, chopped	2
2	garlic cloves, chopped	2
1	green pepper, halved, seeded, deribbed and chopped	1
¼ cup	chopped fresh parsley leaves	50 ml.
2 tbsp.	chopped fresh mint leaves	30 ml.
⅔ cup	yogurt	150 ml.
3 tbsp.	fresh lemon or lime juice	45 ml.
4 tbsp.	clarified butter	60 ml.

Lightly roast the coriander and paprika in a heavy skillet, then grind them with all the other spices, onions, garlic, green pepper and the herbs. Use them to make a paste with the yogurt and lemon or lime juice. Prick the fish all over and rub the paste over the fish, inside and out. Let the fish marinate for 30 minutes to one hour.

Prepare a charcoal fire in a grill; when the coals are medium hot, set a drip pan in the grill and put the rack 4 inches [10 cm.] above the coals. Oil the rack and place the fish on it. Cook the fish for about 15 minutes, or until the paste is dry but not burning. Baste it with the drippings and raise the rack to 6 inches [15 cm.]. Grill the fish, basting it occasionally with the butter and pan drippings, until the flesh flakes easily when pierced with a skewer—about 25 minutes longer for the large fish, 10 to 15 minutes for the small fish. Turn the fish over once halfway through the cooking. Lower the rack to 4 inches again and let the skin crisp for a minute or two, then serve immediately.

DHARAMJIT SINGH
INDIAN COOKERY

Spit-roasted Eel

Anguilla Arrosto

The flesh of eel is rich, and spit-roasting is a good way of cooking it. The skin is left on; it forms a protective crust that prevents the flesh itself from hardening during the cooking and it can easily be peeled off afterward.

	To serve 4	
1	large eel, cut crosswise into sections 3 to 4 inches [8 to 10 cm.] thick	1
	sage leaves, bay leaves or rosemary sprigs	
	salt	

Impale the sections of eel on a spit, with sage, bay leaves or sprigs of rosemary in between. Place a drip pan under the spit and roast the eel for eight minutes, basting it often with its own fatty drippings and plenty of salt. Toward the end of the cooking, the fire should be very hot to brown the skin.

ALAN DAVIDSON
MEDITERRANEAN SEAFOOD

Grilled Eel

To skin the eel use a sharp knife to cut the skin around the head. Using a cloth or clean towel to prevent slipping, pull off the skin with the aid of pliers.

	To serve 6	
2 to 3	eels, heads removed, skinned and cut into 1½- to 2-inch [4- to 5-cm.] pieces	2 to 3
	salt and pepper	
3 tbsp.	fresh lemon juice	45 ml.
2 tbsp.	wine vinegar	30 ml.
6 tbsp.	olive oil	90 ml.
	bay leaves	
½ cup	dry bread crumbs	125 ml.
	lemon quarters	

Put the eel pieces in a flat dish, season them well, and sprinkle over the lemon juice, wine vinegar and 3 tablespoons [45 ml.] of the olive oil—enough to coat the pieces lightly. Let them marinate for two hours.

Thread the eel pieces onto six skewers, alternating them with the bay leaves. Grill the skewered eel over moderate heat until the flesh separates from the bone without too much trouble—about eight minutes. As they cook, brush the pieces from time to time with the remaining marinade. When they are done, brush them with the remaining olive oil and sprinkle them with the bread crumbs. Return the skewers to the grill for a few minutes, until the crumbs are appetizingly browned. Serve the eel with lemon quarters.

JANE GRIGSON
FISH COOKERY

Barbecued Halibut Fillets

If halibut is not available, flounder or sole may be substituted.

	To serve 4	
four ½ lb.	halibut fillets	four ¼ kg.
2 tbsp.	chopped onion	30 ml.
2 tbsp.	chopped green pepper	30 ml.
2 tbsp.	oil	30 ml.
½ cup	dry white wine	125 ml.
¼ cup	soy sauce	50 ml.
½ cup	chopped tomatoes	125 ml.
1	garlic clove, finely chopped	1
2 tbsp.	fresh lemon juice	30 ml.
2 tbsp.	grated fresh ginger or 1 tsp. [5 ml.] ground ginger	30 ml.
½ lb.	fresh mushrooms, sliced and sautéed in 3 tbsp. [45 ml.] butter	¼ kg.

For the marinade, sauté the onion and green pepper in the oil. Add all of the remaining ingredients except the fish and mushrooms. Bring the mixture to a boil and cook it for one minute. Set it aside to cool.

Arrange the fish fillets in a shallow dish and pour the marinade over them. Marinate the fish in the refrigerator for 30 minutes to two hours, turning the fillets twice. Drain the fillets, reserving the marinade, and place them in a hinged basket grill. Grill the fillets over hot coals, turning them once, until the fish flakes easily—about 10 minutes. Meanwhile, add the marinade to the sautéed mushrooms and cook this sauce until it is hot. To serve, pour the sauce over the fish fillets.

JEAN HEWITT
NEW YORK TIMES LARGE TYPE COOKBOOK

Deviled Herring

Arenques a la Diabla

Smelts or mackerel may be substituted for the herring.

	To serve 4	
8	small fresh herring, cleaned and scaled	8
	salt and pepper	
	oil	
¾ cup	dry bread crumbs	175 ml.
	cayenne pepper	
	vinaigrette *(recipe, page 162)*	

Season the herring with salt and pepper, oil them and roll them in the bread crumbs. Dust them with cayenne pepper and grill them for three to four minutes on each side, or until they are browned and cooked through. Place them on a serving dish and serve with vinaigrette sauce.

IGNACIO DOMENECH
PESCADOS Y MARISCOS

Grilled Mackerel

Grillierte Makrelen

If mackerel are not available, bluefish, butterfish or smelts may be substituted.

	To serve 4	
four ½ lb.	mackerel, cleaned	four ¼ kg.
3 tbsp.	fresh lemon juice	45 ml.
	salt	
¼ cup	mixed chopped fresh fennel, parsley, thyme and chervil leaves	50 ml.
2	garlic cloves, finely chopped	2
½ cup	oil	125 ml.
4	slices lemon	4

Cut several deep slashes on each side of each mackerel and sprinkle the fish, inside and outside, with lemon juice and salt. Stuff each fish with chopped herbs mixed with a little of the garlic. Mix together the remaining garlic, lemon juice and the oil. Grill the fish over hot embers for five minutes on each side, or until cooked through, brushing them from time to time with the oil-and-lemon mixture. Serve the mackerel garnished with lemon slices.

FRISCH VOM GRILL

Stuffed Mackerel

Caballas Rellenas

To steam the mussels, first scrub their shells clean and remove the ropelike beards. Put the mussels in a large, heavy pan with a chopped onion, a crushed garlic clove, a bay leaf, some thyme and a splash of white wine. Cover the pan, place it over high heat and cook for three to five minutes, or until all of the shells open.

	To serve 4	
4	small whole mackerel (about ¾ lb. [350 g.] each), cleaned, opened flat and the bones removed	4
12	live mussels, steamed, shucked and chopped	12
3	eggs, hard-boiled	3
1	garlic clove, crushed to a paste	1
2 tbsp.	finely chopped fresh parsley	30 ml.
1 tbsp.	oil	15 ml.
	salt	

Make a paste from the mussels, eggs, garlic, parsley and oil. Add salt to taste. Fill the mackerel with this stuffing. Tie the fish closed with fine string and grill them over a gentle fire, turning them once, until cooked through—about 12 minutes.

MANUEL VAZQUEZ MONTALBAN
LA COCINA CATALANA

Provincetown Mackerel

For this recipe, the fish must be very fresh. If mackerel is not available, bluefish, butterfish or smelts may be substituted.

	To serve 1	
one ½ lb.	whole fresh mackerel, head and tail intact, washed and patted dry but not gutted	one ¼ kg.

Heat the steel blade of a shovel over hardwood coals. When it is hot, place the mackerel on the blade and grill it on both sides. The natural oils from the fish and its innards will furnish the necessary lubrication.

HOWARD MITCHAM
THE PROVINCETOWN SEAFOOD COOKBOOK

Mackerel on Skewers

Makrelen am Spiess

If mackerel are not available, bluefish, butterfish or smelts may be substituted.

	To serve 1	
2	small mackerel, cleaned	2
	salt	
2	bay leaves	2
	olive oil	
	fresh lemon juice	
	parsley sprigs	

Salt the insides of the fish and stick each one lengthwise on a skewer with a bay leaf. Cook the mackerel on the grill, turning them often, and basting them with oil and sprinkling them with lemon juice. When they are ready, after about 10 minutes, pull the fish off their skewers, place them together in a dish, decorate the edge with parsley sprigs and serve.

MARIA HORVATH
BALKAN-KÜCHE

Mackerel Grilled over Embers

Pechena Pryasna Riba

Bluefish or butterfish may be substituted for the mackerel.

	To serve 5	
2 lb.	mackerel fillets	1 kg.
2 tsp.	salt	10 ml.
1 tsp.	freshly ground black pepper	5 ml.
5 tbsp.	vegetable oil	75 ml.
6 tbsp.	fresh lemon juice	90 ml.
2 tbsp.	finely chopped fresh parsley	30 ml.

Prepare a wood or charcoal fire. When it is glowing red, throw some of the ash over it. This will prevent the dripping oil from the fish flaming on the embers.

Season the mackerel fillets with the salt and arrange them in a large, hinged grill. Grill the fish, skin side down, about 4 inches [10 cm.] above the coals until the skin is browned and blistered—about four minutes. Then turn the hinged grill over to let the fillets brown on the other side—about four minutes more.

Remove the fillets carefully from the hinged grill to warmed serving plates. Sprinkle the portions with pepper, vegetable oil and lemon juice to taste, and garnish them with chopped parsley.

GEORGI SHISHKOV AND STOIL VOUCHKOV
BULGARSKI NATSIONALNI YASTIYA

Sea Fish Skewers

Brochettes de Poissons de Mer

These skewers may be made with one kind of fish, or a mixture. If you wish, you may throw twigs of dried fennel onto the coals a few moments before the end of the cooking time. Their smoke will accent the aroma of the fish.

	To serve 4	
2 lb.	monkfish or conger fillets, skinned and cut into 1-inch [2½-cm.] cubes	1 kg.
32	live mussels, scrubbed and debearded	32
2	small shallots	2
4	garlic cloves	4
½ tsp.	dried fennel	2 ml.
½ tsp.	dried thyme leaves	2 ml.
¼ cup	olive oil	50 ml.
2 tbsp.	fresh lemon juice	30 ml.

Combine in a blender the shallots, garlic, fennel, thyme, oil and lemon juice. Process until thoroughly blended. Pour this mixture over the fish cubes and marinate them for two hours. Meanwhile, place the mussels in a saucepan, cover tightly and cook over high heat for five minutes, or until they have all opened. Cool and remove them from the shells.

Thread the fish cubes onto skewers, alternating them with the mussels. Turning them frequently, grill the skewers over coals for eight to 10 minutes.

MARIO V. BONDANINI
GASTRONOMIE DE PLEIN AIR

Grilled Perch

Sandacz z Rusztu

Black sea bass or grouper may be substituted for the perch.

	To serve 4	
1 lb.	perch fillets, cut into 8 pieces	½ kg.
	salt	
3 tbsp.	butter, half melted, the rest cut into small pieces	45 ml.
1 tsp.	finely chopped fresh parsley	5 ml.

Season the fish with salt and let it stand for one hour. Dry the pieces and brush them with the melted butter. Brush the grill rack with oil and grill the fish on it for about 10 minutes, depending on the thickness of the pieces, turning them over after five minutes. Arrange the fish on a serving dish and sprinkle the butter pieces and the parsley over it.

HELENA HAWLICZKOWA
KUCHNIA POLSKA

Mullet in Parcels

Salmonetes Envueltos

The original version of this recipe calls for red mullet, a firm-fleshed, lean Mediterranean fish. If mullet is not available, butterfish, mackerel or perch may be substituted.

	To serve 6	
12	small mullet, cleaned	12
	salt and pepper	
12	thin slices lean bacon	12
6	bay leaves, halved	6

Season the fish with salt and pepper, wrap a bacon slice around each fish and secure it with a wooden pick. Insert half a bay leaf between the bacon and the fish.

Grill the fish over hot charcoal, turning them over several times so that they cook evenly. When the fish are ready, in about 10 minutes, remove the bay leaves and the wooden picks. Serve them hot.

MAGDALENA ALPERI
LA COCINA

Whole Grilled Fish

	To serve 8	
one 6 to 8 lb.	whole salmon or striped bass, cleaned, head and tail removed	one 3 to 4 kg.
	salt and white pepper	
12	slices nitrite-free bacon	12
10	sprigs fresh parsley	10
1½ to 2 cups	dry white wine	375 to 500 ml.

Season the fish inside and out with salt and pepper. Lay eight of the bacon slices and all of the parsley sprigs inside the cavity of the fish. Lay the remaining bacon slices on top of the fish. Place the fish on a double layer of heavy-duty foil large enough to enclose it completely. Shape the edges of the foil up around the fish and pour the wine over the fish. Secure the package tightly and place it 4 to 5 inches [10 to 13 cm.] from medium-hot coals. Cook for 45 minutes to one hour, or until the fish flakes easily when tested. To serve, unwrap the fish and remove the bacon and parsley.

MARIAN BURROS
PURE & SIMPLE

Barbecued Salmon Steaks

To serve 4

four ½ lb.	salmon steaks, cut 1 inch [2½ cm.] thick	four ¼ kg.
½ cup	dry vermouth	125 ml.
⅓ cup	fresh lemon juice	75 ml.
12 tbsp.	butter, melted and cooled	180 ml.
3 tbsp.	finely cut fresh chives	45 ml.
1 tsp.	soy sauce	5 ml.
½ tsp.	dried marjoram leaves	2 ml.
⅛ tsp.	finely chopped garlic	½ ml.
	pepper	

Mix together the vermouth, lemon juice, butter and seasonings, and marinate the salmon steaks in this sauce mixture for at least one hour. Turn the steaks occasionally to be sure they are coated by the sauce. Place the steaks in a well-greased hinged grill, and barbecue them 4 to 6 inches [10 to 15 cm.] above the coals until the steaks are nicely browned and the fish flakes easily when tested with a fork—about five minutes on each side. While cooking, baste with any sauce left in the marinating dish.

DAN AND INEZ MORRIS
THE COMPLETE OUTDOOR COOKBOOK

Grilled Salmon Steaks with Béarnaise Sauce

Darne de Saumon Grillée, Sauce Béarnaise

To serve 6

6	salmon steaks, each cut 2 inches [5 cm.] thick	6
	oil	
	salt and freshly ground black pepper	
	parslied potatoes	
2	lemons, sliced	2
2 cups	béarnaise sauce (recipe, page 166)	½ liter

Brush the steaks with a little oil, season them with salt and pepper, and place them on an oiled, preheated rack set 6 inches [15 cm.] over a bed of medium-hot coals. If you wish a grid design on the steaks, lift each one with a spatula and give it a quarter turn. Cook the steaks for 10 minutes. Turn the steaks and grill them on the other side.

Place the steaks on a long platter lined with a napkin. Surround the steaks with parslied potatoes and place a lemon slice on each steak. Serve with béarnaise sauce.

HENRI LE HUÉDÉ
DINING ON THE FRANCE

Sardines on a Tile

Sardinas a la Teja

Anchovies or herring may be substituted for the sardines. This is a typical dish from the Basque Provinces of Spain.

To serve 4

24	very fresh sardines	24
	salt	
	lettuce leaves	

Salt the sardines. Lay the lettuce leaves on a large earthenware tile that has been placed on top of hot charcoal and allowed to heat through for at least half an hour. Put the sardines, head to tail, on top of the lettuce. Cook the sardines for about three minutes on each side, turning them with tongs. Serve the sardines on the tile.

MAGDALENA ALPERI
LA COCINA

Salted Sardines with Peppers

Sardinas Salpimentonadas

If sardines are not available, smelts, herring or anchovies may be substituted.

The volatile oils in chilies may irritate your skin. Wear rubber gloves when handling them.

To serve 4

24	fresh sardines, cleaned	24
½ cup	salt	125 ml.
1	sweet green pepper, halved, seeded, deribbed and cut into strips	1
6	hot chilies, stemmed, seeded and cut into strips	6

Cover the sardines with the salt and let them stand for 12 to 24 hours. Drain the sardines, pat them dry with paper towels, then slit each one along the back and place strips of green pepper and chilies in the openings. Lay the sardines on a rack over hot coals. When they are cooked on one side, turn them and cook them on the other side—about seven minutes in all. Serve them immediately.

MANUEL M. PUGA Y PARGA
LA COCINA PRÁCTICA

Sardines Grilled over Hot Coals

Sardinas a la Brasa

Herring or anchovies may be substituted for the sardines.

	To serve 4	
12	fresh sardines, cleaned, heads removed, opened out flat	12
⅓ cup	oil	75 ml.
	salt	
1	sprig oregano	1
2	garlic cloves, chopped	2
2 tbsp.	finely chopped fresh parsley	30 ml.
	freshly ground white pepper	

Oil the sardines and grill them, skin side down, over a vigorous fire. When they are cooked, after about five minutes, season them with salt and place them in a serving dish.

Fry the oregano, garlic and parsley and a pinch of white pepper in the remaining oil. Strain the oil and sprinkle it over the sardines before serving them.

M. DEL CARME NICOLAU
CUINA CATALANA

Charcoal-broiled Sardines

If fresh sardines are not available, either herring or anchovies may be used instead.

	To serve 2	
16	fresh small sardines, cleaned and patted dry	16
	coarse salt	
	olive oil	
2	rolls, split into halves	2

In a dish, bury the sardines in coarse salt and let them cure for an hour. Dig them out and brush off most of the salt, but not all of it. Rub them with olive oil. Place the sardines on a grill rack about 3 inches [8 cm.] above hot coals and brown them lightly on both sides.

Serve eight sardines and one roll to each diner. To eat, lay one broiled fish on the bottom half of a roll. Tap the fish gently with the top half of the roll to break the skin, then peel it off. Pick the layer of fish off the bones with your fingers and eat it, then turn the fish over and do likewise to the other side. Use the same roll to hold each new fish. After you eat them all, the roll will be saturated with sardine oil; eat the roll too.

HOWARD MITCHAM
THE PROVINCETOWN SEAFOOD COOKBOOK

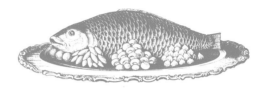

Barbecued Shark

If shark is not available, either swordfish or halibut may be used instead.

	To serve 4	
24	1-inch [2½-cm.] shark meat cubes (about 2 lb. [1 kg.])	24
1 cup	fresh lime or lemon juice	¼ liter
½ cup	peanut oil	125 ml.
	salt and pepper	
24	fresh mushroom caps	24
8	slices bacon, cut into 24 equal pieces	8
	butter, melted	
	fresh parsley, finely chopped	

Marinate the shark in all but 2 tablespoons [30 ml.] of the lime or lemon juice for about 20 minutes. Drain the cubes, brush them with peanut oil and season them with salt and pepper. Arrange the cubes on four skewers alternately with the bacon and mushrooms: first a cube of shark, then a piece of bacon—puncturing the bacon near the end rather than middle, so the bacon will fold over the shark—then a mushroom cap, and so on. Press each mushroom cap tight against the bacon to hold it in place.

Grill the kebabs over a hot charcoal fire for about 10 minutes; the time depends on the heat and distance from the fire, but shark meat cooks quickly. Let the dripping bacon flame up to sear the shark, then move the skewers around the top of the rack to avoid burning. The skewers can be rotated after the bacon adheres to the shark cubes. When serving, sprinkle the skewers with the remaining fresh lime or lemon juice, melted butter and chopped parsley.

A. J. MC CLANE
THE ENCYCLOPEDIA OF FISH COOKERY

Shark Brochettes

Fillets of fresh mackerel may be used instead of shark.

	To serve 4	
1½ lb.	shark fillets, skinned and cut into 1½-inch [4-cm.] cubes	¾ kg.
¼ cup	olive oil	50 ml.
2 tbsp.	finely chopped onion	30 ml.
1 tbsp.	fresh lemon juice	15 ml.
1 tbsp.	chopped fresh basil leaves	15 ml.
¼ tsp.	salt	1 ml.
¼ tsp.	black pepper	1 ml.
2	firm, slightly underripe tomatoes, cut into wedges	2
2	slices bacon, cut into pieces	2

Marinate the cubes of shark for 30 minutes in the olive oil, onion, lemon juice, basil, salt and pepper. Thread pieces of fish, tomato and bacon alternately onto four skewers.

Place the skewers on a preheated rack and grill them—turning them frequently and basting with the marinade—for about 12 minutes.

GRANT BLACKMAN
AUSTRALIAN FISH COOKING

Skewered Fish

Shark, tuna or cod may be substituted for the swordfish.

	To serve 6	
2 lb.	filleted swordfish, skinned and cut into 1½-inch [4-cm.] cubes	1 kg.
2	medium-sized onions, 1 finely chopped, 1 quartered lengthwise and separated into individual layers	2
¼ cup	fresh lemon juice	50 ml.
¾ cup	olive or vegetable oil	175 ml.
¾ tsp.	dried oregano leaves, crumbled	4 ml.
	salt and pepper	
12	bay leaves	12

Put the fish cubes into a large bowl. Cover with the chopped onion, lemon juice, oil, oregano, and salt and pepper. Stirring the cubes occasionally, let the fish marinate for one hour. Thread the cubes onto skewers alternately with the onion pieces and bay leaves. Turning the skewers once or twice and brushing the cubes frequently with the remaining marinade, grill until the fish is tender—10 to 15 minutes. Serve on the skewers.

KAY SHAW NELSON
THE EASTERN EUROPEAN COOKBOOK

Swordfish on Skewers

Xifias Souvlakia

Shark, tuna or cod may be substituted for the swordfish.

	To serve 6	
2 lb.	swordfish, boned, skinned and cubed	1 kg.
	salt and freshly ground pepper	
5 tbsp.	strained fresh lemon juice	75 ml.
¼ cup	olive oil	50 ml.
	chopped fresh thyme leaves	
3	firm, ripe tomatoes, quartered, or 12 cherry tomatoes	3
8	bay leaves	8
2	green peppers, halved, seeded, deribbed and cut into squares	2

Season the cubed swordfish lightly with salt and pepper, and set aside. In a medium-sized bowl, whisk together the lemon juice, oil and thyme leaves to taste. Dip the swordfish in the marinade for a few minutes, then thread the cubes on bamboo or metal skewers, alternating them with the tomatoes, bay leaves and peppers. Grill the fish over coals for approximately 15 minutes, turning the skewers frequently and brushing the fish occasionally with the remaining marinade. Serve hot.

VILMA LIACOURAS CHANTILES
THE FOOD OF GREECE

Grilled Swordfish Steaks

To produce fresh onion juice, squeeze small chunks of onion in a large garlic press. If swordfish is not available, shark, tuna or cod steaks may be substituted.

	To serve 3 or 4	
1½ lb.	swordfish steaks, cut 1 inch [2½ cm.] thick	¾ kg.
2 cups	oil	½ liter
6 tbsp.	fresh lemon juice	90 ml.
1 tbsp.	onion juice	15 ml.
	cayenne pepper	
1 tsp.	chopped fresh parsley	5 ml.
	salt	
	olive oil	

In a shallow dish, mix together the oil, 3 tablespoons [45 ml.] of the lemon juice, the onion juice and a pinch of cayenne pepper. Add the fish steaks, turn them to coat them evenly on all sides, cover and refrigerate. Marinate the fish steaks, turning them occasionally, for five or six hours. Meanwhile, make a sauce from the remaining lemon juice, a little olive oil, salt and the chopped parsley.

Drain the fish steaks and grill them over a charcoal fire for five minutes on each side. Serve with the lemon sauce.

MERIEL BUCHANAN
GOOD FOOD FROM THE BALKANS

Provincetown Broiled Swordfish

If swordfish is not available, shark, tuna or cod steaks may be substituted.

To serve 4

two 1 lb.	swordfish steaks, each cut about 1 inch [2½ cm.] thick	two ½ kg.
1 tbsp.	olive oil	15 ml.
1	small garlic clove, finely chopped	1
2 tsp.	fresh lemon juice	10 ml.
¼ tsp.	dried oregano leaves	1 ml.
¼ tsp.	dry mustard	1 ml.
⅛ tsp.	freshly ground pepper	½ ml.
1 tbsp.	finely chopped fresh parsley	15 ml.
1½ tsp.	anchovy paste	7 ml.
3 tbsp.	butter, softened	45 ml.
	finely cut fresh dill	
	lemon or lime wedges	

Heat the olive oil in a small sauté pan. Sauté the garlic until golden. Transfer the garlic to a small bowl. Cool. Add the lemon juice, oregano, dry mustard, pepper, parsley and anchovy paste to the sautéed garlic. Mix well. Stir in the softened butter with a spoon. Mix until smooth. Coat both sides of the swordfish steaks with the herb mixture. Let them stand for 30 minutes.

Grill the fish until it flakes when pierced with a fork, for about five minutes on each side. Sprinkle with some fresh dill; garnish with lemon wedges.

BERT GREENE
HONEST AMERICAN FARE

Grilled Swordfish

Pesce Spada alla Griglia

If swordfish is not available, shark, tuna or cod steaks may be substituted.

To serve 6

six 7 oz.	swordfish steaks	six 200 g.
3	garlic cloves, slivered	3
	sprigs rosemary	
	olive oil	
	salt and pepper	

Stick garlic slivers and tiny sprigs of rosemary into the fish. Smear the steaks with oil and sprinkle them with salt and pepper. Grill the swordfish over medium-hot coals for about five minutes on each side.

VINCENZO BUONASSISI
CUCINA ALL'ARIA APERTA

Swordfish or Shark Steaks Grilled in Lettuce Leaves

For even more aromatic flavor, toss a handful of fennel seeds or some dried fennel branches over the coals just before putting on the fish.

To serve 4

four ½ lb.	swordfish or shark steaks	four ¼ kg.
3 tbsp.	fresh lemon juice	45 ml.
4 tbsp.	olive oil	60 ml.
2 tbsp.	fennel seeds	30 ml.
½ tsp.	salt	2 ml.
2	garlic cloves, finely chopped	2
2 tbsp.	finely chopped fresh parsley	30 ml.
	Boston or leaf lettuce, separated into individual leaves, washed and drained	

Combine the lemon juice, oil, fennel seeds, salt, garlic and parsley, and marinate the fish in this mixture for several hours at least; all day or overnight is even better.

Make a charcoal fire in an outdoor grill or in a hibachi.

Spread lettuce leaves flat and lift the fish steaks onto them, keeping a fair amount of the marinade on each steak. Spoon some more marinade on top of the fish. Cover each steak with more lettuce, and tie the leaves in place with kitchen string. If you like, place the fish packets in a hinged grilling basket that will hold them snugly. Grill the steaks over white-hot coals for about five minutes on each side, depending on their thickness.

THE GREAT COOK'S GUIDE TO FISH COOKERY

Anchovied Swordfish Steaks

The author suggests that the anchovied butter may be replaced with a mixture of 1½ teaspoons [7 ml.] anchovy paste and ½ teaspoon [2 ml.] peanut oil. If swordfish is not available, shark, tuna or cod steaks may be substituted.

	To serve 2	
two ½ lb.	swordfish steaks, cut 1 inch [2½ cm.] thick	two ¼ kg.
½ tbsp.	butter	7 ml.
1	oil-packed flat anchovy fillet, rinsed and patted dry	1
	cayenne pepper	

Wipe the steaks well. Combine the butter and the anchovy fillet, crushing the fillet as it is blended and adding a scanty pinch of pepper. Coat the steaks with the anchovied butter; grill over bright coals for three minutes on one side, five minutes on the other side.

MEL MARSHALL
COOKING OVER COALS

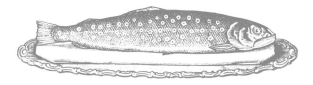

Citrus-barbecued Trout

If trout is not available, bass, whitefish or fresh-water perch may be substituted.

	To serve 4	
four ½ lb.	whole trout, cleaned	four ¼ kg.
4 tbsp.	butter, softened	60 ml.
	salt and pepper	
2½	lemons, halved, 1 half cut lengthwise into 4 wedges	2½
½	small onion, cut lengthwise into 4 wedges	½
2	limes, halved	2

Rub the trout all over with the butter, and sprinkle them with salt and pepper. Insert a wedge of lemon and a wedge of onion into the cavity of each trout. Place each trout on a separate piece of heavy-duty aluminum foil. Squeeze half a lemon and half a lime over each trout. Wrap the foil tightly around the trout and place the packages on the grill rack. Barbecue them over fairly hot coals for 10 minutes; there is no need to turn the fish.

KAREN GREEN AND BETTY BLACK
HOW TO COOK HIS GOOSE (AND OTHER WILD GAMES)

Fisherman's Trout

La Truite du Pêcheur

Perfect accompaniments to this dish are thinly sliced cucumber sprinkled with lemon juice, and a new potato cooked in its skin. The trout can be replaced with mackerel, using fennel tips for flavoring.

	To serve 1	
1	trout, slit down the middle and gutted, leaving the head and tail intact	1
	salt and pepper	
1 tbsp.	butter, kneaded with 1 tsp. [5 ml.] chopped fresh sorrel leaves	15 ml.

Place the trout on a grill rack 6 inches [15 cm.] from ash-covered coals. When the trout skin comes loose from the rack, in about five minutes, turn the trout over and repeat the procedure. When it is done on both sides, season the trout with salt and pepper, and add the sorrel butter to the inside.

JULIETTE ELKON
A BELGIAN COOKBOOK

Trout on a Spit

Khorovadz Ishkhanatsoug

If trout is not available, whitefish, bass or fresh-water perch may be substituted.

The magic of this simple dish depends largely on the quality and flavor of the fish and the glittering tartness provided by the pomegranate seeds.

	To serve 4	
four ½ lb.	trout, cleaned	four ¼ kg.
	salt	
	paprika	
2 tbsp.	butter, melted	30 ml.
2	lemons, sliced	2
	fresh tarragon leaves	
2 cups	fresh pomegranate seeds	½ liter

Carefully cut several gashes on both sides of each trout. Sprinkle them inside and out with salt and paprika. Put a long skewer lengthwise through each trout. Grill the fish over charcoal, brushing them with the melted butter and turning them occasionally until they are golden brown and cooked through—about 10 minutes.

Slide the trout off the skewers onto a heated serving platter and garnish them with the lemon slices, tarragon leaves, and ½ cup [125 ml.] of the pomegranate seeds. Serve the remaining pomegranate seeds in a bowl on the side.

SONIA UVEZIAN
THE CUISINE OF ARMENIA

Grilled Trout
Trota alla Griglia

To serve 6		
6	trout, cleaned	6
½ cup	olive oil	125 ml.
	salt and pepper	
5	garlic cloves, chopped	5
¼ cup	chopped fresh parsley	50 ml.

Brush the insides of the trout with oil and sprinkle the cavities with salt and pepper. Mix the garlic and parsley and use this mixture to stuff the trout. Brush the outsides with oil. Grill the fish for eight to 10 minutes, turning them once.

VINCENZO BUONASSISI
CUCINA ALL'ARIA APERTA

Fish Baked in the Ashes
Keat ot Riba

Costmary is a flat-leaved herb with a slightly bitter, minty flavor. If it is not available, sage or mint leaves may be used instead. Cod, sea bass and mullet are all suitable fish.

To serve 5		
one 1½ lb.	fish, cleaned	one ¾ kg.
	salt and freshly ground pepper	
¾ cup	fresh bread crumbs	175 ml.
⅔ cup	finely chopped onions	150 ml.
¾ cup	walnuts, pounded	175 ml.
1 tsp.	finely chopped fresh costmary leaves (optional)	5 ml.
1 tbsp.	finely chopped fresh parsley	15 ml.
7 tbsp.	butter, melted	105 ml.
	walnut or grapevine leaves	

Start a fire in the fireplace. Season the fish inside and out with salt and pepper. Mix the bread crumbs, onions, walnuts and herbs. Season with salt and stuff the fish with this mixture. Brush the fish with melted butter.

Brush a large sheet of parchment paper with butter. Wrap the fish in the paper, then in the leaves. Finally, cover the packet with a layer of clay about 2 inches [5 cm.] thick.

As soon as the flames of the fire have died down, pull the embers aside to clear a space in the firebox. Place the fish packet on the hot slab. Cover the packet with a layer of hot ash and embers at least 1 inch [2½ cm.] thick. Bake the fish

two hours. Remove the packet from the fire, break the hardened clay and discard it with the leaves. Unwrap the fish onto a heated plate.

GEORGI SHISHKOV AND STOIL VOUCHKOV
BULGARSKI NATSIONALNI YASTIYA

Fish Parcels

The author specifies fillets of white fish. Cod, haddock and sea trout are all suitable.

To serve 8		
8	fish fillets	8
	salt and pepper	
¼ lb.	fresh mushrooms, sliced	125 g.
1	medium-sized onion, chopped	1
¼ cup	capers, rinsed and drained	50 ml.
4 tbsp.	butter	60 ml.
1 cup	light cream	¼ liter
	finely chopped fresh parsley	

Wash the fillets and pat them dry with paper towels. Put each fillet on a buttered square of heavy-duty foil and sprinkle it with salt and pepper. Strew the mushrooms, onions and capers over the fillets and dot them with the butter. Pour the cream over them. Wrap the foil loosely over the fish to make neat parcels. Cook on the grill over hot coals for 15 to 20 minutes. Serve the fish sprinkled with chopped parsley.

BARBARA LOGAN
BARBECUE AND OUTDOOR COOKERY

Barbecued Tuna
Atún a la Brasa

Bonito or swordfish may be substituted for the tuna.

To serve 4		
1½ lb.	tuna steaks, cut 1 inch [2½ cm.] thick	¾ kg.
⅓ cup	oil	75 ml.
2 tbsp.	white wine vinegar	30 ml.
	salt	
1 cup	tomato sauce (recipe, page 163), warmed	¼ liter

Let the tuna marinate in the oil, vinegar and a pinch of salt for one hour. Grill the steaks for 10 minutes, or until they are cooked through, basting them frequently with the marinade and turning them once. Serve the steaks accompanied by the tomato sauce.

MANUEL VAZQUEZ MONTALBAN
LA COCINA CATALANA

Tandoori Fish

The tandoori coloring called for in this recipe may be obtained at Indian food stores. Bluefish, mackerel or butterfish are suitable for this recipe.

The volatile oils in chilies may irritate your skin. Wear rubber gloves when handling them.

To serve 2 or 3

2 lb.	whole fish, cleaned	1 kg.
1	medium-sized onion, finely chopped	1
6	garlic cloves, finely chopped	6
1-inch	piece fresh ginger, peeled and grated	2½-cm.
1	fresh hot green chili, stemmed, seeded and chopped	1
3 tbsp.	fresh lemon juice	45 ml.
1 tbsp.	ground coriander	15 ml.
1 tsp.	ground cumin	5 ml.
2 tsp.	ground fennel or anise	10 ml.
5	whole cardamoms, seeds removed from the pods and crushed to a paste	5
1 tsp.	ground cinnamon	5 ml.
1 tsp.	*tandoori* coloring	5 ml.
⅔ cup	yogurt	150 ml.
	salt and black pepper	

Make a few diagonal incisions in both sides of the skin of the fish. Blend all of the rest of the ingredients to make a paste. Rub the fish with paste inside and out and let it stand at room temperature for at least two hours. Roast the fish on a spit or cook it on a grill, basting it with oil or clarified butter until the flesh begins to flake and the skin is crisp—about 15 minutes in all.

Serve the fish accompanied by onion rings and lemon wedges, and garnished with chopped coriander, mint leaves or flat-leafed parsley.

CLAUDIA RODEN
PICNIC: THE COMPLETE GUIDE TO OUTDOOR FOOD

Skewered Crayfish

Brochetas de Cigalas

To serve 4

12	crayfish, heads removed, tails rinsed and deveined	12
1 each	red and green sweet pepper, halved, seeded, deribbed and cut into 8 pieces	1 each
12	small onions	12
⅓ cup	oil	75 ml.
3 tbsp.	fresh lemon juice	45 ml.
	salt	

Thread the crayfish, peppers and onions onto four skewers in the following order: green pepper, onion, crayfish, red pepper, onion, crayfish, green pepper, onion, crayfish and red pepper. Grill over hot charcoal for five minutes, turning the skewers frequently and basting them with a mixture of the oil and lemon juice, seasoned with a little salt.

IGNACIO DOMENECH
PESCADOS Y MARISCOS

Mussels on the Spit

To serve 4

40	live mussels, scrubbed and debearded	40
4 tbsp.	dry white wine	60 ml.
2	small shallots, chopped	2
	salt and white pepper	
12	mushrooms, each cut into 4 slices	12
2 tbsp.	butter	30 ml.
40	slices salt pork with the rind removed	40
¼ cup	flour	50 ml.
2	eggs, beaten	2
¾ cup	fresh bread crumbs	175 ml.
3 tbsp.	olive oil	45 ml.
	dried fennel	
	fresh parsley sprigs	

Place the mussels, wine, shallots and white pepper in a saucepan. Cover tightly and cook over high heat for three to five minutes until the mussels have opened. Shuck them.
Sweat the mushrooms quickly in the butter and season

them with salt. Wrap a mussel and a mushroom slice in a slice of salt pork, and assemble 10 mussels on each skewer. Roll the skewer first in the flour, then the beaten egg and, finally, the bread crumbs, making sure that the bread crumbs adhere well all around the mussels.

Flavor the olive oil with a pinch each of fennel, salt and pepper. Brush the crumbed mussels gently with the oil and then grill them over slow coals, basting them from time to time with the oil, for about five minutes.

Serve the skewers on a long dish, covered with a napkin and garnished with parsley sprigs.

SYLVAIN CLUSELLS
COOKING ON TURNING SPIT AND GRILL

Spiny Lobster Grilled with Basil Butter

Langouste Grillée au Beurre de Basilic

To serve 2

two 1 lb.	live spiny lobsters (or one 2¼ lb. [1 kg.]), split lengthwise and rinsed under cold running water to remove viscera and intestinal vein	two ½ kg.
20	fresh basil leaves, chopped	20
8 tbsp.	butter	120 ml.
	salt and freshly ground white pepper	
2 tbsp.	olive oil	30 ml.

In a saucepan, combine the freshly chopped basil leaves with the butter. Over very low heat, melt the butter without letting it reach a simmer. Stir it constantly to keep the butter thick and creamy. Set it aside.

Place the lobster halves shell side down on a rack over hot coals. Sprinkle salt and pepper over the lobster meat and brush it with the olive oil. Grill the lobster halves for five minutes, then turn them and grill them meat side down for five minutes more. Turn the lobster halves again and brush the meat generously with the basil butter. Continue to baste the meat frequently with the butter until the lobsters are done—about 10 minutes for two small ones, 20 minutes for one large one.

ROGER VERGÉ
ROGER VERGÉ'S CUISINE OF THE SOUTH OF FRANCE

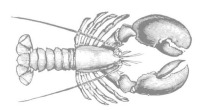

Broiled California Lobster

To serve 2

2 lb.	live lobster	1 kg.
10 tbsp.	butter, 2 tbsp. [30 ml.] softened, 8 tbsp. [120 ml.] melted	150 ml.
1 tsp.	paprika	5 ml.
	salt and black pepper	
1	lemon, quartered	1
	watercress sprigs	

Plunge the live lobster into vigorously boiling water. Boil for four minutes, remove the lobster and allow it to cool sufficiently to be handled. Split the lobster lengthwise through the middle and rinse out its entrails. Make a mixture of the softened butter, paprika, and a dash each of salt and pepper, and brush half of the mixture on the cut flesh of the lobster.

Place the lobster halves, flesh side down, over charcoal and broil for six minutes. Turn over the lobster, brush on the remainder of the butter mixture and finish broiling the halves until the flesh is opaque—about 10 minutes. Garnish the lobster halves with the lemon quarters and watercress. Serve at once, accompanied by the melted butter.

THE BROWN DERBY COOKBOOK

Special Barbecued Lobsters

To serve 8

four 1 lb.	live lobsters	four ½ kg.
8 tbsp.	butter, melted	120 ml.
2	garlic cloves, crushed to a paste	2
3 tbsp.	fresh lemon juice	45 ml.
	salt and pepper	
	watercress sprigs	
	lemon wedges	

Split the lobsters in half lengthwise and remove the intestine, stomach and gills. Twist off the claws where they meet the body. Crush each claw in several places. Remove the flesh from the claws and add it to the flesh in the shells. Combine the butter, garlic, lemon juice, salt and pepper and brush the lobster flesh with this sauce. Set the lobsters cut side up on a grill rack over medium-hot coals, and barbecue them—basting them several times with the sauce—for 15 to 20 minutes, or until the flesh is opaque. Place them on a serving dish and garnish with watercress and lemon wedges.

BARBARA LOGAN
BARBECUE AND OUTDOOR COOKERY

Broiled Oysters au Gratin

To serve 6 to 8

1 quart	shucked oysters, with the liquor reserved	1 liter
2 cups	fine cracker crumbs	½ liter
1 tsp.	salt	5 ml.
½ lb.	butter, melted	¼ kg.

In a shallow dish, mix the cracker crumbs with the salt. Roll the oysters well in a clean napkin to make them as dry as possible. Thrust a fork through the tough muscle of each oyster; dip it into the crumbs, then into the butter, then into the crumbs again. Arrange the oysters in a hinged wire grill and broil them over a bright coal fire for about three minutes, turning the wire grill every five or 10 seconds. When the oysters are plump and the juices run, they are done. Serve them instantly.

DEPARTMENT OF COMMERCE, BUREAU OF FISHERIES

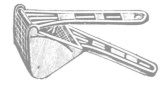

Skewered Oysters

Oysters en Brochette

To serve 1

4	freshly shucked oysters	4
2 tsp.	fresh lemon juice	10 ml.
	salt and freshly ground black pepper	
3 to 4	fresh mushroom caps	3 to 4
1	slice bacon	1
1 tbsp.	butter, melted	15 ml.
	chopped fresh parsley	
	lemon wedges	

Sprinkle the oysters with the lemon juice, salt and pepper. At the end of a skewer place a mushroom cap. Next put the end of the bacon strip, then an oyster, then loop the bacon around the oyster onto the skewer again, add another mushroom, another oyster and continue until you have used four oysters. Brush them with the butter and broil the oysters over charcoal, turning them several times, until they are done—in about three minutes. Sprinkle the oysters with chopped parsley and serve them with lemon wedges.

JAMES BEARD
JAMES BEARD'S NEW FISH COOKERY

Shrimp Kebabs

To serve 4

1 lb.	shrimp, peeled and deveined	½ kg.
6 to 8	slices bacon, cut into halves	6 to 8
4 tbsp.	butter, melted	60 ml.
¼ cup	fresh lemon juice	50 ml.

Wrap each of the shrimp in a piece of bacon, and thread onto bamboo skewers. Combine the melted butter and the lemon juice, and brush the mixture over the kebabs. Barbecue the kebabs over hot coals, turning the skewers frequently, until the shrimp are cooked and the bacon is lightly browned and crisp—five to 10 minutes. Before serving, brush the kebabs again with the butter mixture. Pour any of the remaining butter into a small bowl or pitcher, and serve it with the kebabs.

ELIZABETH SEWELL
BARBECUE COOKBOOK

Barbecued Skewered Shrimp Patties

To serve 4

2 lb.	shrimp, shelled and deveined	1 kg.
1	egg	1
2	scallions, finely chopped	2
2	garlic cloves, crushed to a paste	2
2 tbsp.	fish sauce or light soy sauce	30 ml.
3 tbsp.	oil	45 ml.
1 tsp.	cornstarch	5 ml.
½ tsp.	sugar	2 ml.
	salt and black pepper	

Chop the shrimp into a fine paste or put them through the fine disk of a meat grinder. Add the egg, scallions, garlic, fish sauce or soy sauce, oil, cornstarch, sugar, and salt and pepper. Mix well, and beat with a wooden spoon to form a smooth paste. Shape the shrimp paste into compact 2-inch [5-cm.] balls. Squeeze each ball firmly into an elongated sausage 3 inches [8 cm.] long, and thread a skewer through its length. Prepare a fire for broiling, and broil the patties for 10 minutes on each side, until crisp and brown.

MAY WONG TRENT
ORIENTAL BARBECUES

Barbecued Shrimp

To serve 4

1 lb.	jumbo shrimp in shells (with or without heads), rinsed	½ kg.
¾ lb.	butter, melted	350 g.
1 cup	dry white wine	¼ liter
1	lemon, sliced	1
2	garlic cloves, finely chopped	2
1 tbsp.	chili relish *(recipe, page 164)*	15 ml.
	Tabasco sauce	
	paprika	
	salt and pepper	

Combine the butter, wine, lemon slices, garlic and chili relish. Add a dash of Tabasco sauce, a pinch of paprika, and salt and pepper. Stir in the shrimp and marinate them for at least one hour. Broil the shrimp on a barbecue grill, turning them at least once, until they begin to curl—for about five minutes. Serve the grilled shrimp in soup bowls with the remaining marinade. We eat the shells, heads, tails and all!

THE JUNIOR LEAGUE OF PINE BLUFF, INC.
SOUTHERN ACCENT

Shrimp Satay

To serve 4

1 lb.	shrimp, shelled	½ kg.
1 cup	coconut milk	¼ liter
1 tbsp.	brown sugar	15 ml.
1 tbsp.	Japanese soy sauce	15 ml.
1 tbsp.	fresh lime juice	15 ml.
1 tsp.	salt	5 ml.
½ tsp.	cayenne pepper	2 ml.
⅛ tsp.	ground ginger	½ ml.

In a shallow bowl combine all of the ingredients except the shrimp. Marinate the shrimp in this sauce at room temperature for 30 minutes, turning the shrimp frequently. Remove the shrimp from the marinade with a slotted spoon and thread them, head to tail, onto bamboo or metal skewers, three or four shrimp to each skewer. Broil the shrimp over charcoal until done to your taste—about two minutes on each side. Baste the shrimp liberally with the remaining marinade during the broiling process. Serve them at once.

ALEX D. HAWKES (EDITOR)
THE SHRIMP COOKBOOK

M. C. Charcoaled Shrimp

To serve 4

2 lb.	large shrimp, rinsed and shells snipped down the back	1 kg.
3	garlic cloves, finely chopped	3
1	medium-sized onion, finely chopped	1
1 tsp.	dry mustard	5 ml.
1 tsp.	salt	5 ml.
½ cup	olive or peanut oil	125 ml.
3 tbsp.	fresh lemon juice	45 ml.
½ cup	finely chopped fresh parsley	125 ml.

Place the shrimp in a bowl. Combine the remaining ingredients, and pour them over the shrimp. Cover and marinate the shrimp in the refrigerator for at least five hours. Drain, then arrange the shrimp on a grill rack over hot coals. Cook the shrimp for five to eight minutes, turning them once. Serve the shrimp in their shells.

THE JEKYLL ISLAND GARDEN CLUB
GOLDEN ISLES CUISINE

Garlic-broiled Shrimp

To serve 4 to 6

1 lb.	jumbo shrimp	½ kg.
1 cup	olive oil	¼ liter
3 tbsp.	fresh lemon juice	45 ml.
3	garlic cloves, crushed to a paste	3
2 tbsp.	finely chopped fresh parsley	30 ml.
¼ tsp.	ground cloves	1 ml.

Leaving the shells on, split the shrimp down the back with scissors and remove the veins; wash the shrimp. Make a marinade of the olive oil, lemon juice, garlic, parsley and cloves. Marinate the shrimp for two to three hours; drain—reserving the marinade—and place the shrimp in a hinged grill. Grill the shrimp for three minutes on each side. Let the guests remove their own shrimp from the shells. Serve the marinade as a sauce.

LADIES' HOME JOURNAL ADVENTURES IN COOKING

Charcoal-broiled Shrimp

To serve 4

24	jumbo shrimp or prawns	24
24	oil-packed flat anchovy fillets, rinsed and patted dry	24
12	slices lean bacon	12

Peel the shrimp or prawns. Split them deeply down the back, devein them, and insert an anchovy fillet in each split. Cut the slices of lean bacon into halves lengthwise. Wrap half a slice of bacon around each shrimp or prawn, securing it with a wooden pick. Place the shrimps in a hinged grill basket and grill them over coals until the bacon is crisp—about five minutes or less. Don't overcook them or they will dry out.

NANCY FAIR MC INTYRE
IT'S A PICNIC!

Skewered Scallops and Cucumbers with Dill

Brochettes de Saint-Jacques et Conoombreg à l'Aneth

To serve 4

1 lb.	shucked scallops, halved across the grain if very large, rinsed and patted dry	½ kg.
2	large cucumbers, peeled, halved, seeded, cut into ¾-inch [2-cm.] pieces, blanched for 1 minute in heavily salted water and drained	2
	salt	
	Dill marinade	
1 tbsp.	finely cut fresh dill leaves and tender flower buds, or 1 tsp. [5 ml.] dried dillweed	15 ml.
3 tbsp.	fresh lemon juice	45 ml.
¼ cup	olive oil	50 ml.
	salt and pepper	

Mix together the ingredients for the marinade and marinate the scallops and cucumbers for about one hour. Thread the scallops and cucumber pieces alternately onto skewers, place the skewers in a hinged grill basket and grill them over a fairly intense bed of coals for eight to 10 minutes, basting the skewers regularly with the marinade.

RICHARD OLNEY
SIMPLE FRENCH FOOD

Scallops on Skewers

Coquilles Saint-Jacques en Brochettes

To serve 4

8 or 16	shucked sea scallops, halved if large	8 or 16
7 oz.	salt pork with the rind removed, sliced ¼ inch [6 mm.] thick, cut into 1¼-inch [3-cm.] squares and blanched for 5 minutes in boiling water	200 g.
	salt and pepper	
⅓ cup	olive oil or 4 tbsp. [60 ml.] melted butter	75 ml.
4	shallots, finely chopped	4
¼ cup	finely chopped fresh parsley	50 ml.

Thread the scallops and the salt-pork squares alternately onto four skewers. Sprinkle salt and pepper over the kebabs and brush them generously with half of the oil or melted butter. Grill them over hot coals for about eight minutes, turning them several times.

Meanwhile, fry the chopped shallots and the parsley in the remaining oil or butter. When the scallops are cooked, serve them very hot, covered with the shallots and parsley.

TANTE MARIE
LA VÉRITABLE CUISINE DE FAMILLE

Charcoal-broiled Scallops

To serve 6

2 lb.	shucked sea scallops	1 kg.
½ lb.	sliced bacon	¼ kg.
½ cup	oil	125 ml.
¼ cup	fresh lemon juice	50 ml.
2 tsp.	salt	10 ml.
¼ tsp.	ground white pepper	1 ml.
	paprika	

Place the scallops in a bowl. Combine the oil, lemon juice, salt and pepper. Pour this sauce over the scallops and let them stand for 30 minutes, stirring them occasionally. Cut each slice of bacon in half lengthwise and then crosswise. Remove the scallops, reserving the sauce for basting. Wrap each scallop with a piece of bacon and fasten it with a wooden pick. Baste the scallops with a little of the reserved sauce and place the scallops in well-oiled, hinged wire grills. Cook them about 4 inches [10 cm.] from moderately hot coals for five minutes, basting them with the sauce and sprinkling them with paprika. Turn the scallops and cook them for five to seven minutes longer, or until the bacon is crisp.

JANE CHEKENIAN AND MONICA MEYER
SHELLFISH COOKERY

Broiled Frogs' Legs

	To serve 6	
12	pairs frogs' legs	12
¾ cup	oil	175 ml.
⅓ cup	fresh lemon juice	75 ml.
1	garlic clove, crushed to a paste	1
	salt and freshly ground pepper	
6	slices buttered toast	6

Marinate the frogs' legs in the oil, lemon juice, garlic, salt and pepper for 30 to 45 minutes before cooking. Turn them in the marinade three or four times.

Place the frogs' legs in a hinged grill basket. Fasten the basket, and grill the frogs' legs over low heat, basting them with the marinade every few minutes. Cook them for five to six minutes on each side, or until they are golden brown.

Serve the grilled frogs' legs on crisp buttered toast.

JOHN AND MARIE ROBERSON
THE COMPLETE BARBECUE BOOK

Barbecued Squid

This recipe sounds too easy to be true. It is not. As with any grilled seafood, the fresher the ingredients and the simpler the cooking, the better the end result. Barbecued squid and an anise-flavored apéritif make a wonderful combination.

	To serve 4 to 6	
3 lb.	squid, cleaned, skinned and cut into rings	1½ kg.
1 to 6	garlic cloves, finely chopped	1 to 6
8 tbsp.	butter	120 ml.
⅔ cup	fresh lemon juice	150 ml.

Make a fire, preferably with firewood or Mexican charcoal, started from paper and kindling. In a small saucepan, fry the garlic in 1 tablespoon [15 ml.] of the butter until it is lightly browned. Add the rest of the butter and the lemon juice. Mix well. Set the flavored butter aside.

Skewer the squid rings. When the coals are white, barbecue the rings until they are brown—two to three minutes on each side. Serve the squid with the lemon-garlic butter.

ISAAC CRONIN
THE INTERNATIONAL SQUID COOKBOOK

Sauces and Marinades

Recipes for additional sauces and marinades appear in Standard Preparations, pages 161-167.

Italian Barbecue Sauce

This delicate sauce combines the tart flavor of fresh lemons with fine Italian seasonings to enhance any cut of meat, fish or chicken prepared for barbecuing.

	To make 1 ¼ cups [300 ml.] sauce	
1 cup	fresh lemon juice	¼ liter
¼ cup	olive oil	50 ml.
¼ tsp.	dried oregano leaves	1 ml.
1	sprig fresh parsley, finely chopped	1
1	small garlic clove, finely chopped	1
	salt and pepper	

To the lemon juice, add the olive oil, oregano, parsley and garlic. Season to taste with salt and pepper. Stir the ingredients thoroughly, and let the sauce stand at room temperature for one hour to let the flavors of its ingredients mingle before using it.

JOE CARCIONE
THE GREENGROCER COOKBOOK

Bourbon Marinade

	To make 3 cups [¾ liter] marinade	
½ cup	bourbon	125 ml.
½ cup	brown sugar	125 ml.
⅔ cup	soy sauce	150 ml.
3 tbsp.	fresh lemon juice	45 ml.
1 tsp.	Worcestershire sauce	5 ml.
1½ cups	water	375 ml.

Dissolve the brown sugar in the bourbon. Add the soy sauce, lemon juice, Worcestershire sauce and water. Mix them well. This marinade is very good for flank steak or roasts to be cooked on a grill.

THE JEKYLL ISLAND GARDEN CLUB
GOLDEN ISLES CUISINE

Smoker Special Marinade

This marinade is particularly suitable for beef or chicken.

To make 2½ cups [625 ml.] sauce

1 cup	water	¼ liter
½ cup	dry sherry	125 ml.
½ cup	soy sauce	125 ml.
½ cup	honey	125 ml.
2	garlic cloves, crushed to a paste	2

Combine all of the ingredients and stir well. When marinating foods in the mixture, stir occasionally to keep the honey from settling to the bottom.

GEORGIA ORCUTT
SMOKE COOKERY

Barbecue Sauce

To make about 4 cups [1 liter] sauce

½ lb.	butter	¼ kg.
2½ cups	water	625 ml.
¼ cup	vinegar	50 ml.
¼ cup	chopped onion	50 ml.
2	garlic cloves, chopped	2
1 tbsp.	sugar	15 ml.
1 tbsp.	paprika	15 ml.
2 tsp.	salt	10 ml.
2 tsp.	chili powder	10 ml.
2 tsp.	black pepper	10 ml.
½ tbsp.	Tabasco sauce	7 ml.
1 tsp.	dry mustard	5 ml.

Place all of the ingredients in a nonreactive saucepan. Stirring frequently, bring to a boil. Reduce the heat and simmer, uncovered, for one half hour. In a tightly covered container, the sauce will keep in the refrigerator for about a month.

THE HELEN ALEXANDER HAWAIIAN COOK BOOK

Ferocious Barbecue Sauce

To make about 1½ cups [375 ml.] sauce

1½ cups	tomato ketchup *(recipe, page 163)*	375 ml.
½ cup	distilled white vinegar	125 ml.
1 tsp.	sugar	5 ml.
⅛ tsp.	salt	½ ml.
¼ tsp.	freshly ground black pepper	1 ml.
	cayenne pepper	
¼	lemon, seeded and finely diced	¼
½ tsp.	ground cumin	2 ml.
1 tsp.	ground coriander	5 ml.
⅛ tsp.	paprika	½ ml.
⅛ tsp.	powdered saffron	½ ml.
¼ tsp.	ground ginger	1 ml.

Combine the ketchup, vinegar, sugar, salt, black pepper and a few grains of cayenne pepper in a heavy, nonreactive pan. Bring to a boil, reduce the heat and simmer for 15 minutes, stirring frequently. Stir in the lemon, cumin, coriander, paprika, saffron and ginger, and heat through.

IRMA S. ROMBAUER AND MARION ROMBAUER BECKER
JOY OF COOKING

Hottish Barbecue Sauce

This sauce, ideal for use on grilled spareribs, will keep well in the refrigerator.

To make 2½ cups [625 ml.] sauce

4	garlic cloves	4
1 tbsp.	salt	15 ml.
1 cup	olive oil	¼ liter
1 cup	tomato juice	¼ liter
½ cup	vinegar	125 ml.
1	small onion, finely chopped	1
1	small green pepper, halved, seeded, deribbed and finely chopped	1
1 tbsp.	chili powder	15 ml.
1 tsp.	dried oregano leaves	5 ml.

In a nonreactive saucepan, crush the garlic with the salt. Stir in the oil, tomato juice, vinegar, onion, green pepper, chili powder and oregano. Simmer this mixture for 10 minutes and strain before using.

HELEN EVANS BROWN
HELEN BROWN'S WEST COAST COOK BOOK

Spicy Barbecue Sauce

The author suggests this sauce for spareribs or pork chops.

To make about 3 cups [¾ liter] sauce

¾ cup	tomato ketchup (recipe, page 163)	175 ml.
½ cup	wine vinegar	125 ml.
½ cup	oil	125 ml.
2	slices lemon, seeded	2
1	medium-sized onion, chopped	1
1 cup	water	¼ liter
2 tbsp.	Worcestershire sauce	30 ml.
2 tsp.	dry mustard	10 ml.
1 tsp.	salt	5 ml.
1 tsp.	paprika	5 ml.
⅛ tsp.	Tabasco sauce	½ ml.
¼ cup	honey	50 ml.

Combine all of the ingredients except the honey in a heavy, nonreactive saucepan, and mix them well. Bring them to a boil, reduce the heat, and simmer until the sauce begins to thicken—about 20 minutes. Remove the sauce from the heat and strain it through a fine sieve. Add the honey, stirring until it is well blended.

FREDERICA L. BEINERT
THE ART OF MAKING SAUCES AND GRAVIES

Richmond Barbecue Sauce for Pork or Spareribs

To make about 1 cup [¼ liter] sauce

2 to 3 tbsp.	maple sugar, grated, or substitute other sugar	30 to 45 ml.
1 tbsp.	dry mustard	15 ml.
1 tsp.	celery seeds	5 ml.
1 tsp.	salt	5 ml.
½ to ¾ tsp.	crushed hot red pepper	2 to 4 ml.
1 tsp.	freshly ground black pepper	5 ml.
1 cup	tarragon vinegar	¼ liter

Combine all of the dry ingredients. Pour the vinegar into a heavy, nonreactive pan. Stir in the dry ingredients and boil the sauce for about five minutes.

VERONICA MAC LEAN
LADY MAC LEAN'S BOOK OF SAUCES AND SURPRISES

Standard Preparations

Dry Marinade

To make about 1½ cups [375 ml.] marinade

2 tbsp.	juniper berries	30 ml.
1 tsp.	peppercorns	5 ml.
5	whole allspice	5
1 tbsp.	dried thyme leaves	15 ml.
3	bay leaves, crumbled	3
1 cup	coarse salt	¼ liter

In a large mortar, grind the juniper berries, allspice, peppercorns and thyme to a coarse powder. Then stir in the bay leaves and coarse salt.

Paste Marinade

The volatile oils in chilies may irritate your skin. Wear rubber gloves when you are handling them or wash your hands immediately afterward.

To make about ½ cup [125 ml.] marinade

5	whole allspice	5
3	blades mace	3
15	whole cardamoms, seeds removed and separated	15
2	bay leaves, crumbled	2
10	dried hot red chilies, stemmed and seeded	10
1 to 2 tbsp.	olive oil	15 to 30 ml.

In a mortar, pulverize the allspice and mace with a pestle. Add the cardamom seeds and the bay leaves along with the chilies. Grind them well, then dribble in enough olive oil to form a thick paste.

Cardamom and pepper paste. Grind together ¼ teaspoon [1 ml.] cardamom seeds, ¼ teaspoon black peppercorns and ⅛ teaspoon [½ ml.] crushed red chilies in the mortar. Then add about 2 tablespoons [30 ml.] of olive oil—just enough to make a paste.

Wine and Oil Marinade

To make about 3 cups [¾ liter] marinade

2 cups	dry white or red wine	½ liter
½ cup	olive oil	125 ml.
1	onion, thinly sliced	1
2	carrots, thinly sliced	2
¼ cup	fresh parsley sprigs	50 ml.
¼ cup	fresh dill sprigs	50 ml.
12	blades fresh chives	12
	freshly ground black pepper	

Combine the wine and oil with the onion, carrots, parsley, dill and chives. Season with pepper.

Yogurt Marinade

To make about 2 cups [½ liter] marinade

2 cups	yogurt	½ liter
¼ cup	olive oil	50 ml.
2	garlic cloves, finely chopped	2
2 tsp.	chopped fresh mint leaves	10 ml.
	freshly ground black pepper	

Whisk the yogurt to a smooth consistency, then stir into it the oil, garlic and mint. Season to taste with pepper.

Soy-Sauce Marinade

The volatile oils in chilies may irritate your skin. Wear rubber gloves when handling them or wash your hands immediately afterward.

To make about ¾ cup [175 ml.] marinade

½ cup	soy sauce	125 ml.
¼ cup	oil	50 ml.
4	fresh hot chilies, stemmed, seeded and chopped	4
1 tbsp.	chopped fresh ginger	15 ml.

Combine all of the ingredients in a bowl or shallow dish, and mix thoroughly.

Oil Marinade

To make about ⅔ cup [150 ml.] marinade

¼ cup	olive oil	50 ml.
¼ cup	finely chopped shallots	50 ml.
1 tbsp.	finely chopped garlic	15 ml.
2 tsp.	finely chopped fresh thyme leaves	10 ml.
2 tbsp.	grated orange peel	30 ml.
	coarse salt and freshly ground black pepper	

Combine the oil with the shallots, garlic, thyme and orange peel. Season with salt and pepper.

Oil and ginger marinade. Combine 2 tablespoons [30 ml.] of olive oil with 1 tablespoon [15 ml.] of chopped fresh ginger, 2 tablespoons of grated orange peel and 2 tablespoons of chopped garlic.

Lime, Orange and Garlic Marinade

To prepare enough marinade for a whole small pig as shown on pages 84-87, you will need to double the quantities that are given here.

To make about 3 cups [¾ liter] marinade

1½ cups	fresh lime juice	375 ml.
1 cup	fresh orange juice	¼ liter
½ cup	oil	125 ml.
4	garlic bulbs, cloves peeled and coarsely chopped	4
¼ cup	coarse salt	50 ml.
2 tsp.	freshly ground black pepper	10 ml.
3	bay leaves	3

Combine all of the ingredients together in a bowl.

Vinaigrette

The proportion of vinegar to oil may be varied according to taste. Lemon juice may be substituted for the vinegar.

To make about ½ cup [125 ml.] vinaigrette

2 tbsp.	wine vinegar	30 ml.
½ cup	oil	125 ml.
1 tsp.	salt	5 ml.
¼ tsp.	freshly ground black pepper	1 ml.

Put the salt and pepper into a small bowl. Add the vinegar and stir until the salt dissolves. Finally, stir in the oil.

Tomato Barbecue Sauce

To make 3 to 4 cups [¾ to 1 liter] sauce

6	medium-sized ripe tomatoes, peeled, seeded and coarsely chopped	6
1	large onion, sliced	1
4	large shallots, peeled	4
5	garlic cloves, unpeeled	5
2	bay leaves	2
3	sprigs fresh thyme	3
⅓ cup	molasses	75 ml.
6 tbsp.	Worcestershire sauce	90 ml.
1 tbsp.	olive oil	15 ml.
1 tbsp.	coarse salt	15 ml.
	freshly ground black pepper	

In a large, nonreactive saucepan, combine the tomatoes, onion, shallots, garlic, bay leaves and thyme. Bring the mixture to a boil, reduce the heat and simmer uncovered—stirring occasionally—for about two hours, or until the mixture is thick enough to hold its shape in a spoon. Purée the mixture in a food processor or press it through a food mill, then sieve it into a bowl. Stir in the molasses, Worcestershire sauce, oil, and salt and pepper to taste.

Tomato Sauce

When fresh, ripe tomatoes are not available, use 3 cups [¾ liter] of drained canned Italian plum tomatoes.

To make about 1 cup [¼ liter] sauce

6	medium-sized ripe tomatoes, chopped	6
1	onion, diced	1
1 tbsp.	olive oil	15 ml.
1	garlic clove (optional)	1
1 tsp.	chopped fresh parsley	5 ml.
1 tsp.	mixed dried basil, marjoram and thyme	5 ml.
1 to 2 tbsp.	sugar (optional)	15 to 30 ml.
	salt and freshly ground pepper	

In a large enameled or stainless-steel saucepan, gently fry the diced onion in the oil until soft, but not brown. Add the other ingredients and simmer uncovered until the tomatoes have been reduced to a thick pulp—about 20 to 30 minutes. Sieve the mixture, using a wooden pestle or spoon. Reduce the sauce further, if necessary, to reach the desired consistency. Adjust the seasoning.

Tomato Ketchup

To make about 6 cups [1½ liters] ketchup

6 lb.	firm ripe tomatoes, peeled, seeded and coarsely chopped (about 4 quarts [4 liters])	3 kg.
1 cup	chopped onions	¼ liter
½ cup	chopped sweet red pepper	125 ml.
1½ tsp.	celery seeds	7 ml.
1 tsp.	allspice berries	5 ml.
1 tsp.	mustard seeds	5 ml.
1	cinnamon stick	1
1 cup	sugar	¼ liter
1 tbsp.	salt	15 ml.
1½ cups	vinegar	375 ml.

In a heavy, enameled or stainless-steel pan, combine the tomatoes, onions and sweet pepper. Bring to a boil, stirring constantly, then reduce the heat to low and simmer for 20 to 30 minutes, or until the vegetables are soft. Purée the vegetables, a small batch at a time, through a food mill or strainer into a clean pan. Cook over medium heat, stirring frequently, until the mixture thickens and is reduced to about half of its original volume—about one hour. Tie the whole spices in a cheesecloth bag, and add them to the tomato mixture together with the sugar and salt. Stirring frequently, simmer gently, uncovered, for 30 minutes. Then stir in the vinegar and continue to simmer until the ketchup reaches the desired consistency—about 10 minutes. Remove the bag of spices; taste the ketchup and adjust the seasoning if necessary.

Pour the ketchup immediately into hot, sterilized jars, leaving a ½-inch [1-cm.] headspace. Cover each jar quickly and tightly with its lid. Set the jars on a rack in a water-bath canner. Pour in enough hot water to submerge the jars by 1 inch [2½ cm.], tightly cover the canner and bring to a boil over medium heat. Boil for 10 minutes. Remove the jars with tongs and cool them at room temperature.

Raw Vegetable Relish

Salsa Cruda

The volatile oils in chilies may irritate your skin. Wear rubber gloves when handling them or wash your hands immediately afterward.

To make about 3 cups [³/₄ liter] relish

6	tomatoes, peeled, seeded and coarsely chopped	6
2	medium-sized red or white onions, coarsely chopped	2
2	fresh hot chilies, stemmed, seeded and finely chopped	2
6	garlic cloves, finely chopped	6
²/₃ cup	fresh coriander leaves, coarsely chopped	150 ml.
	coarse salt	
¼ cup	fresh lime juice or wine vinegar	50 ml.
¼ cup	olive oil	50 ml.

Combine the tomatoes, onions, chilies, garlic and coriander in a bowl. Add a large pinch of salt and stir in the lime juice or vinegar. Stir in the olive oil; taste, and add salt if needed. Cover, and let the relish stand for 30 minutes to meld the flavors before serving it.

Tomato and Shallot Relish

To make about 2½ cups [625 ml.] relish

3	medium-sized ripe tomatoes, peeled, seeded and coarsely chopped	3
5	large shallots, finely chopped	5
2 tsp.	chopped fresh thyme leaves	10 ml.
	freshly ground black pepper	
¼ cup	red wine vinegar	50 ml.
⅓ cup	olive oil	75 ml.
	coarse salt	

Place the thyme and the freshly ground pepper in a mixing bowl. Whisk in the vinegar, then the olive oil. Stir in the tomatoes and shallots. Season with salt to taste, and additional pepper, if needed.

Ancho Chili Sauce

To make about 1 cup [¼ liter] sauce

12	dried *ancho* chilies, stemmed and seeded	12
1	large onion, finely chopped	1
8	garlic cloves, finely chopped	8
2 tbsp.	olive oil	30 ml.
1 cup	water	¼ liter

Place the chilies in a food processor and grind them to a fine powder—about 15 minutes. Sieve them through a fine-meshed strainer. Sauté the onion and garlic in the oil for five minutes, or until they are soft but not brown. Stir in the chilies and the water, and simmer the mixture, uncovered, for about one hour, or until shiny and slightly thickened.

Chili Relish

The volatile oils in chilies may irritate your skin. Wear rubber gloves when handling them or wash your hands immediately afterward.

To make about 9 cups [2¼ liters] relish

9 lb.	firm, ripe tomatoes, peeled, seeded and chopped (about 6 quarts [6 liters])	4½ kg.
2 cups	chopped onions	½ liter
1½ cups	chopped sweet green or red peppers	375 ml.
2 to 3	fresh hot chilies, stemmed, seeded and chopped	2 to 3
1 cup	cider vinegar	½ liter
½ cup	brown sugar	125 ml.
1 tbsp.	celery seeds	15 ml.
1 tsp.	mustard seeds	5 ml.
1 tsp. each	ground allspice, cloves, cinnamon and ginger	5 ml. each

Combine all of the ingredients in a nonreactive pot and bring the mixture to a boil. Reduce the heat to low and, stirring frequently, simmer the uncovered mixture until it is very thick—about one and one half to two hours.

Pour the relish immediately into hot, sterilized jars, leaving a ½-inch [1-cm.] headspace. Cover the jars and set them on a rack in a water-bath canner. Add enough hot water to submerge the jars by 1 inch [2½ cm.], cover and bring to a boil over medium heat. Boil for 15 minutes. Remove the jars with tongs and let them cool.

Basil Mayonnaise

To make about 3 cups [¾ liter] mayonnaise

1 cup	fresh basil leaves, loosely packed	¼ liter
4	egg yolks	4
1 to 1½ tbsp.	fresh lemon juice	15 to 22½ ml.
2 to 2½ cups	olive oil	500 to 625 ml.
	salt and freshly ground pepper	

Blanch the basil leaves in boiling water for three seconds; immediately drain them and drop them into cold water to stop the cooking. Pat the leaves dry with paper towels and chop them fine. Combine the basil and egg yolks in a warmed bowl. Whisk them vigorously for a minute, add 1 tablespoon [15 ml.] of the lemon juice and whisk until well mixed.

Whisking constantly, add the oil drop by drop. When the sauce starts to thicken, add the oil in a thin steady stream, whisking rhythmically, until the mayonnaise reaches the desired consistency. Season to taste with salt, pepper and additional lemon juice.

Tomato-basil mayonnaise. Simmer ½ cup [125 ml.] of tomato sauce *(recipe, page 163)* until it is reduced to half its original volume. Cool the sauce to room temperature, then add it to the finished mayonnaise.

Garlic mayonnaise. Replace the basil leaves with three or four garlic cloves that have been combined with a pinch of coarse salt and pounded to a paste. Mix the garlic thoroughly with the egg yolks and lemon juice before adding the oil.

Roe mayonnaise. Replace the basil leaves with 6 ounces [175 g.]—or ¾ cup [175 ml.]—of fresh fish roe that has been poached in lightly salted water for five minutes, drained and mashed with a whisk. Mix the roe thoroughly with the egg yolks and lemon juice before adding the oil. Increase the amount of lemon juice to taste; you may want as much as 5 or 6 tablespoons [75 or 90 ml.]. Striped bass, yellow perch, walleyed pike, shad, herring, mullet, salmon, flounder, tuna or halibut roe are all suitable.

Compound Butter

Compound butter may also be prepared by blending the ingredients together in a food processor. The butter should be chilled, and processed quickly.

To make about 2½ cups [625 ml.] butter

1 lb.	butter	½ kg.
6	sweet red peppers	6
	oil	
	salt and freshly ground black pepper	

Lightly oil the peppers, then grill them for about 20 to 30 minutes, turning them frequently, until the skins are blistered all over but not charred. Stem the peppers and purée them in a food processor or food mill. With a wooden spoon or pestle, press the purée through a sieve into a bowl.

In another bowl, beat the butter with a whisk or wooden spoon until it is light and fluffy. Add the puréed peppers and beat vigorously until the butter is once again light and fluffy. Season with salt and pepper to taste.

Lemon butter. Substitute the grated peel and strained juice of six lemons for the pepper purée.

Olive and anchovy butter. Grate the peel of an orange; squeeze and strain its juice. Remove the pits from 12 oil-cured black olives. Drain eight anchovy fillets. Blanch 15 to 20 sage leaves. Finely chop the peel, olives, anchovies and sage leaves together and combine them with the orange juice. Substitute this mixture for the pepper purée.

Berry butter. Press ¾ cup [175 ml.] of fresh raspberries or strawberries through a sieve. Stir in 1 or 2 tablespoons [15 or 30 ml.] of red wine vinegar—depending on the sweetness of the berries—and add 2 teaspoons [10 ml.] of finely chopped blanched tarragon leaves. Substitute the berry mixture for the pepper purée.

Avocado Sauce

To make about 1½ cups [375 ml.] sauce

2	avocados	2
½ cup	strained fresh lime juice	125 ml.
1 tbsp.	olive oil	15 ml.
	coarse salt	
	freshly ground black pepper	

Cut each avocado in half. Remove the pits, scoop out the avocado flesh with a large spoon, place it in a large bowl and mash it with a fork. Use a whisk to incorporate the lime juice and olive oil, beating until the sauce is light. Add salt and pepper to taste.

Béarnaise Sauce

To make about 1 cup [¼ liter] sauce

½ cup	dry white wine	125 ml.
¼ cup	white wine vinegar	50 ml.
2	shallots, finely chopped	2
	cayenne pepper or 1 small dried red chili	
1	sprig tarragon	1
1	sprig chervil	1
3	egg yolks	3
16 tbsp.	unsalted butter, cut into small bits and brought to room temperature	240 ml.
1 tsp.	finely chopped tarragon	5 ml.
1 tsp.	finely chopped chervil	5 ml.
	salt and freshly ground black pepper	

Put the wine, vinegar and shallots in a fireproof earthenware casserole, a heavy enameled saucepan or the top part of a glass or stainless-steel double boiler set over hot, not boiling, water. Add a pinch of cayenne or the chili, and the sprigs of tarragon and chervil. Place the pan over low heat and simmer the mixture for 15 to 20 minutes, or until only 3 to 4 tablespoons [45 to 60 ml.] of syrupy liquid remain. Strain the liquid into a bowl, pressing the juices from the herbs, then return the liquid to the pan.

Reduce the heat to very low and whisk in the egg yolks. After a few seconds, whisk in one third of the butter and continue whisking until it is absorbed. Repeat this procedure twice more, whisking until the sauce begins to thicken. Remove the pan from the heat and continue whisking: The heat of the pan will continue to cook and thicken the sauce. Stir in the chopped herbs, and season the sauce with salt and pepper to taste.

Cucumber Sauce

To make about 3½ cups [875 ml.] sauce

4	cucumbers, peeled, halved, seeded and cut into ¼-inch [6-mm.] pieces	4
	coarse salt	
1½ tsp.	chopped fresh mint leaves	7 ml.
2	garlic cloves, finely chopped	2
2 cups	yogurt, whisked until smooth	½ liter
	freshly ground pepper	

Place the cucumber pieces in a bowl, sprinkling each layer with a light coating of salt. Let the cucumbers drain for 30 minutes, then scoop the pieces out with your hands—leaving the liquid behind. Pat them dry with paper towels.

In a clean bowl, combine the cucumbers with the mint and garlic. Stir in the yogurt and add pepper to taste.

Stuffed Mushrooms

To make 24

24	large fresh mushroom caps	24
½ cup	olive oil	125 ml.
2 tbsp.	fresh lemon juice	30 ml.
1	sweet red pepper, halved, seeded, deribbed and finely chopped	1
5	garlic cloves, finely chopped	5
6	shallots, finely chopped	6
⅓ cup	finely chopped fresh parsley	75 ml.
2 cups	fresh bread crumbs	½ liter
	salt and freshly ground black pepper	

Combine all but 2 tablespoons [30 ml.] of the olive oil with the lemon juice, and marinate the mushroom caps in this mixture for up to two hours. Drain the mushroom caps, reserving the marinade.

Heat the remaining oil in a skillet and in it sauté the pepper, garlic and shallots for about five minutes, or until they are soft but not brown. Remove them from the heat, add the parsley and reserved marinade and stir in the bread crumbs. Season the stuffing with salt and pepper to taste. Then pack it into the mushroom caps.

Grill the stuffed mushrooms on an oiled rack 4 to 6 inches [10 to 15 cm.] above medium-hot coals for eight to 10 minutes, or until heated through.

Pork Sausages

The technique of making pork sausages is demonstrated on pages 38-39. Finely chopped fennel, parsley, thyme or savory leaves may be substituted for the sage leaves.

To make 5 pounds [2½ kg.] sausages

4 lb.	boneless fatty pork shoulder, cut into pieces and trimmed of connective tissue	2 kg.
1 lb.	pork loin, cut into pieces	½ kg.
5 tbsp.	coarse salt	75 ml.
	freshly ground black pepper	
2 tbsp.	finely chopped fresh sage leaves	30 ml.
6	large garlic cloves, finely chopped (optional)	6
about 4 yards	sausage casing, rinsed	about 4 meters

Using the medium disk, grind the meats in a food grinder. Mix the ground meats with the salt, pepper, sage and garlic, if you are using it. Fry a spoonful of the mixture in a skillet for three to four minutes, or until the juices run clear; taste the fried meat and adjust the seasoning of the remaining sausage mixture if necessary. Grind the mixture a second time before using it to fill the casings.

Mushroom and Bacon Stuffing

To make about 3 cups [¾ liter] stuffing

2 lb.	fresh mushrooms, finely chopped	1 kg.
2 tbsp.	butter	30 ml.
½ lb.	lean bacon, coarsely diced	¼ kg.
2 tbsp.	strained fresh lemon juice	30 ml.
1½ tbsp.	chopped mixed fresh thyme and winter savory leaves	22½ ml.

Melt the butter in a large pan set over medium heat. Add the mushrooms and, stirring occasionally, sauté them until the mushroom liquid has evaporated—about 15 minutes. Place the mushrooms in a mixing bowl and add the lemon juice.

In a skillet, sauté the bacon over medium heat until it is crisp—about five minutes. Drain the bacon and add it to the mushrooms, along with the fresh herbs.

Mixed Meat Stock

This general-purpose strong stock will keep for three or four days if it is refrigerated in a tightly covered container and boiled for a few minutes every day. If frozen, the stock will keep for six months.

To make about 3 quarts [3 liters] stock

2 lb.	beef shank	1 kg.
2 lb.	meaty veal shank, including the shank bone	1 kg.
2 lb.	chicken backs, necks and wing tips plus feet, if obtainable	1 kg.
about 5 quarts	water	about 5 liters
1	bouquet garni, including leek and celery	1
1	garlic bulb	1
2	medium-sized onions, 1 stuck with 2 whole cloves	2
4	large carrots	4

Place a metal rack or trivet in the bottom of a large stockpot to prevent the ingredients from sticking. Fit all of the meat, bones and chicken pieces into the pot and add water to cover by about 2 inches [5 cm.]. Bring slowly to a boil and, with a slotted spoon, skim off the scum that rises. Do not stir, lest you cloud the stock. Keep skimming, occasionally adding a glass of cold water, until no more scum rises—about 10 to 15 minutes. Add the bouquet garni, garlic, onions and carrots, pushing them down into the liquid so that everything is submerged. Skim again as the liquid returns to a boil. Reduce the heat to very low, cover the pot with the lid ajar and simmer for four to five hours, skimming at intervals. If the meat is to be eaten, remove the veal after one and a half hours, the beef after three hours.

Ladle the stock into a large bowl through a colander lined with a double layer of cheesecloth or muslin. Let the strained stock cool completely, then remove any traces of fat from the surface with a skimmer and a paper towel; if the stock has been refrigerated to cool it, remove the solid fat with a knife.

Veal stock. Replace the beef, beef bones and chicken pieces with about 4 pounds [2 kg.] of meaty veal trimmings—neck, shank or rib tips.

Beef stock. Substitute 4 pounds [2 kg.] of beef short ribs or chuck or oxtail for the veal shank and chicken pieces, and simmer for five hours. The veal shank bone can be omitted if a less gelatinous stock is desired.

Chicken stock. Old hens and roosters yield the richest stock. Use about 5 pounds [2½ kg.] of carcasses, necks, feet, wings, gizzards and hearts, and simmer for two hours.

Lamb stock. Use about 6 pounds [3 kg.] of lamb shank, bones and neck, and simmer for seven or eight hours.

Recipe Index

All recipes in this index are listed by their English titles. Foreign recipes are listed by country or region of origin. Recipe credits are on pages 173-175.

General Index/ Glossary

Included in this index to the cooking demonstrations are definitions, in italics, of special culinary terms not explained elsewhere in this volume. The Recipe Index begins on page 168.

Recipe Credits

The sources for the recipes in this volume are shown below. Page references in parentheses indicate where the recipes appear in the anthology.

Ainé, Offray, *La Cuisinier Méridional.* Offray Ainé, Imprimeur-Libraire, Avignon, 1855(109).
Allen, Jana and Margaret Gin, *Innards and Other Variety Meats.* Copyright © 1974 by Jana Allen and Margaret Gin. Reprinted by permission of the publisher, 101 Productions, San Francisco(125).
Alperi, Magdalena, *La Cocina. Tratado Completo de Comidas y Bebidas.* © Magdalena Alperi. First edition June 1977. Second edition December 1978. Translated by permission of the author, Gijon (Asturias)(132, 147, 148).
Beard, James A., *James Beard's American Cookery.* Copyright © 1972 by James A. Beard. Reprinted by permission of Little, Brown and Company(130). *James Beard's New Fish Cookery, A Revised and Updated Edition.* Copyright 1954, © 1976 by James A. Beard. Reprinted by permission of Little, Brown and Company(156).

Beard, James A. and Helen Evans Brown, *The Complete Book of Outdoor Cookery.* Copyright © 1955 by Helen Evans Brown and James A. Beard. Reprinted by permission of Doubleday & Company, Inc.(128, 129).
Beinert, Frederica L., *The Art of Making Sauces and Gravies.* Copyright © 1966 by Frederica L. Beinert. Published by Doubleday & Company, Inc., New York. Reprinted by permission of Frederica L. Beinert(161).
Bertholle, Louisette, *Secrets of the Great French Restaurants.* Translation Copyright © 1974 by Macmillan Publishing Co. Inc. Copyright © 1972 by Opera Mundi, Paris. Reprinted by permission of Macmillan Publishing Co., Inc.(109, 114).
Bickel, Walter and René Kramer, *Wild en Gevolgelte in de Internationale Keuken.* © Copyright 1974, 1980 Zomer en Keuning Boeken B.V. Published by Zomer en Keuning Boeken B.V., Ede. Translated by permission of Zomer en Keuning Boeken B.V.(139).
Blackman, Grant, *Australian Fish Cooking.* © Copyright Grant Blackman 1978. Published by Hill of Content Publishing Company, Melbourne. By permission of Hill of Content Publishing Company(142, 150).
Bondanini, Mario V. (Editor), *Gastronomie de Plein Air.* © Copyright 1970 by Éditions Melior, CH-1020 Renens/Suisse. Published by Éditions Melior. Translated by permission of Éditions Melior, Bussigny-Lausanne(147).

Bonomo, Giuliana, *La Buona Cucina.* © 1976, Curcio Periodici S.P.A. Published by Curcio Periodici S.P.A., Rome. Translated by permission of Curcio Periodici S.P.A.(92, 128).
Böttiger, Theodor, *Das Grill-Buch.* Copyright © 1968 by Wilhelm Heyne Verlag, München. Published by Wilhelm Heyne Verlag. Translated by permission of Wilhelm Heyne Verlag(97).
Brown, Helen Evans, *Helen Brown's West Coast Cook Book.* Copyright 1952 by Helen Evans Brown. Reprinted by permission of Little, Brown and Company(93, 160).
The Brown Derby Cookbook. Published by Doubleday & Company(93, 95, 155).
Buchanan, Meriel, *Good Food from the Balkans.* Copyright © 1965 by Meriel Buchanan. First published by Frederick Muller, Ltd., London. Reprinted by permission of Campbell Thomson & McLaughlin Limited, London(150).
Bugialli, Giuliano, *The Fine Art of Italian Cooking.* Copyright © 1977 by Giuliano Bugialli. Reprinted by permission of Times Books, a division of Quadrangle/The New York Times Book Co., Inc.(129, 130).
Buonassisi, Vincenzo, *Cucina All'Aria Aperta.* © Arnoldo Mondadori Editore 1972. Published by Arnoldo Mondadori Editore S.p.A., Milan. Translated by permission of Arnoldo Mondadori Editore S.p.A.(137, 151, 153).
Burros, Marian, *Pure & Simple.* Copyright © 1978 by

Marian Fox Burros. By permission of William Morrow & Company, Inc.(123, 147).

Burrows, Lois M. and Laura G. Myers, *Too Many Tomatoes, Squash, Beans and Other Good Things.* Copyright © 1976 by Lois M. Burrows and Laura G. Myers. Reprinted by permission of Harper & Row, Publishers, Inc.(94, 115).

Callahan, Ed, *Charcoal Cookbook.* Copyright © 1970 by Pacific Productions. Published by Nitty Gritty Productions. Reprinted by permission of Nitty Gritty Productions(94, 96, 98).

Cantrell, Rose, *Creative Outdoor Cooking.* Copyright © 1979 by Ottenheimer Publishers, Inc. Reprinted by permission of Ottenheimer Publishers, Inc.(113).

Carcione, Joe, *The Greengrocer Cookbook.* Copyright © 1975 by Joe Carcione. Reprinted by permission of Celestial Arts, Millbrae, Calif.(159).

Chablani, Mohan and Brahm N. Dixit, *The Bengal Lancers Indian Cookbook.* Copyright © 1976 by Mohan Chablani and Brahm N. Dixit. Reprinted by permission of Contemporary Books, Inc., Chicago, Ill.(114).

Chandonnet, Ann, *The Complete Fruit Cookbook.* Copyright © 1972 by Ann Chandonnet. Reprinted by permission of the publisher, 101 Productions, San Francisco(133).

Chantiles, Vilma Liacouras, *The Food of Greece.* © 1975 by Vilma Liacouras Chantiles. Published by Atheneum, New York. Reprinted by permission of Vilma Liacouras Chantiles(150).

Chekenian, Jane and Monica Meyer, *Shellfish Cookery.* Copyright © 1971 by Jane Chekenian and Monica Meyer. Reprinted with permission of Macmillan Publishing Co., Inc.(158).

Clark, Morton Gill, *The Wide, Wide World of Texas Cooking* (Funk & Wagnall). Copyright © 1970 by Morton Gill Clark. Reprinted by permission of Harper & Row, Publishers, Inc.(140).

Clusells, Sylvain, *Cooking on Turning Spit and Grill.* English translation © Arthur Barker Limited 1961. Published by Arthur Barker Limited(127, 154). By permission of Arthur Barker Limited(127, 154).

Cocina Regional Española. Published by Editorial Almena, Madrid 1976. Translated by permission of Editorial Doncel, Madrid(94, 108).

Consumer Guide Publications, the editors of, *Smoke Cookery.* Copyright © 1978 by Publications International, Ltd. Published by Crown Publishers, Inc. Reprinted by permission of Publications International, Ltd., Inc.(98, 134, 139).

Cronin, Isaac, *The International Squid Cookbook.* Copyright © 1981 by Isaac Cronin. Reprinted by permission of Aris Books(159).

David, Elizabeth, *Italian Food.* Copyright © Elizabeth David 1954, 1963, 1969. Published by Penguin Books Ltd., London. By permission of Penguin Books Ltd.(108).

Davidson, Alan, *Mediterranean Seafood.* Copyright © Alan Davidson, 1972. Published by Penguin Books Ltd. Reprinted by permission of Penguin Books Ltd.(142, 144).

Day, Irene F., *The Moroccan Cookbook.* Copyright © 1975 by Irene F. Day. Reprinted by permission of The Putnam Publishing Group and Andre Deutsch Limited, London(117).

Department of Commerce, Bureau of Fisheries. By permission of the Department of Commerce, Fishery Utilization & Development Division(156).

D'Ermo, Dominique, *Dominique's Famous Fish, Game & Meat Recipes.* Copyright © 1981 by Acropolis Books Ltd. Reprinted by permission of Acropolis Books(141).

Domènech, Ignacio, *Pescados y Mariscos.* Texto © Archivo Gastronómico Domènech—1979. Published by Editorial Bruguera, S.A., Barcelona. Translated by permission of José C. Balagué Domènech, Barcelona(145, 154).

Domènech, Ignasi, *Apats.* Copyright Archivo Gastronómico Ignasi Domènech. Published by Editorial Laia, S.A., Barcelona 1979. Translated by permission of José C. Balagué Domènech, Barcelona(127).

Donovan, Maria Kozslik, *The Blue Danube Cookbook.* Copyright © 1967 by Maria Kozslik Donovan. Published by Doubleday & Company, Inc. Reprinted by permission of Maria Kozslik Donovan(102).

Dumaine, Alexandre, *Ma Cuisine.* © 1972 by Pensée Moderne, Paris. Published by Éditions de la Pensée Moderne. Translated by permission of Jacques Grancher, Éditeur, Paris(121).

Elkon, Juliette, *A Belgian Cookbook.* Copyright © 1958 by Farrar, Straus and Cudahy, Inc. (now Farrar, Straus and Giroux, Inc.). Reprinted by permission of Farrar, Straus and Giroux, Inc.(152).

Famularo, Joseph and Louise Imperiale, *The Festive Famularo Kitchen.* Copyright © 1977 by Joe Famularo and Louise Imperiale (New York: Atheneum, 1977). Reprinted with permission of Atheneum Publishers(106, 116).

Feast of Italy. Translated from the Italian edition published by Arnoldo Mondadori Editore. Copyright © 1973 by Arnoldo Mondadori Editore. Reprinted by permission of A & W Publishers, Inc.(120).

Finn, Molly, *Summer Feasts.* Copyright © 1979 by Molly Finn. Reprinted by permission of Simon & Schuster, a division of Gulf & Western Corporation(135).

Food Editors of Family Circle and Jean Anderson, *The Family Circle Cookbook.* Copyright © 1974 by The Family Circle, Inc. Reprinted by permission of The Family Circle, Inc.(123).

Frisch vom Grill. © Walter Hädecke Verlag, 7252 Weil der Stadt. Published by Walter Hädecke Verlag. Translated by permission of Walter Hädecke Verlag(95, 145).

Froidl, Ilse, *Das Geflügel-Kochbuch.* Copyright © 1966 by Wilhelm Heyne Verlag, München. Published by Wilhelm Heyne Verlag. Translated by permission of Wilhelm Heyne Verlag(139).

Gin, Margaret and Alfred E. Castle, *Regional Cooking of China.* Copyright © 1975 by Margaret Gin and Alfred E. Castle. Reprinted by permission of the publisher, 101 Productions, San Francisco(123).

The Great Cooks' Guide to Fish Cookery. Copyright © 1977 by David Russell. Published by Random House, New York. Reprinted by permission of Cook's Catalogue, New York(151—Carole Lalli).

Green, Henrietta, *The Marinade Cookbook.* © Text: Henrietta Green. Published by Pierrot Publishing Limited, London, 1978. By permission of the author, London(115).

Green, Karen and Betty Black, *How to Cook His Goose (and Other Wild Games).* Copyright © 1973 by Karen Green and Betty Black. Published by Winchester Press, P.O. Box 1260, Tulsa, Okla. 74101. Reprinted by permission of Karen Green and Betty Black and Winchester Press(141, 152).

Greene, Bert, *Honest American Fare.* Copyright © 1981 by Bert Greene. Reprinted by permission of Contemporary Books, Inc., Chicago, Ill.(132, 151).

Grigson, Jane, *Jane Grigson's Vegetable Book.* Copyright © 1978 Jane Grigson. Reprinted with permission of Atheneum Publishers(134). *Fish Cookery.* Copyright © Jane Grigson, 1973. Published by The International Wine and Food Society. Reprinted with permission of The Overlook Press, Lewis Hollow Road, Woodstock, N.Y.(144).

Hachten, Harva, *Kitchen Safari.* Copyright © 1970 by Harva Hachten (New York: Atheneum, 1970). Reprinted with permission of Atheneum Publishers(103, 107).

Hawkes, Alex D., *The Flavors of the Caribbean & Latin America.* Copyright © The Estate of Alex D. Hawkes, 1978. Published by The Viking Press. Reprinted by permission of John Schaffner Associates, Inc.(100, 106).

Hawkes, Alex D. (Editor), *The Shrimp Cookbook.* Copyright © 1966 by Delair Publishing Company, Inc. Reprinted by permission of Delair Publishing Company, Inc.(157).

Hawliczkowa, Helena, *Kuchnia Polska.* Published by Panstwowe Wydawnictwo Ekonomiczne, Warsaw 1979. Translated by permission of Agencja Autorska, Warsaw, for the author(143, 147).

Hazelton, Nika. *The Picnic Book.* Copyright © 1969 by Nika Hazelton. Published by Atheneum. Reprinted by permission of Nika Hazelton(101, 102).

The Helen Alexander Hawaiian Cook Book. Published by Hawaiian Service (Louise and George T. Armitage)(160).

Hewitt, Jean, *The New York Times Large Type Cookbook.* Copyright © 1968, 1971 by The New York Times

Company. Published by Golden Press, New York, a division of Western Publishing Company, Inc. Reprinted by permission of Times Books, a division of Quadrangle/The New York Times Book Co., Inc.(145).

Hornberg, Ulrike, *Schlemmereien vom Grill.* © Droemer Knaur Verlag Schoeller & Co., Locarno 1976. Published by Droemer Knaur Verlag. Translated by permission of Droemersche Verlagsanstalt Th. Knaur Nachf. GmbH & Co., Munich(101, 109).

Horvath, Maria, *Balkan-Küche.* Copyright © 1963 by Wilhelm Heyne Verlag, München. Published by Wilhelm Heyne Verlag. Translated by permission of Wilhelm Heyne Verlag(107, 126, 146).

Hyun, Judy, *The Korean Cookbook.* Copyright © 1970 by Judy Hyun. Published by Follet Publishing Company. Reprinted by permission of Hollym Corporation: Publishers, Seoul, Korea(92, 107, 135).

Jans, Hugh, *Vrij Nederland* (Dutch magazine). October 4, 1975; June 19, 1976. Translated by permission of Hugh Jans(113, 123).

The Jekyll Island Garden Club, *Golden Isles Cuisine.* Copyright © 1978 by Dot Gibson Publications, Waycross Ga. Reprinted by permission of Dot Gibson Publications(105—Norman Gibson, 124—Mrs. Walter Ravold, 157—Mrs. G. H. Williams Jr., 159—Mrs. Joe Eberhart).

Johnson, Ronald, *The Aficionado's Southwestern Cooking.* © 1968 by the University of New Mexico Press. Reprinted by permission of the University of New Mexico Press(108, 121).

The Junior League of Boston, Inc., *Presenting Boston . . . A Cookbook.* Copyright © 1976 by The Junior League of Boston, Inc. Published by The Junior League of Boston, Inc. Reprinted by The Junior League of Boston, Inc.(125).

The Junior League of the City of New York, *New York Entertains.* Copyright © 1974 by The Junior League of New York City, Inc. Reprinted by permission of Doubleday & Company, Inc.(126).

Junior League of El Paso, Inc., *Seasoned With Sun.* Copyright 1974 by Junior League of El Paso, Inc. Published by the Junior League of El Paso, Inc. Reprinted by permission of the Junior League of El Paso, Inc., 520 Thunderbird, El Paso, Tex. 79912(99).

The Junior League of Pine Bluff, Inc., *Southern Accent.* Copyright 1976 by The Junior League of Pine Bluff, Inc. Published by The Junior League of Pine Bluff, Inc. Reprinted by permission of The Junior League of Pine Bluff, Inc.(140—Vernon T. Tarver, 157—Mrs. Eugene Harris).

Kamman, Madeleine, *Dinner Against the Clock.* Copyright © 1973 by Madeleine Kamman (New York: Atheneum, 1973). Reprinted with permission of Atheneum Publishers(125, 126, 132). *The Making of a Cook.* Copyright © 1971 by Madeleine Kamman (New York: Atheneum, 1971). Reprinted with permission of Atheneum Publishers(143).

Keasberry, Oma, *Oma's Indische Keukengeheimen.* © Copyright 1978 Vermande Zonen bv, IJmuiden. Published by Vermande Zonen bv. Translated by permission of H.J.W. Becht's Uitgevers-Mij. B.V., Amsterdam(118).

Khawan, René R., *La Cuisine Arabe.* © Éditions Albin Michel 1970. Published by Éditions Albin Michel, Paris. Translated by permission of Éditions Albin Michel(118).

Laasri, Ahmed, *240 Recettes de Cuisine Marocaine.* © 1978, Jacques Grancher, Éditeur. Published by Jacques Grancher, Éditeur, Paris. Translated by Jacques Grancher, Éditeur(138).

Ladies' Home Journal (Editors), *Ladies' Home Journal Adventures in Cooking.* Copyright © 1968 by The Curtis Publishing Company & MacLean-Hunter Limited. Published by Prentice-Hall, Inc. Reprinted by permission of Prentice-Hall, Inc., Englewood Cliffs, N.J. and Ladies' Home Journal(124, 127, 157).

Lane, Lilian, *Malayan Cookery Recipes.* © Lilian Lane 1964. Published by Eastern Universities Press Ltd. in association with University of London Press Ltd., London. By permission of Hodder & Stoughton Ltd., Sevenoaks(105).

Le Huédé, Henri, *Dining on the France.* © Editions Menges, Paris. Reprinted by permission of The Vendome Press(137, 148).

Lemnis, Maria and Henryk Vitry, *Old Polish Tradi-*

tions in the Kitchen and at the Table. © Interpress Publishers, Warsaw 1979. Published by Interpress Publishers. By permission of Society of Authors ZAIKS, Warsaw(140).
Logan, Barbara, *Barbecue and Outdoor Cookery.* © Ward Lock Limited, 1978. Reprinted by permission of Ward Lock Limited(153, 155).
McClane, A. J. and Arie DeZanger, *The Encyclopedia of Fish Cookery.* Copyright © 1977 by A. J. McClane and Arie DeZanger. Reprinted by permission of Holt, Rinehart and Winston, Publishers(143, 149).
McIntyre, Nancy Fair, *It's a Picnic!* Copyright © 1969 by Nancy McIntyre. Reprinted by permission of Viking Penguin Inc.(93, 99, 100, 158).
Maclean, Veronica, *Lady Maclean's Book of Sauces and Surprises.* © Veronica Maclean 1978. Published by William Collins Sons and Company Limited, Glasgow and London 1978. By permission of Collins Publishers, London(161).
MacMillan, Diane D., *The Portable Feast.* Copyright © 1973 by Diane DeLorme MacMillan. Reprinted by permission of the publisher, 101 Productions, San Francisco(133).
Mallos, Tess, *Greek Cookbook.* Copyright © Tess Mallos 1976. First published by Paul Hamlyn Pty. Limited, Dee Why West, S.A.W., Australia. Published by The Hamlyn Publishing Group Limited, London. By permission of Lansdowne Press, Dee Why and the author(110).
Mark, Theonie, *Greek Islands Cooking.* Copyright © 1973 by Theonie Mark. Published by Little, Brown and Company. Reprinted by permission of Theonie Mark(140, 142).
Marks, James F., *Barbecues.* Copyright © James F. Marks, 1977. Published by Penguin Books Ltd. Reprinted by permission of Penguin Books Ltd.(96).
Marshall, Mel, *Cooking over Coals.* Copyright © 1971 by Mel Marshall. Published by Winchester Press, P.O. Box 1260, Tulsa, Okla. 74101. Reprinted by permission of Winchester Press(143, 152).
Mitcham, Howard, *The Provincetown Seafood Cookbook.* Copyright © 1975 by Howard Mitcham. Published by Addison-Wesley, Reading, Mass. Reprinted by permission of Howard Mitcham(146, 149).
Morris, Dan and Inez, *The Complete Outdoor Cookbook.* Copyright © 1970 by Dan and Inez Morris. Reprinted by permission of the publisher, E. P. Dutton, Inc. (A Hawthorn Book)(148).
Nelson, Kay Shaw, *The Eastern European Cookbook.* Copyright © 1973 by Kay Shaw Nelson. Published by Dover Publications, Inc., New York. Reprinted by permission of Kay Shaw Nelson(150).
Nicolau, M. del Carme, *Cuina Catalana.* © Editorial Miquel Arimany, S.A. Published by Editorial Miquel Arimany, S.A., Barcelona. Translated by permission of Editorial Miquel Arimany, S.A.(93, 149).
Norman, Barbara, *The Russian Cookbook.* Copyright © 1967 by Bantam Books, Inc. Published by Atheneum, New York. Reprinted by permission of Barbara Norman and her agent Robert P. Mills, Ltd.(104).
Nouveau Manuel de la Cuisinière Bourgeoise et Économique. Published by Bernardin-Bechet, Libraire, Paris, 1868(129).
Novak, Jane, *Treasury of Chicken Cookery.* Copyright © 1974 by Jane Novak. Reprinted by permission of Harper & Row, Publishers, Inc.(135).
The Oaks II Collection. 1981. Reprinted by permission of Carol Fanconi, Laytonsville, Md.(122).
Ochorowicz-Monatowa, Marja, *Polish Cookery.* (Translated and adapted by Jean Karsavina.) Copyright © 1958 by Crown Publishers, Inc. By permission of Crown Publishers, Inc.(99, 119).
Olney, Judith, *Summer Food.* Copyright © 1978 Judith Olney. Reprinted with permission of Atheneum Publishers(100, 110).
Olney, Richard, *Simple French Food.* Copyright © 1974 by Richard Olney. Reprinted with permission of Atheneum Publishers(131, 158).
Orcutt, Georgia, *Smoke Cookery.* Copyright © 1978 by BPS Books, Inc. Reprinted by permission of The New American Library, Inc., New York, New York(102, 160).
Ortiz, Elisabeth Lambert, *The Complete Book of Car-*

ibbean Cooking. Copyright © Elisabeth Lambert Ortiz, 1973, 1975. Published by Penguin Books Ltd., London. By permission of John Farquharson Ltd., London(103).
Ortiz, Elisabeth Lambert with Mitsuko Endo, *The Complete Book of Japanese Cooking.* Copyright © 1976 by Elisabeth Lambert Ortiz. Reprinted by permission of the publisher, M. Evans and Company, Inc., N.Y.(136).
The Outdoor Grill Cookbook. Copyright © 1960 by Spencer International Press, Inc. Reprinted by permission of Grosset & Dunlap, Inc.(96, 131).
Owen, Sri, *Indonesian Food and Cookery.* © 1976, 1980 by Sri Owen. Published by Prospect Books, London and Washington, D.C. By permission of Prospect Books(112).
Paradissis, Chrissa, *The Best Book of Greek Cookery.* Copyright © 1976 by P. Efstathiadis & Sons. Published by Efstathiadis Group, Athens. By permission of P. Efstathiadis & Sons S.A.(114).
Pezzini, Wilma, *The Tuscan Cookbook.* Copyright © 1978 Wilma Pezzini. Reprinted with permission of Atheneum Publishers(119).
Picture Cook Book. Copyright © 1958, 1961 by Time Inc. Published by Time-Life Books, Alexandria(113, 122, 124, 138).
Piepenbrock, Mechthild, *Grill Vergnügen Draussen und Drinnen.* © Gräfe und Unzer GmbH, München. Published by Gräfe und Unzer GmbH. Translated by Gräfe und Unzer Verlag, Munich(94, 138).
Platina (Bartolomeo de Sacchi di Piadena), *De Honesta Voluptate.* Venice 1475(112).
Pourounas, Andreas, *Aphrodite's Cookbook.* Copyright © by Andreas Pourounas and Helene Grosvenor. Published by Neville Spearman (Jersey) Limited, Jersey, Channel Islands 1977. By permission of Neville Spearman Limited, Sudbury, Suffolk(118).
Puga y Parga, Manuel M. (Picadillo), *La Cocina Práctica.* Copyright by Libreria-Editorial Gali. Published by Libreria-Editorial "Gali," Santiago 1966. Translated by permission of Libreria "Gali" Editorial(148).
Ramazani, Nesta, *Persian Cooking.* Copyright © 1974 by Nesta Ramazani. Published by Quadrangle/The New York Times Book Company. Reprinted by permission of The University Press of Virginia(111).
Reiger, Barbara and George, *The Zane Grey Cookbook.* Copyright © 1976 by Zane Grey, Inc., and George Reiger. Published by Prentice-Hall, Inc. Reprinted by permission of Prentice-Hall, Inc., Englewood Cliffs, N.J.(128, 132).
Ripoll, Luis, *Nuestra Cocina: 600 Recetas de Mallorca, Menorca, Ibiza y Formentera.* © by Luis Ripoll. Published by Editorial H.M.B., S.A., Barcelona 1978. Translated by permission of the author, Palma de Mallorca(114).
Roberson, John and Marie, *The Complete Barbecue Book.* Copyright 1951 by Prentice-Hall, Inc. Published by Prentice-Hall, Inc. Reprinted by permission of Marie Roberson Hamm(152, 159).
Roden, Claudia, *Picnic: The Complete Guide to Outdoor Food.* Copyright © Claudia Roden, 1981. First published by Jill Norman & Hobhouse Ltd. Reprinted by permission of Jill Norman(97, 119, 126, 154).
Rombauer, Irma S. and Marion Rombauer Becker, *Joy of Cooking.* Copyright © 1931, 1936, 1941, 1942, 1943, 1946, 1951, 1952, 1953, 1962, 1963, 1964, 1975 by Irma S. Rombauer and Marion Rombauer Becker. Reprinted by permission of the publisher, The Bobbs-Merrill Company, Inc.(106, 160).
Rosselli, Anna Basalini, *Cento Ricette Per La Colazione Sull'Erba.* Copyright © by G. C. Sansoni S.P.A., Firenze. Published by G. C. Sansoni Editore Nuova S.P.A., 1973. Translated by permission of G. C. Sansoni Editore Nuova S.P.A.(96, 103, 127).
Sahni, Julie, *Classic Indian Cooking.* Text Copyright © 1980 by Julie Sahni. By permission of William Morrow & Company(134).
St. Mary's Cathedral Ladies Guild, *Caracas i Buen Provecho!* Copyright St. Mary's Cathedral Ladies Guild. Fifth edition published by The British Ladies' Charities, Caracas 1967. Translated by permission of St. Mary's Cathedral Ladies Guild(95—Elsie K. de Herrera).

Schindler, Roana and Gene, *Hawaii Kai Cookbook.* Copyright © 1970 by Roana and Gene Schindler. Published by Hearthside Press Inc. Reprinted by permission of Roana and Gene Schindler(136).
Schoon, Louise Sherman and Corrinne Hardesty, *The Complete Pork Cook Book.* Copyright © 1977 by Louise Sherman Schoon and Corrinne Hardesty. Reprinted by permission of Stein and Day Publishers(120, 122, 124).
Seidel, Elinor (Editor), *Chefs, Scholars & Movable Feasts.* Copyright © 1978 by the University of Maryland University College. Reprinted by permission of the University of Maryland University College(101—Nancy Coffey).
Semeyno Sukrovishte. Published in Sofia, circa 1916. Translated by permission of Jusautor Copyright Agency, Sofia(141).
Serra, Victoria, *Tía Victoria's Spanish Kitchen.* English text copyright © by Elizabeth Gili, 1963. Published by Kaye and Ward Ltd., London 1963. Translated by Elizabeth Gili from the original Spanish entitled *Sabores: Cocina Del Hogar* by Victoria Serra Suñol. By permission of Kaye and Ward Ltd.(92).
Sewell, Elizabeth, *Barbecue Cookbook.* Copyright 1971 by Paul Hamlyn Pty. Ltd. Published by Paul Hamlyn Pty. Ltd. Reprinted by permission of Lansdowne Press, Australia(129, 156).
Shelton, Ferne (Editor), *Pioneer Cookbook.* Copyright © 1973 by Ferne Shelton. Published by Hutcraft, High Point, N.C. Reprinted by permission of D. D. Hutchinson(93).
Shishkov, Dr. Georgi and Stoil Vouchkov, *Bulgarski Natsionalni Yastiya.* © by the authors 1978 c/o Jusautor, Sofia. First published by Projizdat, Sofia 1959. Translated by permission of Jusautor Copyright Agency(146, 153).
Singh, Dharamjit, *Indian Cookery.* Copyright © Dharamjit Singh, 1970. Published by Penguin Books Ltd., London. By permission of Penguin Books Ltd.(111, 116, 144).
Skipwith, Sofka, *Eat Russian.* © Sofka Skipwith 1973. Published by David & Charles. Reprinted by permission of David & Charles(117).
Tante Marie's French Kitchen. Translated and adapted by Charlotte Turgeon. Originally published in French as *La Véritable Cuisine de Famille* by Tante Marie. Copyright 1950 by Cartes Taride, Éditeurs Libraires, Paris. Published by Kaye & Ward Ltd., London. By permission of Cartes Taride, Paris(158).
Thoughts for Buffets. Copyright © 1958 by Institute Publishing Company. Reprinted by permission of Houghton Mifflin Company(133).
Tiano, Myrette, *Les Meilleures Recettes: Piques-Niques, Barbecues.* © Solar, 1981. Published by Solar, Paris. Translated by permission of Solar(97, 98).
Trent, May Wong, *Oriental Barbecues.* Copyright © 1974 by May Wong Trent. Reprinted with permission of Macmillan Publishing Co., Inc.(138, 156).
Uvezian, Sonia, *The Cuisine of Armenia.* Copyright © 1974 by Sonia Uvezian. Reprinted by permission of Harper & Row, Publishers, Inc.(104, 133, 136, 152).
Valldejuli, Carmen Aboy, *Puerto Rican Cookery.* Copyright © 1977 by Carmen Aboy Valldejuli. Privately published in Santurce. By permission of the author(120).
Vazquez Montalban, Manuel, *La Cocina Catalana.* © Manuel Vazquez Montalban, 1979. Published by Ediciones Peninsula, Barcelona. Translated by permission of Carme Balcells Agencia Literaria, Barcelona(146, 153).
Verge, Roger, *Roger Verge's Cuisine of the South of France.* English translation copyright © 1980 by William Morrow and Company, Inc. Originally published in French under the title *Ma Cuisine du Soleil.* Copyright © 1979 by Editions Robert Laffont, S.A. By permission of William Morrow(155).
Waldron, Maggie, *Fire & Smoke.* Copyright © 1978 by Maggie Waldron. Reprinted by permission of the publisher, 101 Productions, San Francisco(99, 104, 137).
Wolter, Annette, *Das Praktische Grillbuch.* © by Gräfe und Unzer Verlag, München. Published by Gräfe und Unzer Verlag. Translated by permission of Gräfe und Unzer Verlag(92, 95, 97).

Acknowledgments

The indexes for this book were prepared by Louise W. Hedberg. The editors are particularly indebted to Janet Bartucci, Myers CommuniCouncil, New York and Arthur W. Seeds, President, Barbecue Industries Association, Naperville, Illinois.

The editors also wish to thank: Markie Benet, London; Nicola Blount, London; Brinkman Corporation, Dallas, Texas; Tom Calhoun, Culpeper, Virginia; Gail Duff, Maidstone, Kent; Sarah Jane Evans, London; Scott J. Feierabend, National Wildlife Federation, Washington, D.C.; Dr. George J. Flick, Department of Food Science and Technology, Virginia Polytechnic Institute and State University, Blacksburg; Susan Gaible, Consumer Services, Reynolds Aluminum, Richmond, Virginia; Gaines Hardware, Alexandria, Virginia; Hudson Brothers Greengrocers, Washington, D.C.; Maria Johnson, Sevenoaks, Kent; Wanda Kemp-Welch, Nottingham; Larimer's Markets, Washington, D.C.; Ginny McCarthy, Tappan, New York; Norton and Virginia Mailman, New York; Peter Mazzeo, U.S. National Arboretum, Washington, D.C.; MECO (Metals Engineering Corporation), Greeneville, Tennessee; Neam's Market, Washington, D.C.; North Carolina Yam Council, Raleigh; Rosemary Oates, London; Ann O'Sullivan, Deya, Majorca; Anna Maria Perez, Barcelona; Nancy Pollard, La Cuisine, Alexandria, Virginia; Jorge W. Ramirez, Acme Barbecue College, Alhambra, California; Harold Reeves, Beacon Butcher, Alexandria, Virginia; Sylvia Robertson, Surbiton, Surrey; John Sanders, Scott's Barbecue Pit, Washington, D.C.; Santullo's Market, Alexandria, Virginia; Holly Shimizu, Curator, National Herb Garden, U.S. National Arboretum, Washington, D.C.; Straight from the Crate, Alexandria, Virginia; Derek Walker, Port City Seafood, Alexandria, Virginia; Dr. R. L. Wesley, Department of Food Science and Technology, Virginia Polytechnic Institute and State University, Blacksburg.

Picture Credits

All photographs appearing in this book are by Aldo Tutino except page 2, photograph by Louis Klein.
Illustrations: Frederic F. Bigio from B-C Graphics, 6-7.

From the Mary Evans Picture Library and private sources and *Food & Drink: A Pictorial Archive from Nineteenth Century Sources* by Jim Harter, published by Dover Publications, Inc., 1979, 92-167.

Library of Congress Cataloguing in Publication Data
Main entry under title:

Outdoor cooking.
  (The Good cook, techniques & recipes)
  Includes index.
  1. Outdoor cookery. I. Time-Life Books. II. Series.
TX823.O965 1983   641.5′78   82-16735
ISBN 0-8094-2977-2
ISBN 0-8094-2976-4 (lib. bdg.)
ISBN 0-8094-2975-6 (retail ed.)

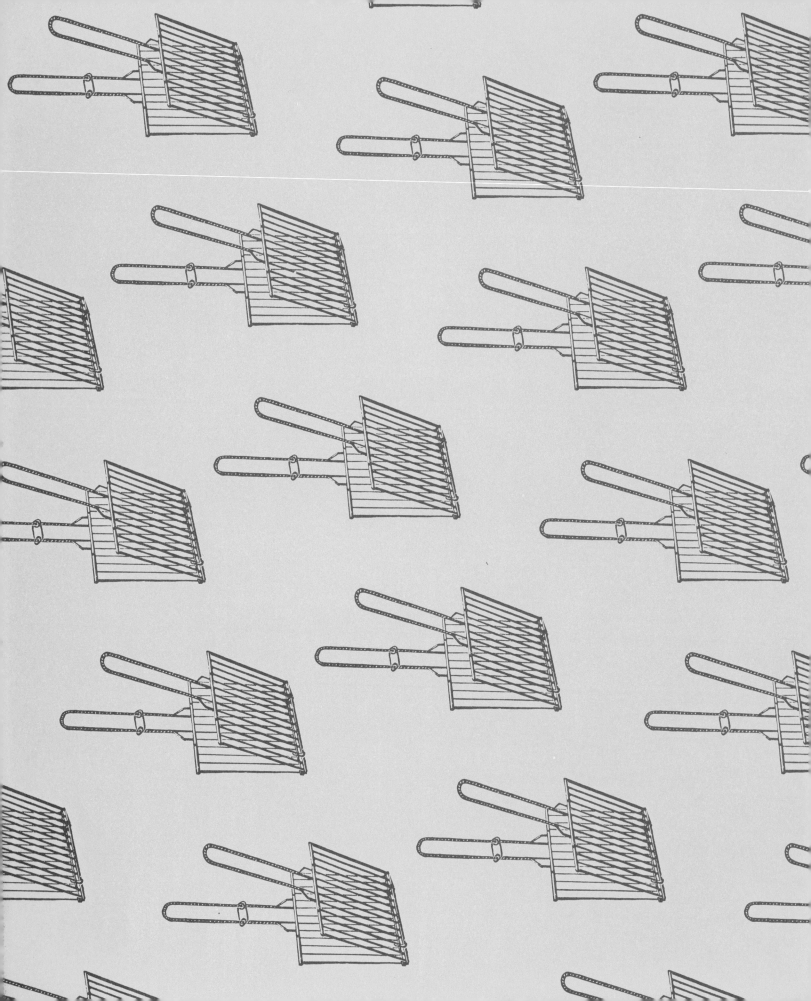